# Mastering Financial Accounting

*The Complete Guide to Financial Statements, Business Finance, and Strategic Decision-Making*

Rob Maxwell

# Copyrights



This publication is designed to provide accurate and authoritative information in regard to the subject matter covered. It is sold with the understanding that neither the author nor the publisher is engaged in rendering legal, investment, accounting or other professional services. While the publisher and author have used their best efforts in preparing this book, they make no representations or warranties with respect to the accuracy or completeness of the contents of this book and specifically disclaim any implied warranties of merchantability or fitness for a particular purpose. No warranty may be created or extended by sales representatives or written sales materials. The advice and strategies contained herein may not be suitable for your situation. You should consult with a professional when appropriate. Neither the publisher nor the author shall be liable for any loss of profit or any other commercial damages, including but not limited to special, incidental, consequential, personal, or other damages.

# TABLE OF CONTENTS

# INTRODUCTION TO FINANCIAL ACCOUNTING

## What is Financial Accounting?

Financial accounting is the structured process of recording, summarizing, and reporting a business's financial transactions in a systematic and standardized manner. It serves as the backbone of financial transparency, allowing stakeholders to assess the company's financial health, operational efficiency, and long-term viability. By documenting and analyzing financial activities, financial accounting enables businesses to track their financial progress, ensure compliance with legal regulations, and support strategic decision-making.

Every business, regardless of size or industry, engages in various daily financial transactions—from purchasing raw materials and paying wages to selling products or services and securing loans. Without a structured accounting framework, businesses would struggle to maintain order in their financial records, leading to inefficiencies, errors, and potential legal consequences. Financial accounting organizes this vast array of economic data into comprehensible reports that provide invaluable insights into a company's profitability, liquidity, and economic stability.

Unlike managerial accounting, which focuses on internal decision-making and operational strategies, financial accounting is primarily designed for external users. These external stakeholders include investors, creditors, regulatory agencies, tax authorities, and financial institutions, who rely on accurate and standardized financial reports to evaluate a company's performance, stability, and risk exposure. Investors assess a company's financial statements to determine whether it represents a sound investment opportunity, while lenders and banks analyze financial data before granting loans or credit lines.

Financial accounting adheres to well-established frameworks such as the Generally Accepted Accounting Principles (GAAP) and the International Financial Reporting Standards (IFRS) to ensure accuracy, reliability, and consistency. These globally recognized accounting standards set forth principles and guidelines that govern financial reporting, ensuring that businesses present their financial statements uniformly. This standardization enhances comparability between companies, industries, and even international markets, making it easier for investors and stakeholders to make informed financial decisions.

Financial accounting is vital in fostering trust and accountability in the business world. It ensures that businesses operate with financial integrity, comply with regulatory requirements, and provide stakeholders with a clear and accurate representation of their economic performance. Financial accounting is not just about crunching numbers; it is a powerful tool that drives business success, facilitates informed decision-making, and supports sustainable financial growth.

At its core, financial accounting answers critical questions such as:

- Is the business profitable?
- Can the company meet its financial obligations?
- How effectively is the business managing its assets and liabilities?
- Is the company growing financially over time?

Understanding financial accounting is essential for any business owner, entrepreneur, or manager who wants to make informed decisions and sustain long-term success.

## The Role of Accounting in Business Success: The Foundation of Growth and Stability

Accounting is often referred to as **the language of business** because it translates every transaction, investment, and financial decision into meaningful data. Whether you are a **small business owner, an entrepreneur scaling a start up, or a CEO managing a multinational**

**corporation**, financial accounting serves as the foundation for **profitability, sustainability, and strategic decision-making**.

A company that ignores accounting operates **blindly**, making decisions based on assumptions rather than facts. On the other hand, businesses that embrace **strong financial accounting practices gain a competitive advantage**, enabling them to forecast trends, mitigate risks, and capitalize on growth opportunities.

## Tracking Financial Performance: The Roadmap to Profitability

A business that does not measure its financial health is **like a pilot flying without instruments**—unaware of potential dangers ahead. **Financial statements serve as the dashboard of a company**, providing a clear view of its revenues, expenses, and overall profitability.

**Why It Matters:**

- Profit and loss statements reveal whether the business is **growing or struggling**.
- Cash flow reports show if a company has enough liquidity to **cover expenses and reinvest** in growth.
- Balance sheets reflect a company's **financial stability and long-term viability**.

By **consistently reviewing financial reports**, business owners and managers can spot patterns, assess performance trends, and make the necessary adjustments to **increase efficiency, cut unnecessary costs, and maximize profitability**.

**Example:** A retail company noticing a **decline in sales over consecutive quarters** may use accounting data to investigate whether the issue is **seasonal, pricing-related, or due to changing customer preferences**. Without proper accounting, they would be **guessing instead of acting strategically**.

## Facilitating Smart Decision-Making: Data-Driven Growth Strategies

Successful businesses do not operate based on **gut feelings**—they rely on **financial data** to make well-informed choices. Every major business decision, from **pricing strategies and market expansion to hiring new employees or cutting costs**, requires accurate financial insights.

**Accounting helps answer key business questions:**

- Can we afford to launch a new product?
- Is it time to expand to a new market?
- Should we invest in technology upgrades to improve efficiency?
- How do we reduce costs without sacrificing quality?

**Example:** A manufacturing company analyzing its **cost of goods sold (COGS)** may decide to **switch suppliers** to improve profit margins, while a tech startup may **invest in automation** after reviewing labor cost trends.

Without reliable accounting, businesses **risk making uninformed decisions that could hurt profitability** and **lead to wasted investments or missed opportunities**.

## Ensuring Legal & Tax Compliance: Protecting Your Business from Costly Mistakes

Tax laws, financial regulations, and compliance requirements can **make or break** a business. Governments and tax authorities require businesses to **maintain accurate financial records**, ensuring that companies **pay the correct taxes, report financial activities honestly, and comply with legal standards**.

**Accounting Helps Businesses Avoid:** Tax penalties and fines from incorrect filings. Audits and investigations from tax authorities. Legal risks associated with financial misreporting.

**Example:** A small business that **fails to properly track deductible expenses** may **overpay taxes**, reducing cash reserves. Conversely, a company that **underreports income** may face **severe penalties and audits**.

Maintaining **accurate financial records is not optional—it is essential** for protecting a business from regulatory risks and ensuring long-term stability.

## Attracting Investors & Securing Loans: The Power of Financial Credibility

Investors and lenders **do not invest in uncertainty**. They want to see **solid financial records that demonstrate stability, profitability, and potential for growth**.

**A business with strong accounting practices can:**

- Secure loans with **favorable interest rates** and repayment terms.

- Attract investors who seek **well-managed companies** with sustainable financial strategies.
- Build credibility with banks and financial institutions for **future funding opportunities**.

**Example:** A start up seeking venture capital funding **must present clear financial statements** showing **growth potential, revenue streams, and profitability trends**. Without accurate financial records, investors will **see the business as high-risk** and look elsewhere.

In contrast, companies with **strong financial transparency gain investor trust** and have better access to capital for expansion.

## Identifying Financial Risks & Opportunities: Gaining a Competitive Edge

Financial accounting is not just about **tracking numbers**—it is about **identifying opportunities and avoiding financial pitfalls**. A well-maintained financial system reveals: Areas of excessive spending that need cost-cutting measures. Cash flow issues that require immediate attention to avoid liquidity crises. Profitable market trends and customer spending habits.

**Example:** An e-commerce business that **analyzes seasonal sales trends** can **optimize inventory purchases**, reducing excess stock while ensuring they meet demand.

A company noticing **high customer acquisition costs** may **adjust marketing strategies** to improve return on investment.

**Accounting transforms financial data into a powerful decision-**

**making tool, allowing businesses to operate with precision, agility, and foresight.**

## Understanding the Three Core Financial Statements

Financial accounting revolves around three primary financial statements, each serving a distinct purpose:

### The Balance Sheet

**Purpose:** Provides a comprehensive snapshot of a company's financial position at a specific moment in time, detailing what the company owns, owes, and the owner's stake.

**Key Components:**

- **Assets**: Represent the economic resources controlled by the company that are expected to provide future benefits. This includes cash, inventory, property, equipment, patents, and other tangible or intangible assets.
- **Liabilities**: The financial obligations a company has towards creditors and suppliers. These include short-term debts like accounts payable and accrued expenses, as well as long-term obligations such as loans and bonds payable.
- **Equity**: Represents the residual interest in the company's assets after deducting liabilities. It includes common stock, retained earnings, and additional paid-in capital.

**Significance:**

- Helps stakeholders assess the company's liquidity, solvency, and overall financial stability.
- Enables comparison of financial position over different periods, facilitating trend analysis and strategic decision-making.

**Example:** If a business has total assets worth $100,000 and liabilities of $40,000, its total equity stands at $60,000 (Assets - Liabilities = Equity). This means the owners have a stake worth $60,000 in the business.

## The Income Statement (Profit & Loss Statement)

**Purpose:** Provides an in-depth analysis of a company's profitability over a defined period (monthly, quarterly, annually) by detailing revenue streams, operating costs, and net earnings. It is a critical tool for assessing financial performance and sustainability.

**Key Components:**

- **Revenue**: Represents the total earnings from core business activities before expenses are deducted. Revenue can be categorized into operating and non-operating income, with operating income stemming from the company's primary business functions.
- **Expenses**: The costs incurred in maintaining business operations, such as wages, rent, utilities, advertising, raw materials, and other overhead costs. Expenses are further divided into fixed and variable costs, affecting business profitability in different ways.
- **Gross Profit**: Calculated as Revenue minus Cost of Goods Sold (COGS). This figure provides insight into a company's ability to

generate profit before operational expenses are deducted.

- **Operating Profit (EBIT - Earnings Before Interest & Taxes)**: This is derived from gross profit after subtracting operating expenses. It indicates the company's efficiency in managing day-to-day expenses.
- **Net Profit/Loss**: The final earnings after deducting all expenses, taxes, interest payments, and depreciation. A positive net profit indicates financial health, while a net loss signals challenges that may require corrective action.

**Significance:**

- Determines a company's profitability and helps in making pricing and cost-reduction decisions.
- Essential for investors and stakeholders to assess financial performance and future growth potential.

**Example:** If a company earns $50,000 in revenue, incurs $10,000 in COGS, and has $20,000 in additional expenses, its net profit is $20,000.

## The Cash Flow Statement

**Purpose:** Tracks the movement of cash in and out of the business, ensuring that it maintains sufficient liquidity to meet financial obligations and operate effectively.

**Key Components:**

- **Operating Activities**: Cash flows related to the primary business operations, including revenue from sales, payments for supplies, employee salaries, and operating expenses.

- **Investing Activities**: Cash flows from acquiring or selling long-term assets, such as purchasing machinery, acquiring real estate, or selling investments.
- **Financing Activities**: Cash flows related to funding the business through debt, equity, or dividend payments, such as issuing shares, repaying loans, or distributing dividends to shareholders.

**Significance:**

- Helps businesses assess their ability to generate cash to sustain operations and manage debt.
- Highlights discrepancies between reported profits and actual cash availability.
- Assists in planning for future investments and business expansion.

**Example:** A business might report a net profit of $30,000 but still experience cash flow problems due to high accounts receivable, which delays cash inflow.

Understanding these three financial statements is crucial for business success. Together, they provide a complete picture of a company's financial health, helping stakeholders make well-informed decisions.

## Real-World Case Study: How Accounting Transformed a Struggling Business

**Background:** Lisa owned a popular small café that struggled financially. Despite having a steady stream of customers, she barely made a profit and often ran out of cash to cover expenses.

**The Problem:** Lisa wasn't tracking her financials properly. She didn't maintain a structured income statement, and her cash flow statement was non existent. She focused only on sales without considering expenses, debt obligations, and profit margins.

**The Solution:** Lisa hired an accountant who implemented proper financial tracking:

- Created an income statement to understand revenue and expenses.
- Developed a cash flow statement to monitor incoming and outgoing cash.
- Identified that rising supplier costs and high rent were reducing profits.
- Adjusted pricing and renegotiated supplier contracts.

**The Outcome:** Within six months, Lisa's café became profitable. She reduced unnecessary expenses, improved cash flow, and used financial data to make smarter decisions, such as introducing a high-margin product line. Proper accounting transformed her struggling business into a thriving one.

## Self-Assessment Quiz

1. What is the primary purpose of financial accounting? **Answer:** To track, summarise, and report financial transactions to provide insights into a company's financial health.
2. Which of the following financial statements shows a company's financial position at a specific point in time? **Answer:** The Balance

Sheet.

3. True or False: The income statement measures a company's financial position on a single day. **Answer:** False. The income statement measures financial performance over a specific period.
4. What are the three main sections of a cash flow statement? **Answer:** Operating Activities, Investing Activities, and Financing Activities.
5. Scenario: A company's income statement shows high profits, but the cash flow statement indicates negative cash flow. What could be the issue? **Answer:** The company might have significant outstanding accounts receivable, high inventory costs, or large capital expenditures impacting cash flow.

# THE ACCOUNTING EQUATION & DOUBLE-ENTRY SYSTEM

## The Fundamental Accounting Equation: Assets = Liabilities + Equity

The financial accounting equation, a fundamental concept in business, offers a structured approach to comprehending a company's financial status. It demonstrates how a business finances its operations through debt (liabilities) and owner's capital (equity), and how these resources are utilized to acquire assets that contribute to the company's growth and sustainability.

Understanding the financial accounting equation is crucial for business management, as it forms the basis of financial statements and accounting records. The dynamic nature of the equation means that every economic transaction affects at least two accounts, ensuring the financial records of the company remain in balance. This guarantees that the company's books accurately reflect its financial standing at any given time.

Furthermore, the equation clearly shows how well a business is leveraging its resources. A higher proportion of equity-financed assets indicates a strong financial position, whereas a high reliance on liabilities may signal potential financial risk. By analysing this balance, business owners, investors, and creditors can make informed decisions regarding growth strategies, investment opportunities, and economic stability.

For instance, if a business reports **$500,000 in assets**, **$200,000 in liabilities**, and **$300,000 in equity**, the equation would be: Assets ($ 500,000) = Liabilities ($ 200,000) + Equity ($ 300,000).

This equation is a powerful tool for understanding a company's financial health and making informed decisions. This breakdown, facilitated by the accounting equation, helps stakeholders assess whether the company is financially healthy, solvent, and prepared for future challenges. By mastering the accounting equation, businesses can maintain financial clarity, ensure compliance with accounting standards, and lay a solid foundation for long-term success, providing a sense of reassurance and security.

Understanding this equation is crucial because it balances a company's financial statements. Every transaction within a business impacts at least two accounts, maintaining this equilibrium.

### Breaking Down the Accounting Equation

6. **Assets** – These are resources controlled by a business that provide future economic benefits. Assets include cash, inventory, accounts receivable, equipment, land, and intellectual property.
7. **Liabilities** – These are obligations a business owes to external parties. Common liabilities include loans, accounts payable, wages payable, and taxes owed.
8. **Equity** – Also known as net worth, equity represents the owner's interest in the business after all liabilities are deducted from assets. This includes common stock, retained earnings, and additional paid-in capital.

For example, if a business has **$100,000 in assets**, **$40,000 in liabilities**, and **$60,000 in equity**, the accounting equation remains balanced:

This equation is the guiding principle of financial accounting, ensuring that every transaction keeps financial records in check.

## Introduction to the Double-Entry Accounting System

The **double-entry accounting system** is the foundation of modern accounting, playing a critical role in ensuring financial integrity, transparency, and accuracy. This system operates on a simple yet powerful principle: every financial transaction affects at least **two accounts** in opposite ways, reinforcing the equilibrium of financial statements. It is the mechanism that keeps the books balanced and allows businesses to maintain an organized, error-free accounting record.

One of the primary advantages of the double-entry system is its ability to prevent and detect errors. Since every transaction requires a corresponding debit and credit entry, discrepancies in financial records become immediately evident. This system reduces the likelihood of misstatements, fraud, and financial manipulation, making it an indispensable tool for accountants, business owners, and financial analysts alike.

The **historical roots** of double-entry accounting date back to the Renaissance period, where Italian mathematician Luca Pacioli formalized its principles in his 1494 work *Summa de Arithmetica*. Since then, this system has become the global standard for financial reporting, forming the basis for financial statements used by corporations, investors, regulators, and financial institutions.

For modern businesses, the double-entry system is essential for generating accurate financial reports, securing loans, attracting investors, and making strategic financial decisions. It provides a complete and accurate picture of an organization's financial health, ensuring compliance with accounting standards such as Generally Accepted Accounting Principles (GAAP) and International Financial Reporting Standards (IFRS).

To illustrate, consider a scenario where a business purchases office equipment for **$5,000 on credit**. This transaction involves both an **increase in assets (debit to Equipment account)** and an **increase in liabilities (credit to Accounts Payable)**. Thus, the balance sheet remains intact, reinforcing the accounting equation:

Mastering the double-entry accounting system enables businesses to develop a robust financial framework, ensuring that every transaction is systematically recorded, categorized, and analyzed. Without it, financial reporting would lack credibility, making it difficult to measure profitability, assess financial health, or meet regulatory requirements. The ability to implement and interpret double-entry accounting effectively is not just a skill—it is a crucial asset in the world of business and finance.

### The Core Principle of Double-Entry Accounting

9. Every financial transaction affects at least **two** accounts.
10. The sum of debits must always **equal** the sum of credits.
11. Transactions must keep the **accounting equation in balance**.

This system provides businesses with a structured way to track their financial activities, making it easier to detect errors and maintain accountability.

For example, if a business **purchases office equipment for $5,000 on credit**, it records:

- A **debit** (increase) of $5,000 to the Equipment account (asset).
- A **credit** (increase) of $5,000 to Accounts Payable (liability).

The total assets increase by $5,000, but the liability also increases, keeping the accounting equation balanced.

## Debit vs. Credit: How Transactions Are Recorded

In double-entry accounting, transactions are meticulously recorded using debits and credits, forming the backbone of an accurate and balanced financial system. Unlike common misconceptions, these terms do not inherently mean "increase" or "decrease" but instead vary in effect depending on the type of account involved. Understanding the application of debits and credits is crucial for maintaining accurate financial records, preventing errors, and ensuring compliance with accounting principles. This method provides transparency, enhances financial control, and allows for precise tracking of business performance. By mastering the distinction and interplay between debits and credits, businesses can build a strong financial foundation, enabling better decision-making, financial stability, and strategic growth.

## Rules of Debits and Credits

- **Assets (Cash, Inventory, Equipment, etc.)**
- **Debit** increases assets
- **Credit** decreases assets
- **Liabilities (Loans, Accounts Payable, etc.)**
- **Debit** decreases liabilities
- **Credit** increases liabilities
- **Equity (Common Stock, Retained Earnings, etc.)**
- **Debit** decreases equity
- **Credit** increases equity
- **Revenue (Sales, Service Income, etc.)**

- **Debit** decreases revenue
- **Credit** increases revenue
- **Expenses (Salaries, Rent, Utilities, etc.)**
- **Debit** increases expenses
- **Credit** decreases expenses

### Example Transaction: Paying Rent

If a company pays **$2,000 in rent**, the journal entry would be:

- **Debit** Rent Expense $2,000 (Expense increases)
- **Credit** Cash $2,000 (Asset decreases)

This method ensures that financial records are accurate and aligned with the fundamental accounting equation.

## Real-World Case Study: A Small Business Owner's First Accounting Mistakes

### Background

Sophia, a small business owner, started an online boutique. While she was passionate about her products, she struggled to manage her financial records. She kept track of sales and expenses informally without using a structured accounting system.

### The Mistakes

12. **Failure to Use Double-Entry Accounting** – Sophia recorded only

cash inflows and ignored the corresponding expenses, leading to an inaccurate view of profitability.

13. **Misclassification of Transactions** – She recorded loan proceeds as revenue, inflating her income.
14. **Ignoring Liabilities** – She didn't track accounts payable, resulting in late fees and damaged relationships with suppliers.

### The Solution

After consulting with an accountant, Sophia implemented the double-entry accounting system. She:

- Used accounting software to track income and expenses correctly.
- Separated business and personal expenses.
- Maintained accurate records of accounts payable and receivable.

### Outcome

Within six months, Sophia's business finances were more structured, and she could make informed decisions based on real financial data. Her improved record-keeping also helped her secure a small business loan.

This case highlights the importance of using an accurate accounting system to prevent costly mistakes.

## Practical Exercise: Recording Transactions in T-Accounts

T-accounts serve as an essential visual aid in accounting, illustrating the movement of financial transactions within a business. Each T-account represents an individual ledger account, with **debits recorded on the left** and **credits on the right**, ensuring that every financial event is accurately documented. This structured approach not only simplifies complex financial data but also enhances error detection, making it easier to identify discrepancies in transaction records. By mastering T-accounts, businesses can develop a deeper understanding of the double-entry system, reinforce fundamental accounting principles, and cultivate a meticulous approach to financial management. This exercise will provide hands-on experience in organizing and analyzing transactions, laying the groundwork for precise and reliable financial reporting.

## Exercise:

Record the following transactions using T-accounts:

15. The business receives **$10,000 cash** from an investor.
16. The company **purchases $3,000 in inventory** on credit.
17. The business **makes a sale of $5,000**, receiving cash immediately.
18. The company **pays $1,500 for utilities**.

**Solution Guide:**

- Transaction 1: Debit Cash $10,000 | Credit Equity $10,000
- Transaction 2: Debit Inventory $3,000 | Credit Accounts Payable $3,000
- Transaction 3: Debit Cash $5,000 | Credit Revenue $5,000
- Transaction 4: Debit Utilities Expense $1,500 | Credit Cash $1,500

By practicing T-accounts, businesses can ensure they properly track their financial transactions and maintain an accurate balance sheet.

## Conclusion

Mastering the **accounting equation** and **double-entry system** is fundamental to understanding financial accounting. These principles form the backbone of financial reporting, ensuring businesses maintain accurate records, avoid costly errors, and make data-driven decisions. Without a strong grasp of these foundational concepts, businesses may struggle with inaccurate financial records, leading to misinformed decisions and potential financial instability.

The accounting equation acts as a financial compass, guiding businesses in structuring their financial statements and ensuring every transaction is accounted for correctly. It enforces the necessity of balancing assets, liabilities, and equity, which in turn aids in assessing financial health and solvency. Additionally, the double-entry system acts as an internal control mechanism, reducing the risk of errors and fraud while enhancing transparency in financial operations.

By adhering to these accounting principles, businesses can confidently prepare for audits, secure loans, attract investors, and maintain regulatory compliance. Moreover, understanding these concepts allows business owners to analyze financial trends, evaluate profitability, and make strategic growth decisions. The ability to interpret financial data with clarity empowers businesses to operate with financial confidence and sustainability.

In the next chapter, we will explore **financial statements** in greater detail, breaking down the balance sheet, income statement, and cash flow statement with real-world applications, reinforcing how these reports are directly linked to the accounting equation and double-entry system.

# FINANCIAL STATEMENTS EXPLAINED

## Understanding Financial Statements

Financial statements are essential tools that provide a comprehensive view of a company's financial well-being, serving as the foundation for informed decision-making and long-term strategic planning. These reports function as both a diagnostic tool and a roadmap, offering businesses a structured and standardized method to evaluate past performance, monitor current financial standing, and project future stability. They facilitate transparency and accountability, ensuring that stakeholders—from executives and investors to creditors and regulatory bodies—have access to accurate financial information that drives confidence and credibility.

Without financial statements, businesses would struggle to measure profitability, assess risk exposure, manage operational efficiency, and secure funding for expansion. These reports not only highlight a company's strengths and weaknesses but also provide key insights into liquidity, debt management, and revenue generation trends. Furthermore, financial statements serve as an early warning system, enabling businesses to identify financial distress signals before they escalate into major issues, thus allowing for timely corrective actions.

Beyond internal use, financial statements play a crucial role in external engagements. Investors analyze these reports to determine a company's growth potential and investment viability, while lenders and creditors rely on them to assess the organization's ability to meet financial obligations. Regulators, too, scrutinize these documents to ensure compliance with financial reporting standards and tax obligations.

The ability to interpret financial statements accurately empowers business owners and decision-makers to optimize resource allocation, streamline operations, and implement strategies for sustainable profitability. By mastering financial reporting and analysis, businesses can navigate economic uncertainties, capitalize on growth opportunities, and strengthen their market position in an increasingly competitive landscape.

The three primary financial statements—**Balance Sheet, Income Statement, and Cash Flow Statement**—each play a unique role in portraying a company's financial activities. Together, they form a comprehensive financial framework that business owners, investors, and creditors rely on to assess risk, profitability, and sustainability. The **Balance Sheet** provides a snapshot of a company's financial position at a specific point in time, detailing its assets, liabilities, and equity. The **Income Statement** tracks revenue, expenses, and profitability over a defined period, offering a dynamic view of financial performance. The **Cash Flow Statement**, often overlooked but equally crucial, reconciles net income with actual cash movement, ensuring businesses have the liquidity needed to sustain operations and growth.

## Historical Evolution of Financial Statements

Financial statements have undergone significant evolution, shaped by economic developments, regulatory changes, and technological advancements. The origins of financial reporting can be traced back to **Luca Pacioli**, the father of accounting, who introduced the double-entry bookkeeping system in **1494**. His method laid the foundation for modern financial record-keeping, enabling businesses to track assets, liabilities, and revenues systematically.

As trade expanded during the Industrial Revolution, financial statements became more standardized to facilitate investment decisions and corporate accountability. In the early **20th century**, regulatory frameworks such as **the U.S. Securities Act of 1933** and **the Securities Exchange Act of 1934** established mandatory financial reporting requirements for publicly traded companies, aiming to protect investors and promote market transparency.

The development of **Generally Accepted Accounting Principles**

**(GAAP)** and **International Financial Reporting Standards (IFRS)** further enhanced financial statement consistency across industries and countries. With the rise of digital finance and automation, businesses now generate real-time financial reports, integrating **artificial intelligence (AI) and big data analytics** into financial analysis to improve accuracy and forecasting capabilities.

## Ethical Considerations & Famous Financial Fraud Cases

The accuracy and integrity of financial statements are paramount, yet history has witnessed numerous **financial scandals** where unethical accounting practices led to catastrophic consequences. Some of the most infamous cases include:

- **Enron Scandal (2001):** Enron's executives engaged in accounting fraud by manipulating financial statements to hide debt and inflate earnings. The scandal resulted in **billions in investor losses** and led to the creation of the **Sarbanes-Oxley Act (SOX)**, which strengthened corporate governance and financial reporting regulations.
- **WorldCom Fraud (2002):** Executives at WorldCom overstated profits by **$3.8 billion** through improper accounting entries. The exposure of this fraud resulted in bankruptcy and stricter financial auditing requirements.
- **Lehman Brothers Collapse (2008):** The investment bank used **off-balance-sheet transactions** to obscure financial risks, contributing to the **global financial crisis**.

These cases underscore the importance of **financial ethics, transparency, and rigorous auditing** to prevent fraudulent activities and ensure corporate accountability.

## The Three Core Financial Statements and Their Interconnection

Each of the three primary financial statements—the **Balance Sheet, Income Statement, and Cash Flow Statement**—plays a unique role in providing a full picture of a company's financial health. Below is a breakdown of their function and how they interconnect:

### *1. Balance Sheet: Understanding Assets, Liabilities, and Equity*

The **Balance Sheet** provides a snapshot of a company's financial position at a specific moment in time, outlining its assets, liabilities, and shareholder equity. This statement adheres to the fundamental accounting equation:

- **Assets:** Resources owned by the company, including cash, accounts receivable, inventory, and fixed assets (e.g., equipment and real estate).
- **Liabilities:** Obligations the company owes, such as loans, accounts payable, and outstanding expenses.
- **Equity:** The residual value of assets after deducting liabilities, representing ownership interest in the business.

The Balance Sheet helps stakeholders assess liquidity, financial stability, and capital structure. **For example, a tech startup** may have high intangible assets (like patents), while a manufacturing company might have significant fixed assets (like machinery and warehouses).

### *2. Income Statement: Revenue, Expenses, and Profitability*

The **Income Statement**, also known as the Profit & Loss (P&L) Statement, details a company's revenues and expenses over a specific period, ultimately determining profitability.

Key components include:

- **Revenue:** Total income generated from sales or services.
- **Cost of Goods Sold (COGS):** Direct expenses incurred in producing goods or services.
- **Gross Profit:** Revenue minus COGS.
- **Operating Expenses:** Costs related to day-to-day operations (e.g., salaries, rent, utilities).
- **Net Income:** The final profit after all expenses and taxes have been deducted.

A business's profitability trends are crucial for investors, who examine revenue growth, operating margins, and net profit margins to determine long-term potential.

### *3. Cash Flow Statement: Operating, Investing, and Financing Activities*

Unlike the Balance Sheet and Income Statement, which use accrual accounting, the **Cash Flow Statement** tracks actual cash movement within the business.

It is divided into three sections:

- **Operating Activities:** Cash flow from core business operations, including sales revenue and supplier payments.

- **Investing Activities:** Cash used in purchasing assets (e.g., property, equipment) or proceeds from asset sales.
- **Financing Activities:** Cash transactions related to debt and equity, such as issuing shares, repaying loans, or paying dividends.

Companies can be profitable on paper but still face liquidity issues if cash inflows do not align with outflows, making this statement vital for financial stability analysis.

## How These Statements Interconnect

Financial statements are not isolated reports; they influence one another:

19. **Net income from the Income Statement** flows into the **equity section of the Balance Sheet** under retained earnings.
20. **Changes in working capital on the Balance Sheet** affect the **Operating Activities section of the Cash Flow Statement.**
21. **Investing and financing activities on the Cash Flow Statement** impact long-term asset and liability accounts on the Balance Sheet.

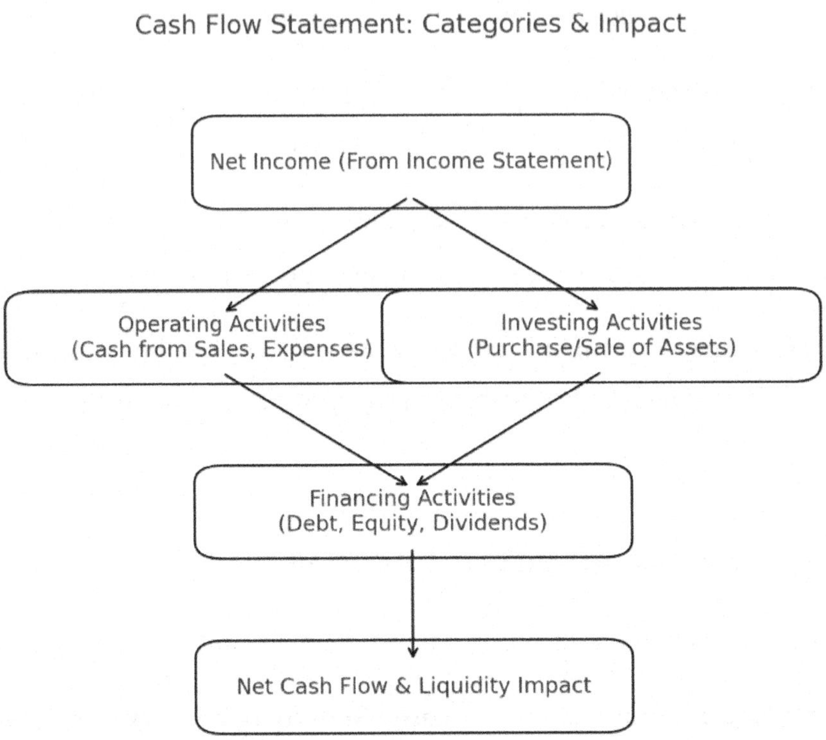


By understanding these connections, businesses can make informed financial decisions that align with their strategic goals.

## Practical Exercise: Analyzing a Sample Set of Financial Statements

### Scenario: Assessing the Financial Health of ABC Retail Ltd.

ABC Retail Ltd. has provided the following financial statements:

***Balance Sheet Snapshot***

***(Year-End)***

- **Assets:** $500,000
- **Liabilities:** $300,000
- **Equity:** $200,000

*Income Statement*

*(Annual)*

- **Revenue:** $1,200,000
- **COGS:** $600,000
- **Operating Expenses:** $300,000
- **Net Income:** $200,000

*Cash Flow Statement*

- **Operating Cash Flow:** $180,000
- **Investing Cash Flow:** -$50,000 (purchase of equipment)
- **Financing Cash Flow:** -$30,000 (loan repayment)

## Questions for Analysis:

22. **Liquidity Check:** Calculate the company's current ratio and quick ratio. Is the company financially stable?
23. **Profitability Assessment:** Determine the gross profit margin and net profit margin.
24. **Cash Flow Analysis:** What does the cash flow statement indicate about the company's liquidity and financial management?

25. **Growth Considerations:** If the company wants to expand, should it seek external financing or reinvest profits?

**Answer Guide:**

26. **Current Ratio = $500,000 ÷ $300,000 = 1.67** → Healthy liquidity.
27. **Gross Profit Margin = ($1,200,000 - $600,000) ÷ $1,200,000 = 50%** → Strong efficiency in production.
28. **Net Profit Margin = $200,000 ÷ $1,200,000 = 16.7%** → Profitable but may need cost controls.
29. **Cash Flow:** Despite profitability, negative investing and financing cash flows suggest reinvestment into business growth.

## How Different Stakeholders Use Financial Statements

Financial statements cater to a diverse set of stakeholders, each with unique objectives:

- **Investors:** Assess profitability, risk, and growth potential before making investment decisions.
- **Lenders & Creditors:** Evaluate a company's ability to repay loans and maintain liquidity.
- **Government & Regulators:** Ensure compliance with tax laws and financial reporting standards.
- **Executives & Managers:** Use financial data for strategic planning, budgeting, and resource allocation.

- **Employees:** Gauge job security and potential for salary increments based on company performance.

For instance, an **investor** analyzing a company's **profit margins and earnings trends** may have different concerns compared to a **bank** assessing its **liquidity ratios** before approving a loan. Understanding these perspectives enhances decision-making efficiency for all parties involved.

## Impact of Economic Conditions on Financial Statements

External economic conditions have a profound influence on financial statements. Key factors include:

- **Recession & Economic Downturns:** Reduced consumer spending leads to lower revenues, increased debt burdens, and declining asset valuations.
- **Inflation:** Rising costs impact profit margins, requiring businesses to adjust pricing strategies.
- **Interest Rate Fluctuations:** Affect borrowing costs, influencing capital investment and leverage decisions.

For example, during the **COVID-19 pandemic**, many companies reported massive losses due to supply chain disruptions and decreased consumer demand, reflecting how macroeconomic conditions shape financial reporting outcomes.

## Technology & Automation in Financial Analysis

Advancements in technology have **transformed financial analysis**, improving accuracy, efficiency, and decision-making capabilities. Key developments include:

- **AI-Driven Analytics:** Automates financial data processing, fraud detection, and predictive forecasting.
- **Cloud Accounting Software:** Enables real-time access to financial data, improving collaboration and transparency.
- **Blockchain & Smart Contracts:** Enhance the security and reliability of financial transactions.

Companies leveraging **AI-powered financial tools** can detect trends, optimize resource allocation, and mitigate financial risks more effectively than traditional manual methods.

## Common Pitfalls in Financial Statement Analysis

Even experienced analysts can misinterpret financial data. Common mistakes include:

- **Over-Reliance on a Single Ratio:** No single metric provides a complete financial picture.
- **Ignoring External Factors:** Economic trends and industry shifts impact financial results.
- **Misinterpreting Non-Recurring Items:** One-time gains or losses can distort profitability analysis.

- **Failing to Adjust for Inflation:** Can lead to inaccurate long-term trend analysis.

For example, a company with a **high profit margin** but negative cash flow may still struggle to meet obligations, highlighting the need for **comprehensive analysis**.

## Industry-Specific Financial Statements

While financial statements follow standardized principles, their structure, presentation, and key focus areas can vary significantly by industry. These differences stem from the unique operational models, revenue streams, regulatory environments, and financial priorities of each sector. Understanding these industry-specific variations is essential for accurate financial analysis, effective benchmarking, and strategic decision-making.

Industry-specific financial statements allow businesses to tailor their financial reporting to highlight critical success factors, such as inventory management in retail, capital expenditures in manufacturing, or loan portfolios in banking. Analysts, investors, and business owners use these tailored financial statements to compare businesses within the same industry, assess profitability, efficiency, and risk exposure, and identify growth opportunities.

Additionally, sector-specific regulations and accounting standards influence financial reporting practices. For example, publicly traded healthcare companies must comply with stringent financial disclosure requirements, while technology firms must account for deferred revenue from subscription-based services. Without a clear understanding of these variations, businesses risk misinterpreting financial data, making inaccurate comparisons, and missing out on industry-specific financial insights.

By recognizing these industry-driven distinctions, businesses and investors can perform more meaningful financial analysis, set realistic performance benchmarks, and make informed strategic decisions. Whether evaluating investment opportunities, assessing competitors, or optimizing business operations, industry-specific financial statement analysis is a crucial tool for financial success.

## 1. Retail Industry

Retail businesses rely heavily on inventory management, sales turnover, and consumer demand patterns. Their financial statements emphasize:

- **Inventory Turnover Ratio:** Measures how efficiently inventory is sold and replenished.
- **Gross Profit Margin:** Key for assessing pricing strategies and cost control.
- **Cash Flow Statement:** Focuses on daily liquidity and seasonality trends, given the cyclical nature of consumer spending.

**Example:** A retail company might experience significant cash flow variations during holiday seasons, requiring careful financial planning.

## 2. Manufacturing Industry

Manufacturers have complex financial statements due to high capital expenditures and inventory valuation challenges. Key financial aspects include:

- **Cost of Goods Sold (COGS):** A major factor in determining profitability.

- **Work-in-Progress Inventory:** Tracks partially completed goods in production.
- **Fixed Asset Turnover:** Evaluates the efficiency of machinery and equipment utilization.

**Example:** A car manufacturer needs to manage raw materials, labor, and production costs efficiently to maintain profit margins.

## 3. Technology Industry

Tech companies, especially start ups, operate in a highly dynamic and innovation-driven environment where traditional financial reporting metrics may not fully capture their value. These businesses rely heavily on intangible assets, such as intellectual property, patents, software, and brand value, which play a crucial role in their financial health. Unlike asset-intensive industries, technology firms often emphasize research and development (R&D) as a core driver of future growth, making it a significant component of their financial statements. Additionally, many tech firms maintain high operating margins, particularly those in the software and subscription-based service sectors, where scalability allows revenue to grow without a proportional increase in expenses.

Their financial statements highlight:

- **R&D Expenses:** A significant portion of costs, crucial for innovation-driven businesses.
- **Deferred Revenue:** Arises from subscription-based business models.

- **Stock-Based Compensation:** A common practice that affects equity and profitability.

**Example:** A SaaS (Software-as-a-Service) company recognizes revenue over time rather than upfront due to subscription billing.

## 4. Real Estate Industry

Real estate firms rely on long-term investments, fluctuating property values, and strategic financial planning to maintain profitability. Their financial statements emphasize key metrics that measure asset appreciation, rental income stability, debt management, and overall financial sustainability. Given the cyclical nature of the real estate market, financial reporting must account for property depreciation, market-driven valuation changes, and leverage levels. Investors and lenders closely examine these financial statements to assess the firm's liquidity, revenue-generating capabilities, and long-term asset growth potential. Additionally, financial statements in real estate often reflect financing structures, including mortgage obligations, lease agreements, and tax implications related to property ownership. Understanding these elements is crucial for evaluating the financial health of real estate enterprises and ensuring sustainable growth.

- **Property Valuation and Depreciation:** Reflects real estate appreciation or loss over time.
- **Debt-to-Equity Ratio:** Since real estate investments involve significant financing.
- **Rental Income vs. Operating Expenses:** Essential for evaluating cash flow sustainability.

**Example:** A commercial real estate company must manage leasing revenue while accounting for property maintenance costs.

## 5. Healthcare Industry

Healthcare businesses, including hospitals, pharmaceutical firms, and private clinics, operate within a highly regulated and complex financial framework. Their financial structures are influenced by insurance reimbursements, government funding, stringent compliance requirements, and significant investments in medical technology and research. Revenue generation in healthcare is unique, as it often involves a mix of direct patient payments, third-party insurance reimbursements, and government programs such as Medicare and Medicaid. Additionally, healthcare organizations must account for high operational costs, including medical staff salaries, facility maintenance, and ongoing research and development expenses. Effective financial management in this industry requires balancing patient care quality with financial sustainability while navigating regulatory challenges and fluctuating reimbursement policies.

- **Accounts Receivable from Insurers:** Payment delays are common in healthcare.
- **Regulatory Compliance Costs:** Significant expenses tied to maintaining industry standards.
- **Operating Margins:** Highly dependent on government policies and insurance agreements.

**Example:** A hospital's revenue cycle management is complex due to varying payment timelines from insurance providers and government agencies.

## 6. Financial Services Industry

Banks, insurance companies, and investment firms have unique financial reporting requirements due to their distinct operational structures, regulatory oversight, and risk exposure. Unlike traditional businesses, these financial institutions generate revenue primarily through interest, investment returns, and risk management services rather than conventional product sales. Consequently, their financial statements emphasize liquidity management, asset quality, capital adequacy, and risk exposure. Regulatory compliance is a significant aspect of their financial reporting, as institutions must adhere to frameworks such as Basel III for banking, Solvency II for insurance, and SEC regulations for investment firms. Given the complexity of their financial instruments, these entities rely on specialized reporting metrics such as loan loss provisions, investment revaluation, and actuarial assumptions to assess financial stability and profitability. Understanding these elements is essential for evaluating the financial health and risk profile of firms in the financial services industry.

- **Loan Loss Provisions:** Essential for assessing credit risk in banks.
- **Liquidity Ratios:** Banks require high liquidity to meet customer withdrawals.
- **Investment Income and Risk Exposure:** Critical for wealth management and insurance companies.

**Example:** A bank's balance sheet differs from other industries due to its large proportion of loan assets and deposit liabilities.

Understanding industry-specific financial statements ensures accurate interpretation and better financial decision-making.

## Advanced Financial Ratio Analysis

Advanced financial ratio analysis is essential for evaluating business performance, identifying risks, and making data-driven decisions. Companies that actively monitor their financial ratios can optimize efficiency, improve profitability, and enhance stakeholder confidence. Beyond short-term financial health, understanding financial ratios enables businesses to anticipate potential financial challenges and implement corrective measures proactively.

Investors and analysts use financial ratios to compare businesses within the same industry, assess creditworthiness, and predict future growth. A company with strong profitability and liquidity ratios is more likely to attract investors, secure loans, and sustain long-term growth. Meanwhile, creditors use leverage and coverage ratios to determine a business's ability to meet its debt obligations and manage financial risk effectively.

Similarly, business owners rely on these metrics to fine-tune operations, manage costs, and strategize for expansion. A company with a declining net profit margin may re-evaluate pricing strategies, reduce unnecessary expenses, or renegotiate supplier contracts to maintain profitability. Financial ratios serve as a powerful diagnostic tool, allowing decision-makers to pinpoint inefficiencies, uncover growth opportunities, and strengthen financial resilience.

Furthermore, financial ratios are integral in strategic planning. They provide valuable insights that influence capital investment decisions, product development initiatives, and market expansion strategies. Businesses that leverage financial ratio analysis to align financial goals with operational performance gain a competitive edge in rapidly evolving markets.

As financial landscapes continue to evolve with advancements in technology, artificial intelligence, and automated financial reporting, businesses must stay ahead by integrating financial ratio analysis into their strategic frameworks. Companies that embrace data-driven decision-making will be better positioned to navigate economic uncertainties, improve operational efficiency, and drive sustainable growth.

## 1. Liquidity Ratios

Liquidity ratios assess a company's ability to meet its short-term obligations. A business with strong liquidity has sufficient assets to cover its liabilities without risking insolvency.

- **Current Ratio:**
- A current ratio above 1 indicates that a company has more current assets than liabilities, suggesting good liquidity.
- **Quick Ratio (Acid-Test Ratio):**
- This ratio removes inventory from current assets since inventory might not be immediately convertible into cash.

**Example:** A company with **$500,000 in current assets**, **$300,000 in current liabilities**, and **$200,000 in inventory** would have:

A quick ratio of 1.0 means the company has just enough liquid assets to cover short-term liabilities.

## 2. Profitability Ratios

Profitability ratios measure a company's ability to generate profit relative to revenue, assets, or equity.

- **Gross Profit Margin:**
- A higher margin indicates better efficiency in producing goods.
- **Net Profit Margin:**
- A high net profit margin indicates strong cost control and pricing strategies.

**Example:** A business generating **$1,000,000 in revenue** with a **$200,000 net profit** would have:

This means the company retains 20% of revenue as profit after all expenses.

## 3. Efficiency Ratios

Efficiency ratios assess how well a company utilizes its assets to generate revenue.

- **Asset Turnover Ratio:**
- A higher ratio suggests effective asset utilization.
- **Inventory Turnover Ratio:**
- A high turnover indicates strong sales and inventory management.

## 4. Leverage Ratios

Leverage ratios measure a company's financial risk by evaluating debt levels relative to assets and equity.

- **Debt-to-Equity Ratio:**
- A higher ratio suggests increased financial risk.

- **Interest Coverage Ratio:**
- This measures how easily a company can cover interest payments on its debt.

## Real-World Case Study: Financial Ratio Analysis

**Company A** and **Company B** operate in the same industry but differ in financial performance.

- **Company A:** Revenue: **$10M**, Net Profit: **$1.5M**, Total Assets: **$20M**, Debt: **$8M**, Equity: **$12M**
- **Company B:** Revenue: **$10M**, Net Profit: **$1M**, Total Assets: **$18M**, Debt: **$10M**, Equity: **$8M**

**Key Ratios:**

- **Net Profit Margin:** Company A **15%**, Company B **10%** → Company A is more profitable.
- **Debt-to-Equity Ratio:** Company A **0.67**, Company B **1.25** → Company B has a riskier debt structure.
- **Return on Assets:**
- Company A: **7.5%**, Company B: **5.5%** → Company A is utilizing assets more effectively.

This example highlights how financial ratios reveal critical insights into company health and risk levels.

## Conclusion: The Importance of Financial Statements in Business Success

Financial statements are the foundation of any successful business, providing a clear and accurate depiction of a company's financial health. They are not just regulatory requirements but essential tools for strategic decision-making, financial planning, and long-term sustainability. By understanding and utilizing the Balance Sheet, Income Statement, and Cash Flow Statement, businesses can effectively manage their resources, track performance, and plan for future growth.

Investors, creditors, and executives rely on financial statements to assess profitability, risk, and operational efficiency. A well-prepared financial statement ensures transparency, builds stakeholder confidence, and enhances the credibility of a company in competitive markets. Furthermore, these statements help businesses identify strengths, address weaknesses, and seize opportunities for expansion.

In an ever-evolving economic landscape, mastering financial statements empowers business owners and financial professionals to navigate challenges, optimize financial performance, and make informed decisions that drive success. Whether used for internal management, investment analysis, or regulatory compliance, financial statements remain one of the most powerful tools in business.

# INDUSTRY-SPECIFIC FINANCIAL ACCOUNTING: PRACTICAL APPLICATIONS FOR DIFFERENT SECTORS

Financial accounting principles apply to every industry, but the way they are implemented varies significantly depending on the sector. Each industry has unique financial structures, operational costs, and regulatory requirements that affect how businesses record revenue, manage expenses, and report financial health. Understanding industry-specific financial accounting applications is essential for businesses looking to optimize financial management, comply with regulatory frameworks, and make informed strategic decisions.

In the technology and start up sector, financial accounting plays a crucial role in managing venture capital funding, revenue recognition for subscription-based business models, and capitalizing research and development costs. Start ups that secure venture funding must properly account for equity investments, convertible notes, and stock-based compensation while ensuring that financial statements accurately reflect burn rates and runway projections. Many technology firms operate on a Software-as-a-Service (SaaS) model, where revenue recognition follows strict guidelines to align with subscription billing cycles, customer contracts, and deferred revenue liabilities. Additionally, companies engaged in research and development must navigate complex accounting rules related to capitalizing R&D costs versus expensing them immediately, which can have a significant impact on financial statements and investor perceptions.

E-commerce and retail businesses face unique accounting challenges related to inventory management, digital payments, and return policies. These businesses operate in a highly competitive landscape with frequent pricing fluctuations, high transaction volumes, and complex logistics. Accurate inventory accounting is critical for maintaining optimal stock levels, preventing losses from overstocking or stockouts, and ensuring the correct valuation of goods sold. Retailers must also manage digital payment processing fees and reconcile online transactions across multiple platforms, which can create discrepancies in revenue recognition and cash flow tracking. Additionally, return policies significantly impact financial statements, as businesses must account for potential refund liabilities and restocking costs while maintaining a customer-friendly return experience. Properly structured accounting processes ensure that these financial components do not distort profitability metrics or misrepresent the business's financial health.

The manufacturing and supply chain industry relies heavily on cost accounting, depreciation of machinery, and financial tracking of global trade operations. Since manufacturers invest in large-scale production equipment and raw materials, they must implement robust cost allocation methods to track direct and indirect costs associated with production. Depreciation of machinery is a key factor in financial reporting, as companies need to account for asset wear and tear while ensuring that production costs remain competitive. Additionally, supply chain financial management requires businesses to track currency fluctuations, import/export duties, and transportation costs, all of which can impact profit margins and cash flow. Global trade finance adds further complexity, as businesses must manage letters of credit, payment terms with international suppliers, and financial hedging strategies to mitigate foreign exchange risk.

In healthcare and pharmaceuticals, financial accounting is highly regulated due to strict compliance requirements and the complexity of insurance reimbursements. Healthcare providers must navigate financial reporting for patient billing, insurance claims, and government reimbursements, which require accurate revenue recognition and accounts receivable management. Pharmaceutical companies, on the other hand, operate in a capital-intensive industry where significant investments are made in drug development, clinical trials, and regulatory approvals before generating revenue. The proper capitalization of research and development costs can determine a company's financial stability and investor confidence. Additionally, pharmaceutical firms must manage financial risks associated with drug patent expirations, pricing regulations, and supply chain disruptions that can affect long-term profitability.

The real estate and hospitality industries require specialized financial accounting approaches to address property valuation, lease accounting, and the seasonality of revenue. Real estate businesses must determine the correct valuation of properties based on market conditions, rental income, and depreciation schedules. The adoption of lease accounting standards such as IFRS 16 and ASC 842 has changed how businesses recognize lease liabilities and right-of-use assets, affecting financial ratios and balance sheet presentations. In hospitality, seasonality plays a major role in revenue cycles, with peak and off-peak periods affecting financial planning. Hotels, resorts, and short-term rental businesses must implement revenue management strategies that account for fluctuations in occupancy rates, maintenance expenses, and booking platforms' commission fees. Managing cash flow during slow seasons is essential to maintaining financial stability and ensuring long-term business sustainability.

Industry-specific financial accounting applications provide businesses with the tools to make informed financial decisions while ensuring compliance with industry regulations. Whether managing venture capital in tech start ups, tracking inventory in retail, or navigating the complexities of global supply chains, businesses must adopt financial accounting practices that align with their operational realities. Properly structured accounting frameworks enable companies to optimize profitability, manage risks, and position themselves for long-term growth in their respective industries.

## Financial Accounting for Non profits and Government Entities: Navigating Fund Management and Compliance

Financial accounting for **non profit organizations (NPOs) and government entities** differs significantly from for-profit businesses. These entities focus on **fund accountability, donor restrictions, and regulatory compliance** rather than profit maximization.

***Key Accounting Considerations for Non profits:***

- **Fund Accounting:** Tracks restricted vs. unrestricted funds separately to comply with donor-imposed conditions.
- **Grant and Donation Accounting:** Revenue recognition must align with donor stipulations and non profit regulations.
- **Statement of Functional Expenses:** Non profits must categorize expenses into **program services, administrative costs, and fundraising** to ensure transparency.

***Key Accounting Considerations for Government Entities:***

- **GASB Standards (U.S.):** Government entities follow **Governmental Accounting Standards Board (GASB) principles** for financial transparency.
- **Modified Accrual Accounting:** Recognizes revenue when measurable and available, and expenditures when incurred.
- **Public Fund Management:** Allocates budgets for public services such as healthcare, infrastructure, and education.

**Case Study:** The **American Red Cross** effectively uses **fund accounting** to track donations for specific disaster relief efforts, ensuring compliance and donor transparency.

## The Role of Environmental, Social, and Governance (ESG) Accounting

Sustainability and **corporate social responsibility (CSR)** reporting are becoming **critical** in financial accounting. Many organizations must integrate **ESG factors** into their financial disclosures due to regulatory requirements and investor demand.

***How ESG Impacts Financial Accounting:***

- **Carbon Credit Accounting:** Businesses in energy and manufacturing must account for **carbon credits, emissions trading, and environmental impact costs**.
- **Sustainability Reporting:** Frameworks such as **Global Reporting Initiative (GRI)** and **Sustainability Accounting Standards Board (SASB)** provide guidelines for financial disclosures related to **social impact and governance**.
- **Long-Term Risk & Cost Analysis:** ESG costs (e.g., environmental fines, supply chain ethics) are increasingly factored into **financial forecasting and valuation models**.

**Case Study:** In 2020, **Unilever** integrated **sustainability metrics** into its financial reporting, showcasing how **climate impact affects financial performance and investment risk**.

## Digital and Cryptocurrency Accounting

As digital assets gain mainstream adoption, financial accountants must

**develop strategies for tracking and valuing cryptocurrencies and blockchain-based transactions**.

*Challenges in Crypto Accounting:*

- **Valuation Fluctuations:** Cryptocurrencies experience **high volatility**, complicating financial statement disclosures.
- **Revenue Recognition & Taxation:** Businesses accepting crypto payments must determine whether to treat transactions as **currency, investment assets, or barter transactions** for tax purposes.
- **Audit and Regulatory Compliance:** GAAP and IFRS guidelines **do not fully address** cryptocurrency valuation, making audit procedures complex.

**Case Study:** Tesla's **2021 Bitcoin investment and subsequent divestment** highlighted how businesses must track crypto assets' fair value changes and account for impairments on financial statements.

## The Influence of Artificial Intelligence (AI) and Automation in Industry-Specific Accounting

AI-driven financial tools are transforming industry-specific accounting practices, allowing businesses to **reduce errors, automate compliance, and improve financial insights**.

*How AI Is Changing Financial Accounting Across Industries:*

- **Retail & E-Commerce:** AI-driven **inventory management** forecasts demand and minimizes carrying costs.
- **Healthcare & Insurance:** Automated **billing and fraud detection**

enhance financial accuracy.

- **Manufacturing:** AI-powered **cost variance analysis** detects inefficiencies in production lines.
- **Banking & Financial Services:** AI enhances **risk assessment models** for loans and investments.

**Case Study:** In 2022, **JP Morgan implemented AI-powered accounting automation** to speed up loan approvals, reducing financial risk while improving decision-making accuracy.

## Forensic Accounting in Industry-Specific Fraud Prevention

Forensic accounting is **critical** in industries prone to financial fraud, such as **banking, real estate, healthcare, and insurance**. Accountants use forensic techniques to **detect financial irregularities and prevent fraudulent activities**.

***Common Fraud Cases in Industry Accounting:***

- **Retail & E-Commerce:** Inventory fraud, vendor kickbacks, and fraudulent return schemes.
- **Healthcare: Medicare and insurance fraud**, including inflated billing and fake patient claims.
- **Real Estate & Construction:** Misreporting project costs and overinflated property valuations.
- **Banking & Finance:** Ponzi schemes and fraudulent financial reporting.

**Case Study:** The **Wirecard scandal (Germany, 2020)** exposed **massive financial fraud**, where auditors failed to detect **$2 billion in missing assets**—demonstrating why forensic accounting is essential in financial auditing.

## The Future of Industry-Specific Financial Accounting: Trends & Predictions

As **financial landscapes evolve**, new regulations, digital transformation, and economic shifts will shape **industry-specific accounting**.

***Key Trends to Watch:***

- **Regulatory Expansion:** Governments are tightening **compliance requirements** for industries such as **finance, crypto, and ESG reporting**.
- **Automation & AI Integration:** AI-driven financial forecasting will **replace manual budgeting and reporting**.
- **Blockchain Adoption:** Smart contracts and **decentralized finance (DeFi)** will redefine **financial tracking and transparency**.
- **Sustainable Finance Growth:** ESG-focused businesses will see **increased investor interest**, requiring accountants to track **sustainability metrics alongside traditional financial KPIs**.

## Strengthening Financial Expertise Across Industries: The Key to Long-Term Success

Financial accounting is not a one-size-fits-all discipline. Every industry—whether technology, healthcare, real estate, manufacturing, or retail—

operates under distinct financial conditions, regulatory requirements, and economic challenges. Understanding **industry-specific financial accounting** is not just about compliance; it is about **strategic financial mastery** that drives sustainable growth, reduces risk, and enhances profitability.

Businesses that tailor their financial accounting practices to their industry's unique demands gain a **competitive advantage**, positioning themselves as financially resilient and prepared for future disruptions. Whether it is a technology startup navigating venture capital funding, a retail company managing inventory fluctuations, or a healthcare provider handling complex reimbursement structures, precise financial accounting ensures operational efficiency and long-term success.

As industries evolve with **emerging technologies, shifting regulations, and global economic changes**, businesses that **embrace innovation, invest in financial expertise, and integrate industry-specific best practices** will thrive. Those that fail to adapt risk falling behind, exposing themselves to inefficiencies, compliance failures, and financial instability.

Mastering financial accounting at an industry level is more than a technical necessity—it is a strategic imperative. **The ability to interpret financial data, anticipate market shifts, and implement sound accounting practices is what separates high-performing businesses from those struggling to keep up.** For accountants, business leaders, and financial professionals, staying ahead means **continuously refining financial expertise, leveraging technology, and applying best practices tailored to their specific industry.** By doing so, they ensure **financial strength, investor confidence, and long-term sustainability**—hallmarks of businesses built to withstand change and lead in their markets.

# REVENUE, EXPENSES, AND THE MATCHING PRINCIPLE

## Introduction: The Role of Revenue and Expenses in Financial Accounting

Revenue and expenses form the foundation of a company's financial health, serving as the key indicators of operational success and long-term viability. These financial elements determine profitability, guide strategic decision-making, and influence business sustainability in a competitive marketplace. Accurate recognition and classification of revenue and expenses ensure that financial statements provide a true and fair view of a company's operations, allowing stakeholders to assess financial stability, investment potential, and future growth prospects.

Beyond mere profit calculations, revenue and expense management play a vital role in cash flow forecasting, budget planning, and financial risk assessment. A company with strong revenue recognition policies and well-managed expenses can better allocate resources, minimize financial inefficiencies, and maintain resilience during economic downturns. Conversely, businesses that fail to properly recognize income and expenses risk misstating their financial position, leading to regulatory scrutiny, diminished investor confidence, and operational challenges.

Furthermore, revenue and expenses impact key financial ratios, such as profit margins, return on investment, and earnings per share. Investors, creditors, and internal management teams rely on these financial figures to evaluate business performance, make strategic funding decisions, and identify areas for cost optimization. By implementing sound accounting practices, companies can ensure compliance with industry regulations, build trust among stakeholders, and position themselves for long-term financial success.

One of the most critical concepts in financial accounting is the **matching principle**, which ensures that expenses are recorded in the same period as the revenue they help generate. This principle supports accurate profit calculations and enhances the reliability of financial reporting.

This chapter will explore the different methods of recognizing revenue, the classification of business expenses, and the importance of the matching principle. We will also discuss real-world applications and common challenges businesses face in applying these concepts.

## Recognizing Revenue: Cash vs. Accrual Accounting

Revenue recognition is one of the most debated topics in financial accounting, as it directly affects a company's reported earnings, financial statements, and tax obligations. The process of determining when and how revenue should be recorded can vary significantly across industries, regulatory environments, and accounting frameworks. Accurate revenue recognition is critical for ensuring financial transparency, building investor trust, and complying with accounting standards such as **GAAP (Generally Accepted Accounting Principles)** and **IFRS (International Financial Reporting Standards)**.

There are two primary methods businesses use to recognize revenue: **cash accounting** and **accrual accounting**. Each method has its advantages and challenges, and the choice between them depends on the size, structure, and financial complexity of the business. Furthermore, revenue recognition has evolved to adapt to modern business models, such as subscription-based services, long-term contracts, and multi-deliverable arrangements, making it even more important to understand the fundamental principles governing revenue recording.

### 1. Cash Accounting: Simple and Immediate

Under the **cash accounting method**, revenue is recognized when cash is received, and expenses are recorded when they are paid. This approach is straightforward and commonly used by small businesses and sole proprietors.

***Example:***

A freelance graphic designer completes a project for a client in November but only receives payment in December. Under cash accounting, the revenue is recognized in December when the cash is received.

**Advantages of Cash Accounting:**

- Simple and easy to implement.
- Provides a clear view of cash flow.
- Suitable for small businesses with straightforward transactions.

**Disadvantages:**

- Does not reflect accounts receivable or accounts payable.
- May distort profitability if revenue and expenses do not match the period in which they occur.

## 2. Accrual Accounting: A More Comprehensive Approach

Accrual accounting, the preferred method for **larger businesses and publicly traded companies**, recognizes revenue when it is **earned**, regardless of when payment is received.

***Example:***

A software company sells an annual subscription to a customer in January. The payment is received upfront, but under accrual accounting, revenue is recognized **monthly** over the 12-month subscription period, as the service is provided.

**Advantages of Accrual Accounting:**

- Provides a more accurate representation of financial health.
- Aligns with Generally Accepted Accounting Principles (GAAP) and IFRS standards.
- Helps businesses manage long-term financial planning.

**Disadvantages:**

- More complex to implement.
- Requires detailed record-keeping.
- Can create cash flow challenges if revenue is recognized before actual payment is received.

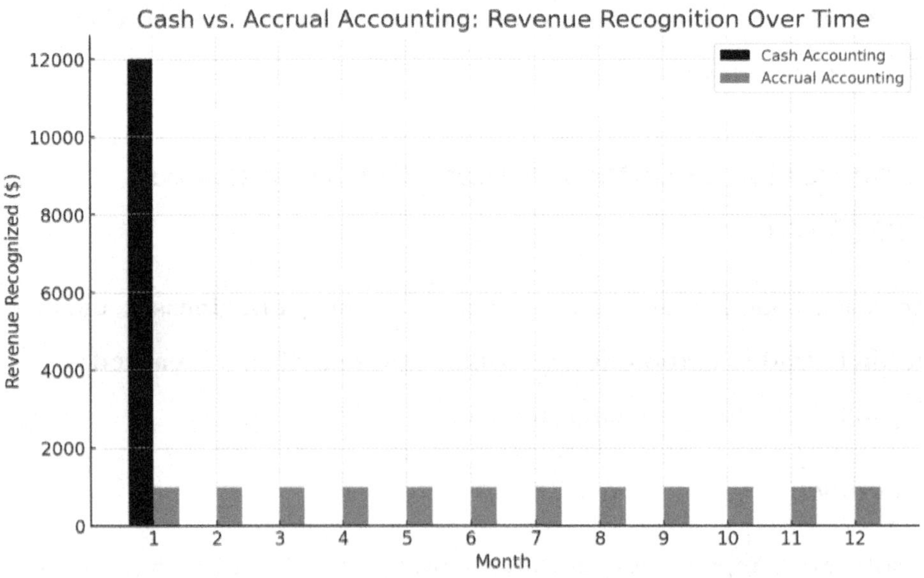

## Understanding Business Expenses and Cost Recognition

Just as revenue needs careful recognition, so do **expenses**. Business expenses encompass a broad range of costs essential for operations, including salaries, rent, utilities, raw materials, depreciation, and research and development. These costs are classified based on their function, behavior, and impact on financial statements, requiring careful recognition to ensure accurate profit measurement and regulatory compliance.

Expense recognition follows similar rules as revenue recognition, ensuring that financial statements present a realistic view of profitability. Accurately categorizing expenses as **fixed or variable, direct or indirect, operating or non-operating** allows businesses to assess cost structures and improve financial efficiency. Failure to recognize expenses correctly can result in misstated financial reports, misleading investors and stakeholders.

Additionally, businesses must account for **prepaid expenses, accrued expenses, and amortization** to ensure expenses align with the periods in which they contribute to revenue generation. For example, if a company pays annual insurance premiums upfront, the expense should be allocated across the entire coverage period rather than being recorded in full when paid. This aligns with the **matching principle**, which ensures expenses are recorded when the corresponding revenue is earned, improving financial statement accuracy and strategic planning.

Understanding expense recognition helps businesses monitor cash flow, optimize spending, and enhance profitability, ensuring sustainable financial management and long-term success.

## 1. Types of Business Expenses

Expenses are categorized into **fixed, variable, direct, and indirect** costs:

- **Fixed Expenses:** Costs that remain constant regardless of production levels (e.g., rent, salaries).
- **Variable Expenses:** Costs that fluctuate with business activity (e.g., raw materials, sales commissions).
- **Direct Expenses:** Costs directly tied to a product or service (e.g., manufacturing costs).
- **Indirect Expenses:** Costs not tied to a specific product but necessary for operations (e.g., utilities, marketing).

## 2. Cost Recognition and Its Importance

The **timing** of expense recognition is crucial, as it directly impacts the accuracy of financial reporting, profitability analysis, and tax obligations. Businesses must align expenses with the revenue they help generate to ensure that financial statements provide a true reflection of financial performance. This is where the **matching principle** plays a vital role, as it prevents misleading financial results and ensures that expenses do not distort profit calculations.

For instance, if a company incurs costs to manufacture products in one period but recognizes revenue from the sales of those products in a later period, failing to match these expenses with the corresponding revenue would result in overstated or understated profits. The matching principle ensures that financial statements provide meaningful insights into a company's cost structure, allowing for better budgeting, forecasting, and performance evaluation.

Additionally, adhering to this principle helps businesses comply with accounting standards such as **GAAP and IFRS**, reducing the risk of financial misstatements and ensuring regulatory compliance. By accurately recognizing expenses, companies can make informed decisions about cost-cutting measures, pricing strategies, and investment opportunities, ultimately driving long-term financial stability and growth.

***Example:***

A clothing manufacturer buys fabric in March to produce shirts that will be sold in June. Under the matching principle, the fabric expense should be recorded in June, aligning with the revenue generated from the shirt sales.

## The Matching Principle: Why Timing Matters in Accounting

The **matching principle** ensures that expenses are recognized in the same period as the revenue they help generate. By adhering to this principle, businesses can present a more accurate and transparent picture of their financial performance, which is essential for effective decision-making, budgeting, and forecasting. This principle is a cornerstone of accrual accounting, enabling businesses to match revenues with corresponding expenses, thus preventing misleading financial results that could distort profitability.

Without the matching principle, companies might either understate or overstate their earnings in a given period, leading to incorrect financial analyses and misinformed business strategies. For example, if a business incurs marketing expenses in December to drive sales in January, failing to apply the matching principle would mean recording the expense in December but recognizing the revenue in January, creating an artificial dip in profitability for one period and an inflated figure in the next.

Additionally, the matching principle helps businesses comply with Generally Accepted Accounting Principles (GAAP) and International Financial Reporting Standards (IFRS), reinforcing financial accountability and credibility. It is particularly crucial in industries with long production cycles, such as manufacturing and construction, where significant costs are incurred well before revenue is realized.

Beyond compliance, applying the matching principle supports long-term financial planning. It allows companies to assess the true cost of revenue generation, optimize resource allocation, and implement more effective cost-control measures. By ensuring that financial statements accurately reflect a company's operational reality, the matching principle strengthens investor confidence, enhances strategic planning, and improves overall financial sustainability.

## 1. Why the Matching Principle Matters

- Prevents misleading financial results.
- Enhances comparability between periods.
- Ensures profitability is accurately reported.

## 2. Real-World Applications of the Matching Principle

- **Subscription-Based Businesses:** A magazine publisher collects a one-year subscription fee upfront but recognizes revenue **monthly** as the magazines are delivered.

- **Manufacturing Companies:** A car manufacturer incurs labor and material costs before selling the final product. These costs are recorded only when the sale occurs.
- **Commission-Based Sales:** A sales agent earns a commission in December but is paid in January. The company records the commission expense in December when the related revenue is earned.

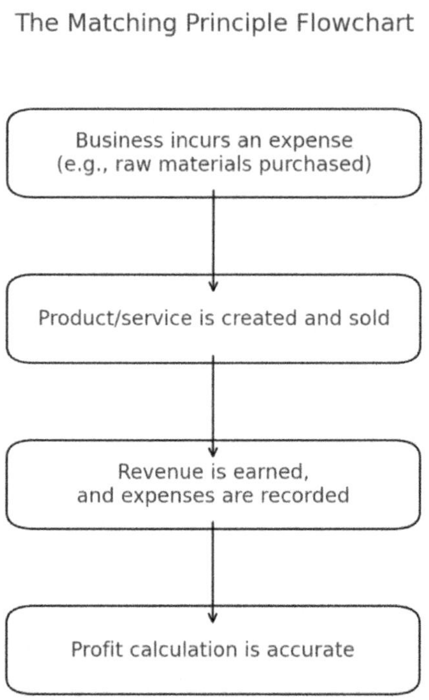

## Scenario-Based Questions: When Should Revenue Be Recognized?

### Scenario 1:

A construction company signs a $500,000 contract in January to build an office. The project will take eight months to complete, and the client pays the full amount upfront. When should the company recognize revenue?

**Answer:** Under accrual accounting, revenue should be recognized gradually over the eight-month project period rather than all at once in January.

### Scenario 2:

A gym offers a one-year membership plan where customers pay upfront for unlimited access. When should the gym recognize revenue?

**Answer:** The gym should recognize revenue monthly as the service is provided rather than recognizing the full amount at the time of payment.

### Scenario 3:

A law firm provides legal services in December but invoices the client in January. When should the revenue be recorded?

**Answer:** Under accrual accounting, revenue should be recorded in December when the service is provided, even though payment is received in January.

## Conclusion: The Role of Revenue and Expense Recognition in Financial Reporting

Accurate revenue and expense recognition is essential for transparent financial reporting and reliable financial analysis. The choice between **cash and accrual accounting** significantly impacts how financial statements reflect business performance, influencing everything from tax reporting to investment decisions.

A well-structured revenue and expense recognition system ensures that businesses remain compliant with regulatory requirements, avoid financial misstatements, and provide a clear financial picture to stakeholders. Proper recognition also helps in **long-term financial planning**, allowing businesses to forecast revenue streams, control operational costs, and align financial goals with business strategy.

Moreover, consistent application of the **matching principle** strengthens investor confidence and enhances the credibility of a company's financial reports. Businesses that fail to adhere to proper revenue and expense recognition standards risk misleading financial statements, which can lead to regulatory scrutiny, loss of investor trust, and financial instability.

In an evolving financial landscape, businesses must stay updated with accounting standards such as **GAAP and IFRS**, ensuring that their financial reports reflect true and fair value. By mastering revenue and expense recognition, organizations can make data-driven decisions, improve financial efficiency, and maintain a competitive edge in their industry.

The **matching principle** ensures that businesses align expenses with the revenue they help generate, preventing distortions in profitability. By applying these accounting principles correctly, companies can provide a **clear, consistent, and truthful financial picture**, enabling investors, managers, and stakeholders to make informed decisions.

# MANAGING ASSETS & LIABILITIES

## Introduction: The Role of Assets & Liabilities in Financial Health

A company's financial stability is largely determined by how well it **manages its assets and liabilities**. Assets represent the **resources** a business owns and utilizes to generate revenue, while liabilities signify the **financial obligations** it must meet. The balance between these two elements directly influences **liquidity, solvency, and**

**long-term financial success**.

Businesses that manage assets efficiently can improve **cash flow, profitability, and return on investment**, while excessive liabilities can lead to **financial strain, reduced creditworthiness, and operational risks**. Whether an organization is investing in new equipment, monitoring inventory levels, or managing debt, understanding the relationship between assets and liabilities is essential for **sustainable growth and risk mitigation**.

This chapter explores **different types of assets and liabilities, the impact of depreciation and amortization, and key financial strategies** to optimize asset utilization and manage debt responsibly.

## Current vs. Non-Current Assets: Understanding Business Resources

Assets are the **economic resources** that businesses use to generate revenue, maintain operations, and expand their market presence. Effective management of **current and non-current assets** is crucial for ensuring **financial stability, liquidity, and long-term profitability**.

- **Current assets** are **short-term** resources that a business expects to **convert into cash within one year**, enabling it to cover **day-to-day expenses and short-term liabilities**.
- **Non-current assets** are **long-term** investments, often requiring significant **capital expenditures**, that businesses use to **support sustained operations and future growth**.

A well-balanced asset strategy ensures that companies have **enough**

**liquidity to meet obligations** while **investing in growth-oriented assets** that generate long-term value.

## Current Assets: Liquid Resources for Short-Term Operations

### Definition & Importance

Current assets provide the financial flexibility that businesses need to **meet payroll, pay suppliers, and handle unexpected expenses**. Managing these assets effectively ensures that a company can **operate without disruptions** and maintain a strong **working capital position**.

A business with **healthy current assets** can **navigate economic downturns**, handle **seasonal fluctuations in revenue**, and seize **new opportunities** without relying excessively on external financing. However, poor current asset management can lead to **cash flow shortages, missed payments, and financial distress**.

### Key Types of Current Assets & Their Role

***1. Cash & Cash Equivalents***

- **Definition:** Includes physical cash, bank balances, and highly liquid investments (e.g., treasury bills, money market funds).
- **Importance:** Businesses must maintain **enough cash reserves** to meet **short-term obligations, unexpected costs, and operational expenses**.
- **Risk:** Holding **too much cash** reduces growth potential, as idle

funds **do not generate returns**. Conversely, **insufficient cash reserves** can lead to financial distress.

**Example:** A retail store keeps **$10,000 in cash reserves** to cover daily expenses and emergency purchases.

***2. Accounts Receivable (A/R): Customer Payments Owed to the Business***

- **Definition:** Money owed by customers for goods/services provided but not yet paid for.
- **Importance:** Efficient accounts receivable management ensures **steady cash flow and reduced risk of bad debts**.
- **Risk: Delayed customer payments** can lead to cash flow problems, making it difficult to pay **suppliers and employees**.

**Example:** A software company provides **cloud services to corporate clients**, billing them **monthly**. If clients delay payments, the company may **struggle to pay server costs**, affecting operations.

***3. Inventory: Products & Raw Materials Available for Sale***

- **Definition:** Goods held for resale (finished products) or production (raw materials).
- **Importance:** Effective inventory management prevents **overstocking (which ties up cash) and understocking (which leads to lost sales opportunities)**.
- **Risk: Slow-moving inventory can create financial strain** by tying up working capital that could be used elsewhere.

**Example:** A clothing retailer carries **$50,000 in inventory** and expects to sell it within three months. If sales are slow, excess stock **occupies storage space and reduces available cash flow**.

***4. Prepaid Expenses: Advance Payments for Future Services***

- **Definition:** Expenses paid in advance for services that will be used over time (e.g., rent, insurance, advertising).
- **Importance:** Prepaid expenses help businesses **secure essential services at fixed costs**, reducing future financial strain.
- **Risk:** If not carefully managed, prepaid expenses may **lock up funds that could be used for other investments**.

**Example:** A consulting firm **prepays office rent for six months** to secure a lower rental rate. The expense is recognized **gradually each month** instead of all at once.

## Non-Current Assets: Long-Term Investments & Fixed Resources

### Definition & Importance

Non-current assets are **essential for business expansion, production efficiency, and strategic growth**. These assets are **not easily converted into cash** but play a crucial role in **long-term financial success**. Businesses that invest wisely in **non-current assets** can **increase efficiency, reduce costs, and enhance profitability over time**.

However, these assets **require careful financial planning** because they **tie up large amounts of capital**. If mismanaged, businesses may **struggle**

**with high maintenance costs, depreciation, or obsolescence risks**.

## Key Types of Non-Current Assets & Their Role

### *1. Property, Plant & Equipment (PPE): Physical Business Infrastructure*

- **Definition:** Includes buildings, machinery, land, vehicles, and equipment used for business operations.
- **Importance:** PPE investments drive **efficiency, production, and revenue generation**.
- **Risk:** Poor maintenance and outdated equipment can **increase operational costs and reduce profitability**.

**Example:** A manufacturing company invests **$500,000 in automated machinery**, improving production speed and reducing labor costs.

### *2. Intangible Assets: Intellectual Property & Brand Value*

- **Definition:** Includes patents, trademarks, copyrights, software, goodwill, and brand reputation.
- **Importance:** Intangible assets provide **competitive advantages** and can significantly **increase company valuation**.
- **Risk:** Intellectual property **must be protected legally** to prevent competitors from benefiting from innovations.

**Example:** A tech start up develops **proprietary AI software** and patents it. This **protects its technology from competitors and adds value to the company**.

***3. Long-Term Investments: Growth-Oriented Financial Assets***

- **Definition:** Includes stocks, bonds, and real estate investments held for long-term growth.
- **Importance:** Helps businesses **generate additional revenue and diversify income streams.**
- **Risk:** Market fluctuations may affect investment value, leading to **financial instability during downturns.**

**Example:** A retail chain invests **$2 million in commercial real estate,** allowing it to expand locations **without relying on leasing agreements.**

## Effective Asset Management: Balancing Liquidity & Growth

A business must balance **current and non-current assets** to achieve **both short-term liquidity and long-term financial security.**

**Key Asset Management Strategies:**

- **Optimizing Inventory Turnover:** Ensuring that stock moves quickly **without excessive holding costs.**
- **Maintaining Adequate Cash Reserves:** Keeping enough liquidity to **cover daily operations and emergencies.**
- **Investing in Productive Fixed Assets:** Purchasing equipment that **enhances efficiency and reduces costs.**
- **Protecting Intellectual Property:** Registering trademarks and patents to **secure competitive advantages.**

## Example: Poor Asset Management & Business Failure

**Case Study: Blockbuster vs. Netflix**

- **Blockbuster relied too heavily on physical store assets** and failed to invest in digital infrastructure.
- **Netflix focused on intangible assets (streaming technology) and long-term investments in AI-driven recommendations**.
- **Blockbuster's physical assets became liabilities** as customer demand shifted toward digital media.

**Lesson Learned:** Businesses must **adapt their asset strategies** to evolving market conditions to remain competitive.

## Conclusion: Strategic Asset Allocation for Sustainable Growth

Managing **current and non-current assets** effectively ensures that a business remains **financially stable and positioned for long-term success**. Companies that **optimize liquidity, invest wisely in long-term assets, and leverage technology** gain a **competitive edge** in their industries.

**Key Takeaways:**

- **Current assets** drive **daily operations** and impact **short-term liquidity**.
- **Non-current assets** support **long-term growth and business expansion**.

- **A well-balanced asset strategy** ensures **stability, profitability, and resilience in a changing market.**

By mastering **asset allocation and financial planning**, businesses can **maximize returns, reduce financial risks, and achieve sustainable success.**

### Understanding Depreciation & Amortization

Properly accounting for **depreciation and amortization** ensures that financial statements reflect the **true cost of assets over time**. These accounting methods help businesses **spread costs across multiple years**, improving **profitability analysis, tax planning, and financial reporting.**

By systematically recognizing the **declining value of tangible and intangible assets**, businesses can accurately report their **financial position, maintain regulatory compliance, and make informed capital investment decisions.**

## What is Depreciation?

### Definition & Purpose of Depreciation

Depreciation is a fundamental **accounting concept** that helps businesses **systematically allocate the cost of tangible assets over their useful life.** When a company purchases a fixed asset such as **machinery, vehicles, equipment, or buildings**, it is typically a **long-term investment** that will be used over several years. Rather than **expensing the entire cost in the year of purchase**, depreciation **spreads the cost** across multiple periods, ensuring that the expense **aligns with the revenue the asset generates.**

This process is essential for **accurate financial reporting, tax planning, and investment decision-making**. By accounting for depreciation, businesses can ensure that their financial statements **reflect the true value of their assets** over time, preventing misrepresentation of profitability.

## Why Depreciation is Important

Depreciation is **more than just an accounting requirement**—it plays a **critical role** in financial management, business strategy, and taxation. Here's why:

### *1. Accurate Profit Measurement & Expense Matching*

Depreciation ensures that an asset's cost is **matched with the revenue it helps generate** over its useful life. This follows the **matching principle** in accounting, which states that expenses should be recognized in the same period as the related revenues.

**Example:** A manufacturing company purchases a **$200,000 machine** that will be used to produce goods for **10 years**. If the company **expensed the entire $200,000 upfront**, its financial statements would show a significant **loss in the first year** and **inflated profits in subsequent years**. By depreciating the machine over **10 years**, the expense is **evenly spread**, giving a **more realistic view of financial performance**.

### *2. Tax Deductions & Cash Flow Benefits*

Depreciation is a **non-cash expense**, meaning it **reduces taxable income without directly impacting cash flow**. Businesses can claim depreciation as a **tax deduction**, which lowers their taxable profit and, consequently, their tax liability.

**Example:** A logistics company buys **20 delivery trucks** for a total cost of **$1 million**. Instead of deducting **$1 million in one year**, they spread the cost over **five years**, claiming an annual depreciation deduction of **$200,000 per year**. This helps them **reduce taxable income and free up cash flow for future investments**.

### *3. Financial Transparency & Investor Confidence*

Investors, creditors, and stakeholders rely on financial statements to **assess a company's financial health and stability**. Depreciation ensures that these statements **accurately reflect the value of assets**, preventing businesses from over-reporting profits.

**Example:** If a company **fails to account for depreciation**, it may appear **more profitable than it actually is**, leading to **misleading financial reports**. This can result in **overvalued stock prices, unexpected financial losses, and diminished investor confidence** when asset values suddenly drop.

### *4. Realistic Asset Valuation & Planning for Reinvestment*

Depreciation helps companies **track the true value of their assets** over time. Fixed assets **lose efficiency and productivity** as they age, so businesses must plan for **eventual replacements**.

**Example:** An airline purchases **five aircraft** with a lifespan of **20 years**. As depreciation is recorded annually, the company can **forecast when new aircraft will be needed** and set aside funds for replacement, ensuring seamless operations.

Without depreciation, companies might **unexpectedly face massive capital expenses**, leading to financial strain.

## What Happens Without Depreciation?

If depreciation **is not recorded**, a business may face **several financial and operational issues**, including:

**Overstated Profits:** Without depreciation, financial statements would show **inflated profits**, misleading stakeholders about the company's true financial position.

**Tax Overpayments:** Companies would pay **higher taxes** since they wouldn't be deducting depreciation expenses, **reducing available cash for reinvestment**.

**Financial Instability:** Businesses may **fail to plan for asset replacements**, leading to **unexpected capital expenditures** that strain liquidity.

**Reduced Investor Confidence:** Investors may question a company's **financial management and long-term planning** if assets are not accurately valued.

## Depreciation in Different Industries

Different industries **use depreciation in unique ways** based on **the type of assets they rely on**.

**Manufacturing & Construction:** High depreciation due to heavy machinery, which wears down quickly with constant use. **Technology & Software Companies:** Rapid depreciation of **computer equipment** and software due to fast-changing technology. **Retail & Hospitality:** Buildings and store fixtures depreciate over time but at a slower rate than machinery. **Energy & Utilities:** Depreciation of power plants and infrastructure can span **decades**, with companies using **accelerated depreciation** for tax benefits.

### Conclusion: The Strategic Role of Depreciation

Depreciation is not just a **technical accounting requirement**—it is a **critical tool** for businesses to **accurately report financial performance, reduce tax liabilities, and plan for future investments**. By spreading asset costs over time, companies can **smooth out expenses, maintain cash flow, and ensure long-term financial stability**.

**Key Takeaways:** Ensures that asset costs align with revenue generation (**Matching Principle**). Provides **tax savings**, improving **cash flow and reinvestment potential**. Helps companies **plan for asset replacements**, preventing financial shocks. Increases **financial transparency and investor confidence**.

By understanding and applying depreciation correctly, businesses can **optimize financial performance, make better investment decisions, and achieve long-term success**.

## 2. What is Amortization?

### Definition & Purpose

Amortization is similar to depreciation but applies to **intangible assets** such as patents, trademarks, copyrights, goodwill, and software. Since these assets **do not have a physical form**, their value **decreases over time due to market changes, expiration, or legal limitations**.

Like depreciation, amortization helps businesses: Spread the cost of intangible assets over time. Reduce taxable income. Reflect accurate asset values on financial statements.

**Key Difference: Depreciation applies to tangible assets (buildings, equipment, vehicles). Amortization applies to intangible assets (patents, trademarks, software).**

## Amortization: Accounting for Intangible Assets

Amortization is a fundamental accounting concept used to **gradually reduce the book value of intangible assets** over their useful life. Unlike depreciation, which applies to **physical assets**, amortization applies to **intangible assets**, such as:

**Patents** (legal protection for inventions) **Trademarks** (brand identity and logos) **Copyrights** (intellectual property rights for creative works) **Franchises & Licensing Agreements** (exclusive rights to operate under a brand) **Goodwill** (business reputation and customer loyalty) **Software Development Costs** (capitalized technology investments)

Intangible assets **do not physically deteriorate**, but they do have a **finite useful life**, after which they become obsolete, expire, or lose value due to **market changes, industry competition, or legal limitations**.

Properly amortizing intangible assets ensures that financial statements accurately reflect their **declining economic benefit**, allowing businesses to **spread costs over multiple years** instead of taking a large, one-time expense.

## Why Businesses Use Amortization

Amortization is an essential part of financial management and reporting. Businesses apply amortization to:

**Match Expenses with Revenue Generation** Just like depreciation for physical assets, amortization ensures that **the cost of intangible assets is allocated over the period they provide value** to the company.

**Example:** A pharmaceutical company holds a **10-year patent** for a new medication. Instead of recording the **entire cost in the first year**, the company **spreads the cost across 10 years**, reflecting the long-term benefit of the patent.

**Improve Tax Efficiency** Amortization provides **tax benefits**, as companies can **deduct the amortized amount** each year, reducing taxable income. This improves cash flow and allows businesses to **allocate funds to other investments**.

**Example:** A tech company develops a **new software system**, which is classified as an **intangible asset**. By amortizing the cost over several years, the company can **reduce taxable income annually**, improving financial flexibility.

**Ensure Financial Transparency** Accurate amortization reporting ensures that **financial statements reflect the true value of intangible assets**. Investors and stakeholders need reliable financial data to assess a company's **long-term financial health**.

**Example:** A media company owns **multiple copyrights** for original content. Over time, these copyrights **lose market value**, so amortization ensures that their declining worth is reflected in financial statements.

## Amortization in Different Industries

Industries rely on amortization differently, depending on how intangible assets contribute to their operations.

**Pharmaceutical & Biotech:** Patents for new drugs are amortized over their legal lifespan, typically **10-20 years**. Once expired, generic versions flood the market, reducing the patent's value.

**Technology & Software:** Companies amortize **software development costs**, licenses, and proprietary technology over their expected useful life, usually **3-5 years**.

**Retail & Franchising:** Franchise agreements and brand licensing are amortized over the contract duration, ensuring that the cost aligns with business operations.

**Entertainment & Media:** Film production companies amortize copyrights over their commercial lifespan, ensuring costs align with the **expected revenue from licensing and distribution**.

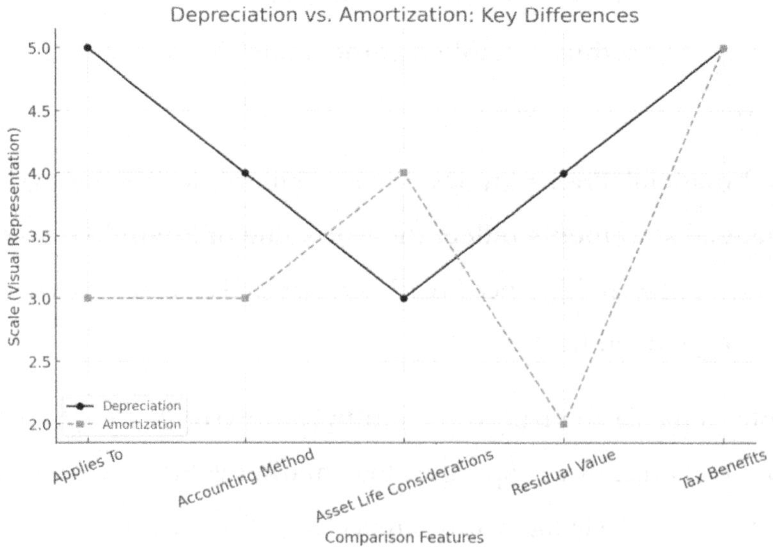

### The Impact of Poor Amortization Practices

**Overestimating Asset Life**: If a company assumes an intangible asset will last **longer than its actual value period**, it may **delay expense recognition**, making profits appear **inflated** in early years.

**Underestimating Asset Value**: If a company amortizes an asset **too quickly**, it **increases expenses unnecessarily**, lowering reported profits and affecting investor confidence.

**Failing to Amortize Key Assets**: Ignoring amortization for assets like **trademarks and intellectual property** can lead to **overstated financial statements**, causing regulatory compliance issues.

### Conclusion: Why Amortization Matters

Amortization is **more than just an accounting process**—it ensures that **businesses recognize the true economic value of their intangible assets over time**. Proper amortization:

Aligns **asset costs with revenue generation**. Provides **tax benefits** and improves **cash flow management**. Ensures **accurate financial reporting and transparency**.

By properly amortizing **intellectual property, software, patents, and other intangible assets**, companies can **make informed financial decisions, manage risks, and maintain investor confidence**.

## The Role of Depreciation & Amortization in Financial Planning

Properly managing **depreciation and amortization** allows businesses to

**accurately reflect asset values, reduce taxable income, and improve financial decision-making.**

**Depreciation ensures that businesses recognize the gradual decline of physical assets, improving long-term budgeting and capital investment planning. Amortization helps businesses allocate costs for intangible assets, protecting intellectual property investments and ensuring compliance with financial reporting standards.**

By applying the right **depreciation and amortization strategies**, businesses can: Maintain accurate financial records. Optimize tax deductions. Ensure long-term financial stability.

In the next chapter, we will explore **how businesses assess financial performance using key accounting ratios**, providing deeper insights into **efficiency, profitability, and financial stability**.

## Types of Liabilities: Understanding Financial Obligations

### Key Short-Term Liabilities

***1. Accounts Payable: Outstanding Payments to Suppliers***

- Represents **unpaid invoices** for goods or services received.
- Businesses must **pay suppliers on time** to maintain **good relationships and avoid late payment fees**.
- Managing accounts payable efficiently helps businesses **negotiate better terms and improve cash flow**.

**Example:** A retail store purchases inventory on credit and has **30 days to pay the supplier**. If payment is delayed, the supplier may **refuse future orders** or charge **late fees**.

**Risk:** Failing to pay suppliers on time can **strain supplier relationships, disrupt supply chains, and lead to legal disputes**.

***2. Short-Term Loans: Immediate Business Borrowing Needs***

- Includes **business lines of credit, working capital loans, and other short-term financing solutions**.
- Often used for **temporary cash flow shortages, emergency expenses, or seasonal fluctuations**.
- Short-term loans typically have **higher interest rates** due to their short repayment period.

**Example:** A small business **takes out a 6-month loan for $50,000** to cover **inventory purchases** before the holiday season. The business repays the loan after generating revenue from holiday sales.

**Risk:** If sales are lower than expected, the business **may struggle to repay the loan on time**, leading to **penalties or higher interest costs**.

***3. Wages Payable: Salaries Owed to Employees***

- Represents employee salaries and wages **earned but not yet paid**.
- Businesses must **ensure timely payroll payments** to maintain employee satisfaction and avoid legal issues.
- Payroll liabilities also include **tax withholdings, benefits, and bonuses** owed to employees.

**Example:** A company pays employees on the **15th and 30th of each month**. Any wages earned between pay periods are classified as **wages payable** until disbursed.

**Risk:** If a company faces **cash flow issues and delays payroll**, employee morale and productivity may decline, leading to **turnover and reputational damage**.

***4. Taxes Payable: Government Tax Obligations***

- Businesses are required to pay **income taxes, payroll taxes, sales taxes, and other government-mandated fees**.
- Failing to pay taxes on time can result in **penalties, interest charges, and legal consequences**.
- Many businesses **set aside a portion of revenue** to cover tax liabilities and avoid last-minute cash flow shortages.

**Example:** A business collects **sales tax from customers** and must remit **quarterly payments** to the government. Proper **tax planning ensures compliance and avoids penalties**.

**Risk:** If a company **fails to pay its tax obligations**, it may face **fines, audits, and even legal action** from tax authorities.

## The Importance of Managing Short-Term Liabilities

Short-term liabilities play a **crucial role in financial planning** and require businesses to maintain **strong cash flow management**. Companies must **balance short-term debts with available liquid assets** to prevent financial distress.

**Effective Strategies for Managing Short-Term Liabilities: Cash Flow Forecasting:** Monitoring **incoming revenue and outgoing expenses** ensures businesses **can meet short-term obligations on time.** **Prioritizing High-Interest Liabilities:** Businesses should focus on repaying **high-interest short-term loans** first to reduce financing costs. **Negotiating Better Payment Terms:** Extending **supplier payment deadlines** while accelerating customer collections improves liquidity. **Maintaining an Emergency Cash Reserve:** A financial cushion helps **cover short-term liabilities during unexpected downturns.**

## Example: Restaurant Cash Flow Crisis

**Scenario:** A restaurant has **$20,000 in accounts payable** to a food supplier, due in **30 days**. However, sales have been slow, and the business does not have enough cash on hand to make the payment.

**Potential Consequences: Supplier Relationship Strain:** Late payments may cause the supplier to **refuse future orders**, limiting access to necessary ingredients. **Late Fees & Interest:** The restaurant may **incur additional financial penalties**, worsening its cash flow issues. O**perational Disruptions:** If the restaurant cannot restock ingredients, it may **struggle to serve customers, leading to revenue loss.**

**Solution: Negotiate Extended Payment Terms:** The restaurant contacts the supplier and **requests a 15-day extension** to avoid late fees. **Increase Revenue:** The business **launches a marketing campaign** to **boost sales and generate immediate cash flow. Secure Short-Term Financing:** A **small business line of credit** helps bridge the cash flow gap and prevent supply chain disruptions.

By **actively managing short-term liabilities**, businesses can **avoid financial distress, improve cash flow, and strengthen supplier relationships**.

## The Role of Short-Term Liabilities in Business Success

Managing short-term liabilities is **critical for financial stability and business continuity**. Companies that **maintain liquidity, prioritize debt repayments, and plan for short-term obligations** are more resilient to financial challenges.

While short-term liabilities are **essential for operational funding**, excessive reliance on them **without a proper repayment strategy** can lead to **cash flow crises, penalties, and business failure**. Companies must carefully balance **their short-term liabilities with available assets** to ensure they can **meet obligations without jeopardizing financial health**.

By implementing **strong financial planning, effective cash flow management, and proactive debt strategies**, businesses can **leverage short-term liabilities responsibly while maintaining long-term sustainability**.

## Long-Term Liabilities: Funding Growth and Managing Financial Risk

Long-term liabilities are **financial obligations that extend beyond one year** and play a crucial role in **business expansion, asset acquisition, and financial stability**. These liabilities help businesses **fund major investments**, such as acquiring **real estate, purchasing equipment, financing large-scale projects, or entering new markets**. While they provide the **necessary capital for long-term growth**, excessive or poorly managed long-term liabilities can **lead to financial distress, liquidity issues, and high-interest burdens**.

Businesses strategically utilize **long-term debt** to spread out large expenditures over time, ensuring they maintain **operational liquidity while investing in future profitability**. Companies that manage long-term liabilities wisely **balance leverage with sustainable cash flow**, ensuring they can meet their financial obligations **without compromising day-to-day operations**.

## Key Types of Long-Term Liabilities

### *1. Mortgages & Bonds Payable*

- **Mortgages:** Long-term loans used to finance **real estate or business properties**, typically repaid over **10 to 30 years** with interest.
- **Bonds Payable:** Companies issue bonds to raise capital from investors, promising **fixed interest payments** over a specified period.

**Example:** A retail company takes out a **$10 million mortgage** to open a new store. The mortgage allows for expansion without using all available cash reserves.

**Risk:** If real estate values decline, the company may **owe more than the property is worth**, creating financial strain.

### *2. Long-Term Bank Loans & Corporate Debt*

- Used to finance **large capital projects, research & development,**

**or business expansion**.

- Can have **fixed or variable interest rates**, affecting the cost of borrowing.

**Example:** A manufacturing company borrows **$50 million** to expand production capacity. Over **10 years**, it repays the loan using profits from increased sales.

**Risk:** High interest payments can reduce profitability, especially during **economic downturns**.

### *3. Pension Liabilities & Employee Benefit Obligations*

- **Pension Liabilities:** Companies offering retirement plans must **account for future pay outs** to employees.
- **Post-Retirement Benefits:** Includes **healthcare benefits** for retired employees.

**Example:** A Fortune 500 company estimates **$500 million** in pension liabilities over the next **20 years**.

**Risk:** If pension funds are underfunded, companies must **cover shortfalls,** impacting cash flow.

### *4. Deferred Tax Liabilities*

- Arise when a company **delays tax payments** due to differences in financial reporting vs. tax rules.
- Often seen when businesses use **accelerated depreciation methods**, deferring tax obligations to future years.

**Example:** A tech company claims **depreciation deductions** on its equipment, reducing taxable income now but **increasing tax obligations in the future**.

**Risk:** If tax laws change, deferred liabilities may increase unexpectedly.

## Strategies for Effective Long-Term Liability Management

To ensure that long-term liabilities are **managed strategically**, companies must implement **proactive financial planning and debt management techniques**.

***1. Align Debt Financing with Business Growth***

- Businesses should take on long-term debt **only when there is a clear return on investment (ROI)**.
- Ensuring that borrowed funds are used to **generate revenue** and **expand operations** prevents unnecessary financial strain.

**Example:** A manufacturing firm secures long-term financing to **upgrade production facilities**, resulting in **higher output and increased revenue**.

***2. Maintain a Healthy Debt-to-Equity Ratio***

- A balanced **debt-to-equity ratio** ensures that a company is **not overly dependent on borrowed funds** for growth.
- This ratio helps determine whether a business can **comfortably service its long-term liabilities** without compromising liquidity.

**Example:** A tech company with a **low debt-to-equity ratio** can **secure better financing terms**, as lenders view it as a **low-risk borrower**.

*3. Evaluate Fixed vs. Variable Interest Rates*

- Businesses must carefully **choose between fixed and variable interest rate loans**, depending on market conditions.
- Fixed-rate loans provide **stability**, while variable-rate loans may offer **lower initial rates** but carry the risk of **rising interest costs**.

**Example:** A hotel chain taking on a **$100 million expansion loan** may opt for a **fixed interest rate** to avoid the risks of fluctuating borrowing costs.

*4. Conduct Regular Financial Assessments*

- Businesses must continuously **monitor cash flow, repayment schedules, and overall debt structure** to adjust their financial strategies.
- Proactive assessments help companies **identify potential liquidity issues before they become critical**.

**Example:** A logistics company facing **declining revenue** restructures its debt by **renegotiating repayment terms**, reducing its financial burden.

## Practical Exercise: Depreciation Calculations

### Scenario 1: Straight-Line Depreciation

A company purchases a **delivery truck** with a projected **useful life of five years**.

**Question:** How should the company allocate the cost of the truck over its useful life?

✅ **Hint:** The company will recognize an **equal expense each year**, ensuring the asset's cost is **evenly spread over time**.

### Scenario 2: Declining Balance Depreciation

A corporation acquires **specialized equipment** for manufacturing and plans to use an **accelerated depreciation method** to account for the asset's higher wear in its early years.

**Question:** How will the depreciation expense be recorded in the first few years compared to later years?

✅ **Hint:** The company will recognize **higher depreciation expenses in the earlier years**, reflecting the asset's **rapid initial decline in value**.

## Conclusion: Managing Long-Term Liabilities & Asset Depreciation

Effectively managing long-term liabilities ensures that businesses can **leverage debt responsibly**, enabling expansion and investment while maintaining financial health. **Depreciation calculations** further support financial planning by **tracking asset values, reducing taxable income, and ensuring accurate financial reporting**.

**Key Takeaways:**

**Strategic debt management ensures long-term business sustainability.**

**Balancing debt with cash flow is crucial to avoid financial distress.**

**Depreciation helps businesses allocate asset costs efficiently over time.**

**Regular financial reviews improve risk management and operational efficiency.**

By adopting these best practices, businesses can effectively **manage liabilities, optimize asset investments, and maintain financial resilience** in changing market conditions.

## Real Case Studies

### Case Study 1: Apple Inc. – Efficient Asset Utilization & Long-Term Growth

**Background:** Apple Inc. is one of the most valuable companies in the world, with a market capitalization exceeding **$3 trillion**. A major contributor to Apple's success is its **efficient management of assets and liabilities**, particularly in how it **allocates capital, invests in innovation, and maintains financial flexibility**.

**Key Strategies in Asset & Liability Management:**

- **High Cash Reserves:** Apple maintains significant cash and cash equivalents, allowing it to **fund R&D and acquisitions without relying on excessive debt**.
- **Intangible Assets & Innovation:** Apple's **trademarks, patents, and software ecosystem** (e.g., iOS, App Store) are its most valuable assets, contributing to its long-term dominance.
- **Debt Strategy:** Despite holding billions in cash, Apple strategically issues **long-term bonds** to take advantage of **low-interest rates** for financing new projects and stock buybacks.

**Financial Impact:**

- **Efficient asset turnover** has helped Apple generate **consistent revenue growth** and industry-leading profit margins.
- **Minimal reliance on short-term liabilities**, ensuring **strong liquidity** and financial stability during economic downturns.

**Lesson Learned:**

- **Strategic asset investment and well-managed liabilities lead to financial sustainability and growth.**

## Case Study 2: General Electric (GE) – Poor Asset & Liability Management Led to Decline

**Background:** General Electric (GE) was once one of the **largest and most successful conglomerates** globally, but in recent years, it has struggled due to **poor financial management and excessive liabilities**.

**What Went Wrong?**

- **Over-Leveraging & High Debt:** GE accumulated **massive long-term liabilities**, taking on **too much debt for acquisitions that didn't generate expected returns**.
- **Asset Mismanagement:** The company expanded into **too many industries**, resulting in **inefficient asset utilization** and difficulties in maintaining profitability across divisions.
- **Cash Flow Shortages:** GE struggled to generate enough **operating cash flow** to cover **debt repayments and business investments**, leading to **dividend cuts and layoffs**.

**Financial Impact:**

- GE's **stock price collapsed from over $30 per share to under $10**, as investors lost confidence in its **ability to manage assets and liabilities** effectively.
- The company was forced to **sell off major business divisions** to reduce debt, significantly shrinking its market influence.

**Lesson Learned:**

- **Taking on too much long-term debt without sustainable cash flow can lead to financial distress.**

## Case Study 3: Tesla's Asset Investment & Risk-Taking Approach

**Background:** Tesla Inc., led by **Elon Musk**, took a **high-risk, high-reward approach** to asset management. Unlike Apple, Tesla operated with **aggressive debt financing** to fund its expansion.

**Key Strategies in Asset & Liability Management:**

- **Heavy Investment in Manufacturing Assets:** Tesla **invested billions** into its **Gigafactories**, despite initially struggling with **cash flow shortages and high production costs**.
- **Debt-Funded Expansion:** The company took on **significant long-term liabilities** to fund **battery technology development and autonomous driving research**.
- **Rapid Asset Turnover & Innovation:** Despite its **high-risk model**, Tesla managed to **turn its assets into revenue growth**

**quickly**, improving cash flow over time.

**Financial Impact:**

- Initially, Tesla **struggled with financial losses** due to high debt, but its **asset investments paid off**, making it one of the **most valuable automakers in the world**.
- Effective use of long-term financing enabled Tesla to **survive early financial struggles and scale globally**.

**Lesson Learned:**

- **Strategic long-term debt can be beneficial if assets are turned into revenue effectively.**

## Conclusion: Strategic Asset & Liability Management

Effective management of **assets and liabilities** is essential for maintaining financial stability, optimizing cash flow, and ensuring long-term growth. Businesses that invest in **productive assets, track depreciation, and manage debt responsibly** can improve their profitability and strengthen their financial position.

By understanding **current vs. non-current assets**, companies can **allocate resources efficiently** and determine the best strategies for investing in **new equipment, expanding operations, and improving financial health**. Similarly, recognizing **short-term vs. long-term liabilities** enables businesses to **balance financial obligations while maintaining liquidity**.

# DEPRECIATION AND AMORTIZATION

## Introduction: Understanding Depreciation and Amortization

Every business acquires assets—whether **tangible** (e.g., buildings, machinery, vehicles) or **intangible** (e.g., patents, trademarks, copyrights). Over time, these assets **lose value or become obsolete**, making it necessary to allocate their costs systematically. This process is known as **depreciation for tangible assets** and **amortization**

**for intangible assets**.

Depreciation and amortization serve critical functions in business finance:

- **They allow businesses to match asset costs with the revenue they generate**, ensuring financial statements reflect realistic profitability.
- **They reduce taxable income**, allowing businesses to optimize tax savings.
- **They provide a clear financial picture for investors, lenders, and decision-makers**, helping assess the company's long-term financial stability.

In this chapter, we will explore:

- **How depreciation and amortization work** and why they are critical in financial reporting.
- **Different depreciation calculation methods and their applications.**
- **Amortization of intangible assets and how businesses account for them.**
- **The financial statement impact of depreciation and amortization.**
- **Tax strategies using depreciation for financial benefits.**
- **Real-world case studies of businesses that successfully use depreciation and amortization to their advantage.**

## Understanding Depreciation

### What is Depreciation?

Depreciation is the **systematic allocation of an asset's cost over its useful life**, ensuring that financial statements reflect a realistic valuation of business assets. Since **fixed assets** such as machinery, buildings, and vehicles **lose value over time** due to **wear and tear, obsolescence, or decreasing efficiency**, businesses must account for this gradual reduction.

If depreciation were not recorded, a company's **financial statements would overstate profitability**, leading to **inaccurate tax calculations, misleading investor reports, and poor financial decision-making**.

### Why is Depreciation Necessary?

Depreciation is essential for several reasons:

30. **Accurate Financial Reporting** – Allocating asset costs over time ensures that **financial statements reflect a true and fair view of a company's performance**.
31. **Profitability Alignment** – Businesses **match the cost of an asset with the revenue it helps generate**, ensuring that expenses are **spread evenly over its productive life**.
32. **Tax Benefits** – Depreciation is a **non-cash expense**, meaning businesses can deduct it from taxable income, reducing overall tax liability.
33. **Capital Budgeting** – By tracking depreciation, companies can **plan for asset replacements and upgrades**, ensuring **efficient use of**

**financial resources.**

## Depreciation Example: The Impact on Financial Statements

Consider a **manufacturing company** that purchases **machinery for $500,000** with an expected useful life of **10 years**. If the company **immediately records the full cost** of the machine in one year, the financial reports would **show a massive expense**, making it appear as if the company was **operating at a loss**.

However, by **depreciating the cost over 10 years**, the company **gradually spreads the expense**, allowing for a more **accurate reflection of financial performance**. This means that:

- Instead of recording a **one-time $500,000 expense**, the company records **$50,000 per year** (assuming straight-line depreciation).
- Net income is **not artificially reduced** in the year of purchase.
- The company **maintains a more stable profit trend**, improving investor confidence.

## How Depreciation Impacts Different Stakeholders

34. **For Business Owners:** Depreciation helps manage **asset replacement schedules**, ensuring that machinery, buildings, and equipment are **replaced before they become obsolete**.
35. **For Investors & Analysts:** Investors assess **depreciation trends** to understand whether a company **invests sufficiently in its long-term assets** or is at risk of **outdated infrastructure**.

36. **For Tax Authorities:** Governments allow depreciation deductions because they recognize that businesses **incur real costs for asset deterioration over time**.

## Depreciation vs. Immediate Expense Recognition

If businesses were required to record the full cost of assets immediately:

- **Profitability would fluctuate dramatically**, making financial statements **inconsistent year over year**.
- **Taxable income would be artificially reduced** in asset-purchase years, then **artificially inflated** in following years.
- **Companies would struggle to budget for future capital expenditures**, as asset values would disappear from the books too quickly.

## Real-World Example of Depreciation in Action

### *Amazon's Use of Depreciation in Warehouse Expansion*

Amazon, one of the world's largest e-commerce companies, **invests billions in warehouses, distribution centers, and robotics**. Instead of recording the full cost of these investments in the year of purchase, Amazon **depreciates these assets over time**, reducing tax liabilities and ensuring long-term financial stability.

- By **depreciating warehouse facilities over 30-40 years** and **robotics over 5-7 years**, Amazon maintains a **stable net income** and **maximizes cash flow** for reinvestments.
- This strategy **minimizes taxable income in early years**, allowing

Amazon to continuously expand its infrastructure **without excessive tax burdens**.

## Conclusion

Depreciation is **not just an accounting formality**—it is a **critical financial strategy** that impacts **profitability, tax planning, and capital management**. Businesses must carefully choose **depreciation methods** that align with their industry standards, financial goals, and tax strategies to ensure **long-term financial sustainability and asset optimization**.

# Methods of Calculating Depreciation

There are **several methods** for calculating depreciation, each with its unique advantages. Businesses choose the method that best fits their **industry, asset usage, and financial goals**.

## 1. Straight-Line Depreciation (SLD) – Simple & Consistent

This method spreads depreciation **evenly** over an asset's useful life.

- Best for: Assets that have **consistent usage** over time (e.g., office furniture, buildings).
- **Advantage:** Predictable and simple, making it widely used for financial reporting.

**Example:** A company purchases a **$100,000 machine** with a useful life of **10 years** and a **salvage value of $10,000** (expected resale value at the end of its life). The annual depreciation expense would be calculated by subtracting the salvage value from the purchase cost and dividing it by the useful life.

### 2. Declining Balance Depreciation (DBD) – Faster Write-Offs

The **double-declining balance (DDB) method** depreciates assets faster in their **early years**, which is useful for tax benefits.

- Best for: Assets that **lose value quickly** (e.g., vehicles, computers).
- **Advantage:** Reduces taxable income **more aggressively in the first few years**.

### 3. Units of Production Method (UoP) – Usage-Based Depreciation

Instead of using time, this method **bases depreciation on asset usage**, such as hours operated or miles driven.

- Best for: **Manufacturing equipment, trucks, airplanes**—where value depends on output rather than time.
- **Advantage: More accurate reflection** of asset wear and tear based on actual usage.

## Amortization of Intangible Assets

### What is Amortization?

Like depreciation, **amortization spreads an asset's cost over its useful life**, but it applies to **intangible assets** instead of physical ones.

### Examples of Intangible Assets:

- **Patents** – Typically amortized over **20 years**, since patents have a **legal expiration date.**
- **Copyrights & Trademarks** – Amortized based on their **legal lifespan** or business use.
- **Software Development Costs** – Spread over an estimated period of **technological usefulness.**

### Key Differences Between Amortization and Depreciation

37. **Depreciation applies to tangible assets**, while **amortization applies to intangible assets.**
38. **Depreciation often considers salvage value**, but **amortization usually assumes complete asset exhaustion.**
39. **Depreciation allows for various methods (e.g., straight-line, declining balance)**, whereas **amortization is almost always straight-line.**

## Financial Statement Impact of Depreciation & Amortization

### 1. Income Statement Effects

Both depreciation and amortization are recorded as **operating expenses, reducing net income.**

### 2. Balance Sheet Implications

- Depreciation lowers an asset's **book value** over time.
- Intangible assets appear as **net book value**, reflecting amortization deductions.

### 3. Cash Flow Impact

Depreciation and amortization are **non-cash expenses**, meaning businesses **add them back** when calculating net cash flows.

## Tax Implications & Strategies

### 1. Depreciation Tax Deductions

Governments allow businesses to **deduct depreciation from taxable income**, lowering tax liability.

### 2. Special Tax Programs for Depreciation

- **Bonus Depreciation** – Businesses can deduct **a large portion of an asset's cost upfront** instead of over several years.
- **Section 179 Deduction** – Allows small businesses to **fully expense qualifying asset purchases immediately**.

### 3. Strategic Tax Planning Using Depreciation

- **Using Accelerated Depreciation** – Helps defer taxes, keeping more cash within the business in early years.

- **Optimizing Asset Purchase Timing** – Buying assets near year-end allows for **faster tax deductions**.

## Real-World Case Studies

### 1. Amazon's Warehouse Depreciation Strategy

Amazon invests billions in **warehouses and automation equipment**, using depreciation to offset tax burdens while expanding aggressively.

### 2. Tesla's Gigafactory Write-Offs

Tesla uses depreciation deductions to **lower reported taxable income**, reinvesting savings into R&D.

## Conclusion: The Power of Depreciation & Amortization

Depreciation and amortization are **more than just accounting entries**—they are **powerful financial tools** that influence a company's **profitability, tax obligations, investment decisions, and long-term financial strategy**. Businesses that strategically manage depreciation and amortization can **enhance cash flow, optimize tax benefits, and ensure financial statements accurately reflect business performance**.

## Why Depreciation & Amortization Matter

Effective depreciation and amortization strategies allow businesses to:

40. **Ensure Financial Accuracy** – Assets do not last forever, and businesses must account for their diminishing value to **present realistic financial statements**. Proper depreciation methods

ensure that **profitability is reported accurately**, allowing for **clearer financial comparisons over time**.

41. **Optimize Tax Efficiency** – Depreciation and amortization **reduce taxable income**, allowing businesses to **retain more earnings for reinvestment**. Companies that use **accelerated depreciation methods** or **bonus depreciation provisions** can significantly **lower tax burdens in early years**, freeing up cash for growth.

42. **Improve Capital Planning** – Depreciation and amortization help businesses **forecast when assets need to be replaced** and how much to allocate for future investments. Without proper depreciation tracking, businesses **risk underestimating capital needs**, leading to **unexpected costs or operational disruptions**.

43. **Enhance Business Valuation & Investment Appeal** – Investors and stakeholders **assess a company's asset management efficiency** when determining valuation. Companies that **effectively manage asset depreciation schedules** signal **strong financial discipline**, increasing investor confidence.

44. **Strengthen Long-Term Financial Stability** – Businesses that align depreciation and amortization with their financial strategy can **balance expenses, stabilize cash flow, and create predictable financial outcomes**. This is particularly important for **capital-intensive industries** like manufacturing, real estate, and technology, where asset depreciation plays a significant role in long-term financial planning.

## The Role of Depreciation in Business Decision-Making

- **Manufacturing companies** strategically use **units of production depreciation** to ensure that machinery depreciation aligns with **actual usage levels**, preventing over- or under-depreciation.
- **Retailers and e-commerce businesses** depreciate **warehouse infrastructure, IT equipment, and logistics assets** to maintain operational efficiency.
- **Technology firms** amortize **software development costs and intellectual property**, ensuring that investments in innovation are **spread over their useful lifespan**.
- **Service-based companies** rely on amortization to track the **value of acquired customer lists, contracts, and goodwill** from mergers and acquisitions.

By tailoring depreciation and amortization approaches to their industry, businesses can **align asset valuation with business performance, enhance tax planning, and improve cash flow management**.

## Depreciation & Amortization: A Strategic Advantage in Financial Management

Depreciation and amortization are more than just accounting concepts—they are powerful financial tools that directly impact business profitability, tax efficiency, and capital investment strategies. **Failing to account for asset depreciation accurately can distort financial reports, inflate profits, and result in tax miscalculations that weaken a company's financial position.** On the other hand, businesses that **proactively**

**manage asset depreciation and amortization gain a significant advantage** in financial planning, investment decisions, and long-term growth.

In this chapter, we explored how different depreciation methods—such as **straight-line, declining balance, and units-of-production—affect financial statements, tax obligations, and asset valuations.** We also examined amortization's role in spreading out the cost of intangible assets, ensuring that businesses align their expenses with revenue generation in a way that reflects economic reality.

Businesses that strategically leverage depreciation and amortization:

- **Optimize cash flow and tax deductions**, ensuring they retain capital for reinvestment and expansion.
- **Strengthen investor and lender confidence** by maintaining accurate, transparent financial reporting.
- **Enhance long-term financial planning** by aligning asset expenditures with business cycles and revenue streams.
- **Ensure regulatory compliance** by following accounting standards and industry best practices.

Mastering depreciation and amortization allows companies to make **data-driven decisions** about asset acquisition, replacement, and financial structuring. By understanding the economic lifespan of both tangible and intangible assets, businesses can position themselves for **sustained profitability, reduced financial risk, and long-term competitive advantage.**

# THE IMPORTANCE OF EQUITY & RETAINED EARNINGS

## Introduction: The Role of Equity in Business Stability and Growth

Equity is one of the most fundamental components of a company's financial structure. It represents the **ownership interest** in a business and reflects the **net worth** of the company after liabilities are deducted from total assets. Unlike debt, which must be repaid, equity provides businesses with a **sustainable source of funding** that does not carry the burden of interest payments or repayment obligations.

Equity plays a crucial role in **business expansion, investment opportunities, and financial decision-making**. For start ups and growing companies, equity is often used to **attract investors, raise capital, and fund operations**. Established businesses rely on equity to **strengthen their financial position, reinvest in operations, and distribute earnings to shareholders**.

This chapter explores the **difference between owner's investment and retained earnings**, the impact of dividends on financial health, and how start ups use equity for growth. It also includes a **practical exercise** to reinforce key equity concepts.

## Understanding Equity: Owner's Investment vs. Retained Earnings

### Definition and Components of Equity

Equity represents the **ownership stake** in a business and is recorded in the company's financial statements as **shareholder's equity or owner's equity**, depending on the type of business structure. Equity consists of two primary components:

- **Owner's Investment (Paid-in Capital)** – Funds contributed by the business owner(s) or investors.
- **Retained Earnings** – Profits that have been accumulated and

reinvested in the business rather than distributed as dividends.

Equity can be **raised through private investment, public stock offerings, or reinvesting earnings from operations**. The balance of equity fluctuates over time based on **business performance, investment decisions, and dividend payments**.

## Owner's Investment: Capital Contributions and Stock Issuance

Owner's investment, also known as **paid-in capital**, refers to the funds contributed to the business by its owners or shareholders. This investment can take different forms depending on the business structure:

- **Sole Proprietorship and Partnerships** – The owner(s) contribute **personal funds** to start and grow the business.
- **Corporations** – Companies issue **common stock and preferred stock** to investors in exchange for capital.

New businesses often rely heavily on **equity financing** since they may not have the credit history or revenue required to secure loans. In contrast, established companies may issue **additional shares** to raise capital for expansion.

**Example:** A technology start up raises funds from private investors by issuing **equity shares**. The funds are used for **product development, hiring employees, and expanding operations**.

### Retained Earnings: The Accumulation of Profits Over Time

Retained earnings represent **profits that a business reinvests instead of distributing to shareholders as dividends**. These earnings are used to **finance business growth, purchase new equipment, pay down debt, or build reserves for future stability**.

Unlike paid-in capital, which comes from external investments, retained earnings are **generated internally through business operations**.

Retained earnings can be **increased or decreased** based on the company's financial decisions:

- **Increased when the company earns a profit and retains those earnings instead of distributing them.**
- **Decreased when the company incurs losses or distributes earnings to shareholders in the form of dividends.**

**Example:** A retail company earns significant profits and chooses to reinvest its retained earnings to **open new store locations** rather than pay dividends to shareholders.

## Dividends and Their Impact on Financial Health

### What Are Dividends?

Dividends are **payments made to shareholders** from a company's profits. These distributions can take the form of **cash payments, stock dividends, or property dividends**. While dividends provide shareholders with a return on investment, they also **reduce the amount of retained earnings**

**available for reinvestment.**

A company's **dividend policy** depends on factors such as profitability, growth objectives, and financial stability.

## Types of Dividends

45. **Cash Dividends** – The most common form, where shareholders receive cash payments per share.
46. **Stock Dividends** – Shareholders receive additional shares instead of cash, increasing ownership stakes.
47. **Property Dividends** – Non-cash dividends distributed in the form of company assets.

A **high dividend payout** may attract investors seeking regular income, but it can also **limit a company's ability to reinvest profits for growth**. Conversely, companies that **retain most of their earnings** may experience higher stock price appreciation, benefiting investors in the long run.

**Example:** A pharmaceutical company experiencing rapid growth reinvests most of its profits into **research and development** rather than issuing large dividends, ensuring continued expansion.

## The Impact of Dividend Decisions on Financial Health

The decision to pay dividends influences several key financial aspects:

- **Liquidity** – Cash dividends reduce a company's available cash reserves, which can impact its ability to meet operational expenses.
- **Growth Potential** – Companies that reinvest profits into expansion

projects can enhance their market position and long-term sustainability.

- **Investor Perception** – A company with a **consistent dividend policy** is often seen as financially stable, while irregular or reduced dividends may signal financial distress.

**Case Study:** A telecommunications company faced financial challenges but continued issuing dividends to maintain investor confidence. However, this decision strained the company's cash flow and limited its ability to **invest in new infrastructure**, ultimately affecting long-term growth.

## Case Study: How Start Ups Use Equity for Growth

Start ups often rely on **equity financing** to fund their early stages of development. Unlike established businesses that can leverage profits or bank loans, start ups issue **equity shares to investors** in exchange for funding.

### Key Ways Start ups Use Equity Financing

- **Seed Funding and Venture Capital** – Investors provide capital in exchange for an equity stake in the company.
- **Initial Public Offerings (IPOs)** – High-growth start ups issue public shares to raise large-scale funding.
- **Employee Stock Options** – Start ups offer shares to employees as incentives, aligning company success with employee motivation.

**Example:** A software start up raises equity funding from venture capital firms to develop its product. Instead of taking on debt, the start up offers **a percentage of ownership to investors** in return for capital, allowing it to scale operations without immediate repayment obligations.

## Practical Exercise: Calculate Equity Based on Business Transactions

Consider the following scenario:

A business has the following financial activities during the year:

- The owner invests capital into the business.
- The company generates revenue and incurs operating expenses.
- Some of the profits are retained, while the rest is paid out as dividends.

**Exercise:**

Based on these activities, determine:

48. **Total equity at the end of the year.**
49. **The impact of dividends on retained earnings.**
50. **How equity changes with new investments or losses.**

This exercise helps reinforce how **equity is built, retained, and distributed**, shaping a company's long-term financial health.

## The Impact of Equity and Retained Earnings on Business Growth

To understand how **equity management, retained earnings, and dividend policies** influence a company's financial success, let's explore **real-world examples** of businesses that have effectively leveraged equity—or suffered consequences due to mismanagement.

## Case Study 1: Apple Inc. – Balancing Retained Earnings and Shareholder Value

### Background

Apple Inc. is one of the most successful technology companies in the world, with a strong focus on **retained earnings and shareholder value**. The company generates **billions of dollars in profit each year** and has historically reinvested earnings to fund **product innovation, research and development, and market expansion**.

### Equity Strategy

- Apple has used **retained earnings** to develop and launch ground breaking products like the iPhone, iPad, and Apple Watch.
- The company maintains a **strong cash reserve** while strategically issuing **dividends and share buybacks** to reward investors.
- Rather than relying on external financing, Apple uses its **high equity reserves to fund acquisitions, expand its global retail presence, and improve technology infrastructure**.

### Financial Impact

- Apple's strategic use of retained earnings has resulted in **consistent revenue growth and high profit margins**.
- Investors remain confident in Apple's financial health due to its **balanced approach to dividend payments and reinvestment**.
- The company's **stock buyback program** has increased shareholder value, reducing outstanding shares and boosting earnings per share.

### Key Takeaway

A **well-balanced approach to equity management**—including **retaining earnings for innovation while rewarding investors with dividends and stock repurchases**—is a proven strategy for **long-term success and market leadership**.

## Case Study 2: Tesla Inc. – Using Equity to Fund Growth and Expansion

### Background

Tesla, the electric vehicle (EV) giant, has relied heavily on **equity financing** to support its **rapid expansion and technological advancements**. Unlike traditional automakers that finance projects through long-term debt, Tesla has consistently raised capital through **equity offerings and retained earnings**.

## Equity Strategy

- Tesla issued new shares multiple times to **raise billions of dollars**, using the funds for **gigafactory construction, battery innovation, and international market expansion**.
- The company initially **did not pay dividends**, choosing instead to **reinvest all profits into research and development** to improve EV technology and autonomous driving capabilities.
- By maintaining a **high equity ratio**, Tesla avoided excessive debt, giving the company greater **financial flexibility**.

## Financial Impact

- Tesla became **one of the most valuable companies in the world**, despite operating at a loss for many years.
- Investors supported Tesla's **aggressive equity financing strategy**, believing in its long-term vision for EV dominance.
- The company's strong **retained earnings and reinvestment model** led to significant breakthroughs in battery technology and vehicle production efficiency.

## Key Takeaway

Start ups and high-growth companies can use **equity financing as a strategic tool** to fund expansion, develop new technologies, and scale operations without accumulating excessive debt.

## Case Study 3: General Electric (GE) – The Consequences of Poor Equity and Dividend Management

### Background

General Electric (GE), once an industrial powerhouse, struggled due to **poor equity management, excessive dividend payouts, and a failure to reinvest earnings strategically**.

### Equity Strategy Gone Wrong

- GE **prioritized dividend payments over reinvesting profits**, distributing a significant portion of earnings to shareholders instead of strengthening its balance sheet.
- The company also engaged in **aggressive stock buybacks**, using available cash to repurchase shares instead of investing in its core industrial businesses.
- During economic downturns, GE **faced cash flow challenges**, but since much of its earnings had already been paid out as dividends, it lacked the retained earnings necessary to stabilize operations.

### Financial Impact

- GE's inability to **maintain a sustainable dividend policy** led to **a dividend cut**, which damaged investor confidence.
- Without sufficient **retained earnings**, the company was forced to **sell off key business units** and take on significant debt to cover

operational costs.

- GE's stock price plummeted as investors lost trust in the company's **equity strategy and financial management.**

### Key Takeaway

An **unsustainable dividend policy** and failure to reinvest retained earnings can lead to **financial distress, reduced shareholder value, and long-term instability.**

## Case Study 4: Amazon – Prioritizing Growth Over Dividends

### Background

Amazon, the global e-commerce and cloud computing giant, has built its financial empire by **reinvesting nearly all its profits instead of paying dividends.** Since its inception, Amazon has **focused on scaling operations, expanding into new markets, and innovating in multiple industries.**

### Equity Strategy

- Amazon does not pay dividends, instead **reinvesting earnings into business expansion, technology development, and acquisitions.**
- The company has used **retained earnings to fund projects** like Amazon Web Services (AWS), which now generates a significant portion of its profits.

- By consistently prioritizing reinvestment, Amazon has grown into one of the **most valuable and influential companies in the world**.

## Financial Impact

- Amazon's **aggressive reinvestment strategy** led to massive infrastructure expansion, strengthening its market position.
- Investors continued supporting Amazon despite its **lack of dividend payments**, as they recognized the company's **long-term vision for sustained growth**.
- The decision to **retain profits instead of distributing dividends** allowed Amazon to **remain competitive and dominate multiple industries**.

## Key Takeaway

For companies focused on **long-term expansion, retaining earnings rather than distributing dividends** can fuel **innovation, global market entry, and business diversification**.

## Key Lessons from These Case Studies

A well-balanced equity strategy is fundamental to a company's ability to achieve sustainable growth while maintaining financial stability. Businesses that carefully manage their retained earnings can reinvest in innovation, fund expansion, and create a financial cushion that enables them to navigate economic downturns without relying excessively on debt or external funding. Companies that prioritize reinvestment, such as Amazon and

Tesla, have demonstrated how leveraging retained earnings can fuel long-term success, allowing them to scale operations and maintain a competitive advantage in their respective industries.

For start ups and high-growth companies, equity financing plays a critical role in securing the necessary capital to scale quickly. Instead of accumulating debt, which comes with the burden of interest payments and repayment schedules, these businesses can issue equity to raise funds while maintaining financial flexibility. Tesla's ability to raise capital through equity rather than relying on excessive borrowing illustrates how this approach can support long-term expansion and technological advancement.

On the other hand, companies that fail to manage their dividend policies effectively risk depleting their financial reserves and weakening their ability to sustain long-term growth. General Electric's financial struggles serve as a cautionary example of how excessive dividend payments and aggressive stock buybacks can drain essential capital, leaving the company vulnerable to financial distress when revenue declines. A poorly structured dividend strategy can limit a company's ability to reinvest in core operations, reduce its capacity to fund new initiatives, and ultimately erode investor confidence.

Investor confidence is directly tied to how a company manages its equity, dividends, and retained earnings. Businesses that reinvest profits wisely and maintain a disciplined approach to capital allocation are more likely to attract long-term investors who recognize the value of financial stability and growth potential. Apple's balanced approach—paying dividends while retaining significant earnings for reinvestment—has enabled it to maintain industry leadership while keeping investors engaged.

By adopting a strategic approach to equity and retained earnings, businesses can optimize financial growth, strengthen their market position, and build lasting investor trust. The most successful companies strike a careful balance between rewarding shareholders, reinvesting in innovation, and maintaining financial resilience, ensuring they can withstand market fluctuations and continue to grow in an increasingly competitive landscape.

## Conclusion: The Role of Equity in Financial Growth

Equity is a **fundamental pillar of financial stability and business expansion**, serving as both a **source of funding** and an **indicator of a company's financial health**. Whether through **owner contributions, retained earnings, or strategic issuance of shares**, equity enables businesses to **fund operations, invest in growth opportunities, and sustain long-term financial success**.

Unlike debt, which requires **regular interest payments and eventual repayment**, equity provides a **more flexible and sustainable source of capital**. Businesses that effectively manage their equity structure can **strengthen investor confidence, enhance financial resilience, and create long-term value for stakeholders**.

Equity financing is particularly crucial for **early-stage companies and high-growth enterprises**, allowing them to **access capital without the burden of debt financing**. For established corporations, maintaining a **well-balanced equity structure** ensures that funds are allocated **efficiently between reinvestment, dividend payments, and financial reserves**.

However, mismanagement of equity can lead to **financial instability, shareholder dissatisfaction, and limited access to future capital**.

Companies that distribute too much of their profits as **dividends** may find themselves lacking **sufficient retained earnings for reinvestment**, while those that **issue excessive shares** risk **diluting ownership and reducing stock value**.

## Key Takeaways

- **Equity financing provides businesses with capital for expansion without the obligations of debt repayment.** Companies can raise funds through **private investments, venture capital, or public stock offerings**, ensuring they have the resources needed to **scale operations and innovate**.
- **Retained earnings serve as a critical resource for reinvestment and financial security.** Companies that reinvest a **portion of their profits** can fund **new projects, expand infrastructure, and improve operational efficiency**, reducing reliance on external financing.
- **Dividend policies significantly impact financial liquidity, growth potential, and investor perception.** A company that **consistently pays dividends** may attract **income-seeking investors**, but excessive distributions can **limit reinvestment potential**, affecting **long-term financial stability**.
- **Start ups strategically use equity to fund operations and attract investors.** New businesses often rely on **venture capital and private equity funding**, exchanging **ownership stakes for financial support**. This allows them to **scale quickly** while maintaining operational flexibility.

- **Balancing owner's investment, retained earnings, and dividend distributions is essential for financial sustainability.** Companies must carefully evaluate **how much of their earnings should be reinvested, distributed, or used to strengthen financial reserves**, ensuring long-term **profitability and competitiveness**.

## The Long-Term Impact of Equity Management

A company's approach to **equity management** determines its **financial trajectory and competitive positioning**. Businesses that establish a **strong equity foundation** are better equipped to **navigate economic fluctuations, seize growth opportunities, and adapt to market changes**.

For investors, a well-managed equity structure reflects **financial discipline, strategic foresight, and commitment to long-term value creation**. Businesses that maintain **stable retained earnings, carefully structured dividends, and balanced equity financing** are more likely to **attract investors, secure favorable financing, and achieve sustainable growth**.

As businesses evolve, their equity management strategies must adapt to **market conditions, regulatory changes, and evolving financial goals**. By maintaining a **disciplined approach to equity and retained earnings**, companies can ensure their **long-term financial health, investor confidence, and market leadership**.

# INTRODUCTION TO MANAGERIAL ACCOUNTING

## Introduction: The Role of Managerial Accounting in Business Success

In today's fast-paced business environment, making **informed financial decisions** is critical to **staying competitive, maximizing profitability, and ensuring long-term sustainability**. While financial accounting focuses on reporting past performance to **external stakeholders**, managerial accounting is **internally focused**, providing managers with the **data and tools needed to make strategic decisions**.

Managerial accounting is not just about recording numbers; it is about **using financial data to drive business success**. Through budgeting, forecasting, cost analysis, and performance measurement, managerial accounting equips businesses with the **insights needed to optimize operations, control costs, and set achievable financial goals**.

This chapter will introduce the fundamentals of **managerial accounting**, highlighting its **scope, objectives, and how it differs from financial accounting**. We will also explore **how businesses use managerial accounting for decision-making, budgeting, and cost management**, ensuring that financial resources are **allocated efficiently** to support growth.

## Purpose and Scope of Managerial Accounting

### What is Managerial Accounting?

Managerial accounting is a branch of accounting that focuses on **internal business operations**, helping companies **plan, control, and evaluate financial performance**. Unlike financial accounting, which follows **strict reporting regulations** (such as GAAP or IFRS), managerial accounting is **flexible and tailored to a company's specific needs**.

At its core, managerial accounting provides **financial and non-financial data** that assists with:

- **Strategic Planning** – Setting financial goals and aligning resources accordingly.

- **Budgeting & Forecasting** – Estimating future revenue, costs, and profit margins.
- **Performance Measurement** – Analyzing profitability, efficiency, and cost-effectiveness.
- **Operational Decision-Making** – Determining pricing strategies, cost control, and investment opportunities.

## Scope of Managerial Accounting

Managerial accounting encompasses a **wide range of financial activities** that assist businesses in making **informed decisions, controlling costs, and optimizing performance**. Unlike financial accounting, which focuses on **historical reporting and compliance**, managerial accounting is **flexible, forward-looking, and customized to the needs of the organization**. It provides **real-time financial insights** that help managers set **strategic goals, allocate resources efficiently, and measure success**.

## Key Areas of Managerial Accounting

### *1. Budgeting & Forecasting: Planning for Financial Stability*

**Budgeting and forecasting are critical for financial planning**, helping businesses set goals, allocate resources, and anticipate future financial needs.

- **Budgeting** involves creating a **detailed financial plan** that outlines projected revenue, expenses, and cash flow over a specific period. Businesses use **operating budgets, capital budgets, and cash flow budgets** to ensure financial stability.

- **Forecasting** predicts future financial performance using **historical data, market trends, and economic indicators**. This allows businesses to **anticipate potential risks and opportunities**, ensuring they can respond proactively.

**Example:** A retail company uses sales forecasts to determine **inventory purchasing plans**, ensuring they stock enough products to meet demand without overstocking.

### *2. Cost Analysis: Understanding and Optimizing Costs*

Managerial accounting helps businesses analyze **cost structures** to maximize efficiency and reduce unnecessary expenses. Cost analysis involves:

- **Fixed Costs** (e.g., rent, salaries) – Costs that remain constant regardless of production levels.
- **Variable Costs** (e.g., raw materials, commission) – Costs that fluctuate with production and sales volume.
- **Mixed Costs** (e.g., utilities, maintenance) – Costs that have both fixed and variable components.

Understanding cost behavior enables businesses to **identify inefficiencies, optimize pricing strategies, and improve profitability**.

**Example:** A manufacturing company conducting a cost analysis may **switch suppliers** or negotiate better contracts to reduce material costs while maintaining quality.

### *3. Profitability Analysis: Measuring Business Performance*

Businesses must regularly evaluate profitability to ensure they are generating

**sufficient returns on investment (ROI)**. Managerial accounting helps assess profitability by:

- **Calculating Gross & Net Profit Margins** – Helps managers understand **how much revenue remains after covering costs**.
- **Evaluating Return on Investment (ROI)** – Measures how efficiently a business **turns capital into profit**.
- **Analyzing Product & Service Profitability** – Identifies **which products or services contribute the most to the company's bottom line**.

**Example:** A restaurant chain uses profitability analysis to determine **which menu items generate the highest profit margins** and adjust its offerings accordingly.

### *4. Break-Even Analysis: Determining Financial Viability*

Break-even analysis is a crucial tool that helps businesses understand the **minimum sales volume required to cover costs**. This analysis allows businesses to:

- **Determine the break-even point (BEP)** – The sales level where total revenue equals total costs.
- **Set pricing strategies** based on cost structures and target profits.
- **Make investment decisions** by assessing the feasibility of expanding operations or launching new products.

**Example:** A tech start up uses break-even analysis to determine **how many units of a new software subscription must be sold** before covering development costs.

***5. Variance Analysis: Measuring Financial Performance Against Expectations***

Variance analysis compares **actual financial performance to budgeted or forecasted figures**, identifying **discrepancies and areas for improvement**. This analysis is used to:

- **Pinpoint cost overruns or savings** in production and operations.
- **Improve financial planning** by refining future budget assumptions.
- **Hold departments accountable** for performance and spending.

**Example:** A hotel chain identifies that **actual utility costs are significantly higher than budgeted**, prompting an investigation into **energy efficiency improvements**.

## Why Managerial Accounting is More Flexible Than Financial Accounting

Unlike financial accounting, which is governed by **GAAP (Generally Accepted Accounting Principles) or IFRS (International Financial Reporting Standards)**, managerial accounting:

- **Does not have strict reporting guidelines** – Businesses can tailor reports to meet specific needs.
- **Is designed for internal use** – Unlike financial statements, which are meant for investors and regulators, managerial accounting reports are for **business owners, managers, and executives**.
- **Focuses on operational decision-making** – Financial accounting

reports **past performance**, while managerial accounting helps businesses **predict and improve future performance.**

## How Businesses Benefit from Strong Managerial Accounting Practices

**Increased Profitability** – By analyzing revenue streams and cost structures, businesses can **maximize profit margins and reduce waste. Better Cash Flow Management** – Effective budgeting and forecasting help businesses **maintain financial stability** and **avoid cash shortages. Data-Driven Decision Making** – Managerial accounting provides actionable insights that **help businesses scale, invest, and adapt to market changes. Improved Cost Control** – Businesses can **identify and eliminate unnecessary expenses**, ensuring resources are used efficiently.

**Example:** A multinational corporation uses **real-time financial dashboards** to track profitability across different markets, allowing executives to make **quick, informed decisions** on pricing and expansion.

## Conclusion: Why Managerial Accounting is Essential for Business Success

The **scope of managerial accounting is vast**, covering essential functions like **budgeting, forecasting, cost control, profitability analysis, and financial planning.** Unlike financial accounting, which is focused on **compliance and external reporting**, managerial accounting provides businesses with **the tools they need to make strategic decisions that drive growth and efficiency.**

By implementing strong managerial accounting practices, companies can:

- **Improve financial stability** through better budgeting and cash flow management.
- **Increase profitability** by analyzing cost structures and setting optimal pricing strategies.
- **Make smarter investment decisions** by using financial data to forecast revenue and expenses.
- **Achieve long-term business growth** through proactive planning and strategic financial management.

Understanding **the full scope of managerial accounting** ensures that business owners and managers have the **insights they need to optimize operations, improve decision-making, and stay ahead in competitive markets**.

## Key Differences Between Managerial and Financial Accounting

Although both managerial and financial accounting deal with **financial data**, they serve **different purposes and audiences**.

### 1. Audience & Purpose

- **Financial Accounting:** Reports information for **external stakeholders** such as investors, creditors, and regulatory agencies.
- **Managerial Accounting:** Provides insights for **internal stakeholders**, such as executives, department managers, and operational teams.

## 2. Focus & Timeframe

- **Financial Accounting:** Focuses on **historical data**, summarizing a company's past performance.
- **Managerial Accounting:** Focuses on **future-oriented** financial planning, forecasting, and decision-making.

## 3. Reporting Standards

- **Financial Accounting:** Must follow established regulations such as **GAAP or IFRS** to ensure consistency across industries.
- **Managerial Accounting:** Is **not bound by formal regulations**, allowing companies to **customize reports based on internal needs.**

## 4. Report Format & Frequency

- **Financial Accounting:** Produces **standardized reports** (e.g., income statements, balance sheets) on a **quarterly or annual basis.**
- **Managerial Accounting:** Generates **real-time, customized reports** as often as necessary for **operational and strategic decision-making**.

By understanding these differences, businesses can ensure that they **leverage the right accounting approach for the right purpose**, using financial accounting for **external transparency** and managerial accounting for **internal efficiency and profitability**.

# Role of Managerial Accounting in Decision-Making

## How Managerial Accounting Supports Decision-Making

Managerial accounting is essential for **day-to-day business decisions**, helping companies:

- **Evaluate profitability** of different product lines.
- **Optimize operational efficiency** by tracking expenses and reducing waste.
- **Make data-driven investment decisions** that align with long-term goals.

## Types of Business Decisions Influenced by Managerial Accounting

51. **Operational Decisions**

- Determining **cost-cutting measures** without affecting product quality.
- Evaluating supplier contracts to **reduce production costs**.
- Deciding **when to hire additional staff** based on revenue trends.

52. **Strategic Decisions**

- Assessing whether to **expand into new markets** based on profitability projections.
- Determining whether to **outsource production** or keep it in-house.

- Pricing strategies based on **cost analysis and market demand**.

A **data-driven decision-making approach** ensures that companies **maximize profitability while minimizing financial risks**.

**Budgeting and Forecasting Essentials**

## Why Budgeting Matters in Business

A budget serves as a **financial blueprint** that enables businesses to **plan, monitor, and control financial performance effectively**. Without a structured budget, companies risk **overspending, cash shortages, and inefficient resource allocation**. A well-structured budget allows businesses to:

53. **Control Expenses and Allocate Resources Efficiently**

- Budgets ensure that businesses **spend within their means**, preventing unnecessary expenditures.
- They help managers prioritize spending by allocating funds to **high-impact areas** like product development, marketing, and operational improvements.
- Effective budgeting ensures that a company **maintains liquidity while investing in future growth opportunities**.

54. **Predict Cash Flow Needs and Avoid Liquidity Shortages**

- A budget provides a **roadmap for incoming and outgoing cash**, ensuring that businesses can meet financial obligations like payroll, supplier payments, and loan repayments.
- Businesses with unpredictable cash flow, such as seasonal

businesses, can use **budgeting to prepare for low-revenue periods** and avoid cash shortfalls.

55. **Measure Performance by Comparing Actual vs. Budgeted Financial Outcomes**

- Comparing actual financial performance against a budget allows managers to **identify areas where spending exceeded or fell below projections**.
- This analysis helps businesses adjust strategies **to improve efficiency, reduce costs, or increase revenue**.
- Budget variances can signal **operational inefficiencies, changing market conditions, or potential risks that need to be addressed**.

## Real-World Example: The Importance of Budgeting

A **small restaurant chain** creates a **quarterly budget** to plan for expenses like food inventory, employee wages, and marketing campaigns. By **monitoring actual expenses against the budget**, the owner discovers that food costs are **10% higher than projected** due to supplier price increases. The business responds by:

- **Negotiating new contracts with suppliers to reduce costs.**
- **Adjusting menu prices slightly to maintain profitability.**
- **Exploring cost-saving measures such as reducing food waste.**

By using budgeting to **identify financial inefficiencies**, the restaurant avoids unnecessary losses and improves its **financial health**.

## Common Budgeting Techniques

Businesses use different budgeting approaches depending on their **size, industry, and financial strategy**. Choosing the right budgeting method ensures that businesses **allocate funds effectively, plan for uncertainties, and stay financially stable**.

### Incremental Budgeting – Adjusting Past Budgets for Expected Growth

Incremental budgeting involves **taking last year's budget and making adjustments** based on expected revenue changes, inflation, or company goals.

- **Advantages:**
- Simple and easy to implement.
- Works well for **stable businesses with predictable expenses**.
- **Disadvantages:**
- **Does not encourage cost efficiency**—departments may continue receiving unnecessary funding.
- Can **fail to account for changing business needs** or market shifts.

**Example:** A manufacturing company increases its budget by **5% annually** to account for **inflation and labor costs**, without reviewing whether all previous expenses are still necessary.

## 2. Zero-Based Budgeting – Justifying Every Expense from Scratch

Zero-based budgeting (ZBB) requires businesses to **re-evaluate all expenses each year, rather than automatically increasing budgets based on previous spending**.

- **Advantages:**
- Forces managers to **justify every expense**, preventing wasteful spending.
- Encourages **cost-cutting and efficiency**.
- **Disadvantages:**
- Time-consuming, requiring **detailed analysis** and justification of all costs.
- Can disrupt business operations if **essential expenses are overlooked**.

**Example:** A software company using ZBB may decide to **eliminate low-performing marketing channels** while increasing investment in **social media ads that generate higher ROI**.

## 3. Rolling Budgets – Continuous Updates Based on Real-Time Financial Data

Rolling budgets are **dynamic budgets that are updated periodically (monthly, quarterly) instead of being fixed for an entire year**.

- **Advantages:**

- Allows businesses to **adjust spending based on actual performance** and market conditions.
- Reduces **forecasting errors** by continuously revising financial projections.
- **Disadvantages:**
- Requires **constant monitoring** and financial adjustments, making it resource-intensive.

**Example:** A tech start up **updates its budget every three months**, adjusting marketing and hiring plans based on its latest sales growth and funding status.

## Forecasting for Financial Planning

Budgeting alone is **not enough**—businesses must also **forecast future financial trends** to stay ahead of **market shifts and economic fluctuations**. Forecasting provides a **data-driven approach** to predicting future revenue, expenses, and profitability.

### Qualitative vs. Quantitative Forecasting

56. **Qualitative Forecasting – Expert Opinions & Market Research**

- Used when **historical data is unavailable or unreliable** (e.g., launching a new product).
- Involves input from **industry experts, customer surveys, and market trends**.
- Commonly used in **startups, emerging industries, and fast-**

**changing markets.**

**Example:** A new electric car manufacturer consults **industry experts and analyzes consumer demand trends** to estimate future sales.

57. **Quantitative Forecasting – Statistical & Financial Data Analysis**

- Uses **historical financial data** to predict future revenue and expenses.
- Includes **trend analysis, regression models, and time-series forecasting.**
- More accurate for **established businesses with consistent financial trends.**

**Example:** A retail chain uses past sales data and seasonal trends to forecast **holiday sales projections** for inventory planning.

## How Budgeting and Forecasting Work Together

**Budgeting and forecasting are complementary tools:**

- **Budgeting** sets **spending limits** and helps businesses **allocate resources** based on planned financial goals.
- **Forecasting** provides **updated financial predictions** based on real-time data, allowing businesses to **adjust their budgets as needed.**

### Example: Retail Business Budgeting & Forecasting Integration

A **clothing retailer** creates an **annual budget** based on last year's sales. However, after **six months**, market trends indicate that **consumer demand for sustainable fashion is rising**. The company **updates its sales forecast** and **shifts marketing and inventory budgets toward eco-friendly clothing**, ensuring they **capitalize on market trends rather than sticking to outdated projections**.

## Best Practices for Effective Budgeting & Forecasting

58. **Use Real-Time Data** – Businesses should leverage **modern accounting software and financial dashboards** to track spending and update forecasts.
59. **Involve Multiple Departments** – Collaboration between **finance, marketing, operations, and HR** ensures budgets reflect **real business needs**.
60. **Set Flexible Budgets** – Companies should **leave room for unexpected costs** or revenue fluctuations.
61. **Review and Adjust Regularly** – A budget is a **living document** that should be revisited **monthly or quarterly** to reflect changing market conditions.

## Conclusion: How Budgeting & Forecasting Drive Business Success

Budgeting and forecasting are **foundational elements of financial planning** that allow businesses to **stay competitive, manage cash flow, and allocate resources effectively**.

### Key Takeaways:

**Budgeting** ensures financial discipline, cost control, and performance tracking. **Different budgeting techniques** (incremental, zero-based, rolling) help businesses **adapt to their specific needs. Forecasting** provides valuable insights into **future revenue and expenses**, allowing for **proactive decision-making**. Businesses that integrate **budgeting and forecasting** can **respond to market changes, reduce financial risks, and maximize profitability**.

By implementing **strong budgeting and forecasting strategies**, companies can **optimize financial stability, make smarter investment decisions, and drive long-term growth**.

## Cost Behavior & Cost-Volume-Profit (CVP) Analysis

### Understanding Cost Behavior

Every business incurs different types of costs:

- **Fixed Costs** – Remain constant regardless of production levels (e.g., rent, salaries).

- **Variable Costs** – Change with production volume (e.g., raw materials, commissions).
- **Mixed Costs** – Have both fixed and variable components (e.g., utility bills).

### Cost-Volume-Profit (CVP) Analysis & Breakeven Point

**CVP analysis** helps businesses **understand how costs, revenue, and profit interact**, allowing them to:

- Determine the **breakeven point** (when total revenue equals total costs).
- Assess how **changes in sales volume affect profitability**.
- Adjust **pricing strategies** to maximize profits.

A strong understanding of **cost structures and break-even points** helps businesses **reduce risk and make profitable operational decisions**.

## The Value of Managerial Accounting in Business Success

Managerial accounting is an **indispensable tool** for businesses that want to **optimize financial decision-making, control costs, and plan strategically**. Unlike financial accounting, which focuses on historical data for external reporting, managerial accounting provides **real-time insights for operational efficiency and long-term growth**.

In this chapter, we covered:

- **The purpose and scope of managerial accounting** and its **role**

**in financial planning**.

- **The key differences between managerial and financial accounting**, highlighting their distinct audiences and objectives.
- **How managerial accounting drives strategic decision-making** in areas such as **cost control, budgeting, and forecasting**.
- **The fundamentals of cost behavior and cost-volume-profit analysis**, providing valuable tools for **profitability assessment and financial optimization**.

By mastering managerial accounting principles, business owners, managers, and financial professionals can **make data-driven decisions, enhance operational efficiency, and drive business profitability**.

## Looking Ahead: Budgeting & Financial Planning

Now that we have established a strong foundation in financial management, the next logical step is understanding how businesses plan for future financial success. While financial accounting provides a snapshot of a company's past and present performance, budgeting and financial planning allow businesses to anticipate challenges, allocate resources efficiently, and position themselves for long-term stability.

Budgeting is not just about controlling expenses; it is a strategic tool that helps businesses optimise profitability, improve decision-making, and align financial goals with operational priorities. A well-structured budget ensures that companies can manage cash flow effectively, mitigate financial risks, and make informed investments in growth opportunities.

In the next chapter, we will explore:

- **Developing Effective Budgets:** How businesses create structured financial plans that control expenses while maintaining flexibility for market shifts.
- **Financial Forecasting Techniques:** The importance of anticipating future revenue, costs, and market trends to ensure financial preparedness.
- **Ensuring Financial Discipline:** How businesses can use budgeting as a tool to improve accountability, reduce inefficiencies, and optimise resource allocation.
- **Strategic Planning for Growth:** The role of budgeting in securing funding, scaling operations, and making long-term investment decisions.

Mastering budgeting and financial planning ensures that businesses are not just tracking their performance but actively shaping their financial future. Whether a company is a start up seeking financial stability or an established enterprise planning for expansion, a sound budgeting framework is essential for sustainable success.

By understanding and implementing advanced budgeting strategies, businesses can gain financial clarity, improve profitability, and create a roadmap for growth. Let's dive into the next chapter to explore the essential tools and techniques needed to build a strong financial future.

# STRATEGIC BUDGETING & FINANCIAL PLANNING

## Introduction: The Role of Budgeting in Business Success

Budgeting is a fundamental pillar of financial planning, ensuring that businesses allocate resources efficiently, control costs, and drive long-term profitability. A well-structured budget serves as a roadmap for financial success, helping businesses **forecast revenue, manage expenses, and plan for future investments**. Whether a company is a start up, a mid-sized enterprise, or a multinational corporation, budgeting is crucial for **financial stability and strategic decision-making**.

A business without a budget operates **without direction**, making it vulnerable to **cash flow problems, uncontrolled spending, and inefficient resource allocation**. Companies that fail to implement proper budgeting strategies often struggle to scale, mismanage their working capital, and find themselves unable to react effectively to financial challenges.

A well-designed budget does more than track income and expenses—it aligns financial resources with **business objectives, optimizes capital allocation, and provides a clear framework for evaluating financial performance**. Organizations that embrace advanced budgeting techniques can **anticipate future financial trends, identify potential risks, and allocate funds strategically to maximize growth opportunities**.

This chapter explores the **importance of budgeting, how to create an effective budget, cost control strategies, and real-world applications**. We will also introduce a **scenario-based budgeting exercise** to reinforce the application of these concepts.

## The Role of Budgeting in Business Success

Budgeting plays a **multifaceted role** in business success, influencing **financial management, strategic planning, and operational efficiency**. The most successful businesses use budgeting as a **proactive financial tool**, rather than merely as an accounting requirement.

### 1. Financial Control and Cash Flow Management

A well-structured budget **ensures that expenses do not exceed revenues**, preventing businesses from operating in financial distress. Proper budgeting allows companies to **forecast cash flow fluctuations, prepare for seasonal variations, and set aside funds for contingencies**.

For instance, a **retail business** may see a surge in revenue during the holiday season but experience slower sales during other periods. Without effective budgeting, the business may struggle to cover expenses during slower months. A properly planned budget **accounts for fluctuations and ensures liquidity throughout the year**.

## 2. Resource Allocation and Investment Planning

Businesses operate with **limited resources**, making **efficient allocation of capital essential for growth**. A budget provides clarity on where to **invest in growth opportunities, optimize operating expenses, and avoid unnecessary spending**.

For example, a **manufacturing company** may need to decide whether to **invest in new machinery or expand its workforce**. A detailed budget **helps assess potential returns on investment (ROI) and determine the most cost-effective strategy**.

## 3. Risk Management and Financial Stability

Economic downturns, supply chain disruptions, and unexpected market shifts can **severely impact a business's financial health**. Budgeting enables businesses to **prepare for uncertainties** by maintaining **emergency reserves, monitoring debt levels, and creating contingency plans**.

Companies that operate **without a budget** are often caught off guard by sudden financial challenges, leading to **reactive decision-making** that can harm profitability. **Proactive budgeting reduces uncertainty and strengthens long-term financial resilience**.

### 4. Performance Evaluation and Accountability

A budget provides **clear financial targets** that enable businesses to measure actual performance against expected outcomes. By comparing **budgeted vs. actual results**, companies can identify **financial inefficiencies, control costs, and improve decision-making**.

For example, if a company budgeted **$500,000 for marketing but only generated $100,000 in additional revenue**, it can analyze the **ROI of marketing efforts and adjust future allocations**. This process enhances **accountability and operational efficiency**.

## Creating an Effective Business Budget

An effective business budget is more than just a list of projected revenues and expenses. It involves a **systematic approach to financial forecasting, risk assessment, and performance monitoring**. Below are the key steps in developing a **robust and actionable budget**.

### Step 1: Define Financial Goals and Business Objectives

Before creating a budget, businesses must establish **clear financial goals** aligned with their broader **strategic objectives**. These goals may include:

- **Revenue growth targets**
- **Expense reduction plans**

- **Profitability benchmarks**
- **Debt repayment strategies**
- **Investment in new projects or equipment**

Having a well-defined goal ensures that **budgeting decisions support long-term business success**.

## Step 2: Identify Revenue Sources and Forecast Income

Accurate revenue forecasting is critical for developing a realistic budget. Businesses should consider:

- **Historical sales trends**
- **Market demand and economic conditions**
- **Pricing strategies and competitive positioning**
- **New product launches or expansion plans**

Revenue projections should be **realistic**—overestimating income can lead to **overspending**, while underestimating revenue can result in **missed opportunities for investment**.

## Step 3: Categorize Fixed and Variable Expenses

Understanding business costs is essential for effective budgeting. Expenses are generally divided into **fixed and variable categories**:

- **Fixed Costs**: Expenses that remain constant regardless of business activity (e.g., rent, salaries, insurance).
- **Variable Costs**: Expenses that fluctuate based on production levels

or sales volume (e.g., raw materials, utilities, marketing).

Businesses should **prioritize essential expenses while identifying opportunities to reduce unnecessary costs**.

### Step 4: Implement Budgeting Methods

There are several budgeting techniques that businesses can use, depending on their **financial structure and objectives**:

- **Incremental Budgeting**: Adjusting last year's budget based on expected growth or changes.
- **Zero-Based Budgeting (ZBB)**: Justifying each expense from scratch rather than basing it on previous budgets.
- **Activity-Based Budgeting**: Allocating funds based on specific business activities and expected outcomes.

Each method has its advantages, and businesses should choose the one that **best aligns with their financial goals**.

## Cost Control Strategies to Improve Profitability

Cost control is **one of the most effective ways** to improve profitability. Businesses that actively manage expenses can **increase profit margins, optimize cash flow, and allocate resources efficiently**.

### 1. Identifying and Eliminating Unnecessary Costs

Regularly reviewing financial statements helps **spot unnecessary expenses**. Businesses should eliminate or renegotiate:

- **Non-essential subscriptions or services**
- **Inefficient marketing campaigns with low ROI**
- **Excess office space or underutilized resources**

## 2. Improving Supply Chain and Vendor Management

Negotiating better contracts with suppliers and **sourcing alternative vendors** can lead to **significant cost reductions**. Businesses should evaluate:

- **Bulk purchasing discounts**
- **Strategic supplier partnerships**
- **Reducing waste and inefficiencies in production**

## 3. Investing in Automation and Technology

Many businesses reduce operational costs by implementing **automated processes, AI-driven financial management tools, and data analytics.** Investing in technology can **streamline accounting, inventory management, and customer service**, reducing long-term labor costs.

## 4. Controlling Labor and Payroll Expenses

While employees are a business's greatest asset, **uncontrolled labor costs** can reduce profitability. Cost-saving measures may include:

- **Optimizing work schedules to improve productivity**
- **Offering performance-based incentives instead of across-the-board raises**

- **Outsourcing non-core functions to reduce overhead**

## Scenario-Based Exercise: Creating a Budget for a Small Business

Imagine you are managing a **new coffee shop start up**. You have **$100,000 in start up capital**, and your projected monthly revenue is **$30,000**. Your key expenses include:

- Rent: **$4,000**
- Employee salaries: **$10,000**
- Cost of goods sold (coffee beans, milk, supplies): **$6,000**
- Utilities: **$2,000**
- Marketing: **$2,500**

Using this data, develop a **six-month budget** that accounts for revenue growth, seasonal fluctuations, and unforeseen expenses. After completing your budget, analyze:

62. Are there **cost areas that can be reduced**?
63. How much should be **set aside for unexpected expenses**?
64. What revenue milestones must be met to ensure **profitability by month six**?

### Advanced Budgeting Techniques for Business Growth

Budgeting is not just about predicting revenues and expenses; it is a **strategic tool** that businesses use to optimize financial planning, **improve**

**forecasting accuracy**, and **prepare for long-term expansion**. To stay competitive in dynamic markets, companies must go beyond traditional budgeting approaches and implement **advanced techniques** that allow them to adjust their financial strategies based on real-time data and external conditions.

These **advanced budgeting methods** help businesses **reduce financial risks, plan for uncertainties, and allocate capital efficiently** to maximize profitability and long-term growth.

***Rolling Budgets: A Dynamic Approach to Financial Planning***

A rolling budget is a **continuously updated financial plan** that adjusts every **month or quarter** to reflect the latest business and economic conditions. Unlike static annual budgets, rolling budgets provide **greater flexibility and real-time accuracy** by incorporating the most recent **market trends, operational performance, and financial forecasts**.

For example, a **fast-growing technology startup** might struggle with **unpredictable revenue fluctuations and shifting customer demand**. By using a rolling budget, the company can **adjust its financial plans frequently**—allocating more resources to high-performing areas and cutting costs in underperforming sectors.

Rolling budgets are particularly beneficial for industries with **rapid innovation cycles, fluctuating market demand, or seasonal variations**, such as **retail, e-commerce, and software companies**.

***Scenario Planning Budgets: Preparing for the Unexpected***

In uncertain business environments, relying on a **single financial projection** can be risky. **Scenario planning budgets** help companies prepare for various potential outcomes by creating multiple budget variations based on different assumptions.

Companies typically develop:

- **Best-case scenario** – Strong revenue growth, low costs, high market demand.
- **Moderate scenario** – Steady growth, stable expenses, no major disruptions.
- **Worst-case scenario** – Economic downturn, declining sales, higher operating costs.

For example, a **manufacturing company** might create different budget plans based on **raw material price fluctuations**. If supply chain disruptions cause **higher material costs**, the business can shift to a more **cost-efficient production method** to maintain profitability.

By using scenario-based budgeting, companies can anticipate **financial risks, adjust spending plans, and remain agile in unpredictable markets**.

***Capital Budgeting: Making Smart Long-Term Investment Decisions***

Capital budgeting is the process of **evaluating long-term investment opportunities** to determine whether they will provide a **positive return on investment (ROI)**. Businesses use capital budgeting to decide whether to invest in:

- **New product development**
- **Equipment and machinery upgrades**

- **Infrastructure expansion**
- **Acquisitions or mergers**

For example, a **logistics company** deciding whether to invest in **electric delivery trucks** would conduct a **capital budgeting analysis** to determine whether the long-term cost savings (fuel and maintenance reduction) outweigh the initial investment.

Capital budgeting ensures that businesses allocate their resources **strategically**, prioritizing investments that will drive **long-term growth and profitability**.

## Budgeting for Different Business Stages

A company's budgeting needs vary depending on **where it is in its lifecycle**. From start ups to established corporations, each business stage requires a **different financial approach** to ensure sustainability and profitability.

***Start up Budgeting: Managing Limited Capital Efficiently***

Start ups operate with **tight financial constraints** and often **lack predictable revenue streams**. Budgeting at this stage focuses on:

- **Minimizing unnecessary costs** – Prioritizing essential spending on product development and marketing.
- **Securing funding** – Managing external capital from investors, loans, or crowdfunding.
- **Setting realistic revenue expectations** – Avoiding overly optimistic projections that could lead to cash flow shortages.

For example, a **new e-commerce store** should **carefully budget for inventory, advertising, and logistics** to ensure it does not overspend before achieving steady sales.

***Growth-Stage Budgeting: Scaling While Maintaining Profitability***

Businesses in the **growth phase** must balance **expansion and profitability**. At this stage, budgets focus on:

- **Increasing production capacity to meet demand.**
- **Investing in marketing and sales strategies to drive growth.**
- **Ensuring positive cash flow to sustain operations.**

A **software company** experiencing rapid user growth might need to **expand its server infrastructure** while carefully budgeting to **avoid overspending on unnecessary upgrades**.

***Mature Business Budgeting: Maintaining Efficiency and Profitability***

Mature companies focus on **maximizing efficiency, optimizing costs, and maintaining profitability**. This stage involves:

- **Reducing operational inefficiencies** – Streamlining expenses without affecting product quality.
- **Optimizing pricing models** – Ensuring competitive yet profitable pricing strategies.
- **Planning for future investments and innovations.**

For example, a **fast-food franchise** may use budgeting to **introduce automation technology** in stores to reduce labor costs and improve service efficiency.

### *Crisis Budgeting: Managing Financial Challenges*

During economic downturns or unexpected financial crises, businesses must **quickly adjust their budgets** to survive. Key strategies include:

- **Reducing discretionary spending (e.g., advertising, bonuses).**
- **Negotiating better payment terms with suppliers.**
- **Delaying non-essential capital expenditures.**

A **travel agency affected by a global recession** might cut marketing expenses and **focus on cost-effective customer retention programs** instead of launching new products.

## The Psychological Aspects of Budgeting and Financial Discipline

Budgeting is not just about numbers; it also involves **human psychology, financial discipline, and decision-making behavior**. Many businesses make poor budgeting decisions due to **emotional biases** rather than rational financial planning.

### *Common Psychological Biases That Impact Budgeting*

- **Over-Optimism Bias** – Overestimating revenue and underestimating expenses, leading to unrealistic financial projections.
- **Anchoring Bias** – Sticking to old budgets without adjusting for new market conditions.
- **Sunk Cost Fallacy** – Continuing to invest in failing projects because of past financial commitments.

For example, a **fashion retailer** might **overestimate future sales growth** due to a few successful product launches, leading to **excessive spending on inventory and advertising**.

***Creating a Budgeting Culture Within a Company***

To ensure financial discipline, businesses must:

- Encourage **cross-departmental accountability** for spending.
- Set **realistic financial goals** based on historical performance.
- Use **data-driven decision-making** instead of emotional spending.

A **company with strong budgeting culture** sees **higher profitability, better cash flow management, and reduced financial risks**.

## The Relationship Between Budgeting and Tax Planning

Tax planning is an essential component of budgeting that **many businesses overlook**. Poor tax management can lead to **unexpected liabilities, cash flow issues, and compliance risks**.

***Key Tax Planning Strategies***

- **Tax-Efficient Budgeting** – Businesses should proactively plan tax deductions, depreciation, and credits to **minimize taxable income**.
- **Setting Aside Tax Reserves** – Ensuring sufficient funds are available for **quarterly and annual tax payments**.
- **Understanding Depreciation Benefits** – Properly budgeting for capital investments to take advantage of tax write-offs.

For example, a **construction company investing in heavy machinery** must budget for **depreciation deductions** to reduce taxable income over multiple years.

## How AI and Automation Are Transforming Budgeting

Artificial intelligence (AI) is revolutionizing financial planning, making budgeting **more accurate, automated, and predictive**.

### *How AI Enhances Budgeting*

- **AI-Driven Expense Forecasting** – Machine learning algorithms predict future spending patterns.
- **Automated Budgeting Software** – Platforms like **QuickBooks and Xero** dynamically adjust budgets based on financial trends.
- **Real-Time Budget Monitoring** – AI-driven dashboards provide **instant updates on financial performance**.

For example, a **large retail chain** might use AI to **analyze sales data and adjust inventory budgets in real-time**, ensuring efficient stock levels while avoiding overstocking.

## The Strategic Power of Budgeting and Financial Planning

Budgeting is far more than just a financial exercise—it is a **strategic tool that determines the success or failure of a business**. As we have explored in this chapter, businesses that implement **structured, forward-thinking budgeting systems** gain a significant competitive advantage, ensuring **long-term financial stability, scalability, and profitability**.

Throughout this chapter, we have examined **the evolution of budgeting techniques**, moving from traditional static budgets to **advanced, data-driven financial planning methods**. Businesses today must **embrace rolling budgets, scenario planning, and capital budgeting** to navigate uncertain market conditions while making well-informed financial decisions. With an increasingly volatile business environment, the ability to **adapt and refine financial plans in real-time** has become an essential survival skill.

We also explored **how budgeting changes at different business stages**. Start ups must be laser-focused on **efficient cash flow management and securing funding**, while growth-stage companies must **balance reinvestment with profitability**. Mature businesses must **focus on cost optimization, expansion, and long-term sustainability**, while crisis budgeting provides a **safety net for businesses during economic downturns**. Understanding how financial planning evolves with a company's lifecycle enables businesses to **adjust their strategies and mitigate risks at every stage of growth**.

Beyond the technical aspects, this chapter highlighted **the human and psychological factors** that influence financial decision-making. Budgeting is not just about numbers—it requires **discipline, accountability, and rational financial thinking**. Businesses often fall into **behavioral traps**, such as **over-optimism, sunk cost fallacies, and emotional spending**, which can derail financial plans. By fostering a **strong budgeting culture**, organizations can **reduce wasteful spending, improve resource allocation, and enhance financial resilience**.

Another key takeaway is the **relationship between budgeting and tax planning**. Many businesses overlook tax obligations when preparing their budgets, leading to unexpected liabilities and cash flow constraints. By integrating **tax-efficient budgeting strategies, forecasting tax liabilities, and leveraging depreciation benefits**, businesses can maximize profits while remaining compliant with regulations.

Moreover, the future of budgeting is rapidly changing with the integration of **AI, automation, and real-time data analytics**. Businesses that adopt **AI-driven forecasting tools** can enhance accuracy, **automate expense tracking, and optimize cost allocations based on predictive analytics**. Companies leveraging AI for budgeting will gain **unmatched financial agility**, allowing them to **respond proactively to market shifts** rather than reacting to crises.

The **practical budgeting exercise** in this chapter reinforced the importance of **financial foresight, contingency planning, and cost control**. Businesses must not only prepare realistic budgets but also **continuously monitor performance, adjust financial plans as needed, and ensure every dollar spent aligns with long-term business goals**.

## Final Thoughts: The Future of Financial Planning

The evolution of budgeting techniques has made financial planning **more dynamic, data-driven, and adaptable**. Businesses that integrate **advanced budgeting strategies, embrace AI-powered financial automation, and align tax planning with their financial frameworks** will be better positioned to **thrive in competitive and uncertain markets**.

Budgeting is not a **one-time exercise**—it is a **continuous process of refinement, analysis, and strategic decision-making**. Companies that develop **flexible, forward-thinking budgeting systems** will ensure **long-term sustainability, financial security, and scalable growth**.

Mastering budgeting and financial planning is **essential for any business striving to maintain profitability, withstand financial uncertainties, and drive long-term success**. By controlling costs, optimizing resource allocation, and making data-driven decisions, businesses can unlock new opportunities for **expansion, innovation, and financial prosperity**.

# CASH FLOW MANAGEMENT & FORECASTING

## Introduction: The Lifeline of Business – Understanding Cash Flow

Cash flow is the **lifeblood of any business**. While profitability is important, **a company can be profitable on paper and still fail due to poor cash flow management**. Many businesses, especially start ups and small enterprises, make the mistake of focusing **only on revenue and profit margins** while ignoring the movement of cash in and out of their operations. A business that does not have enough cash to cover its **day-to-day expenses, loan repayments, or unexpected costs** is at risk of financial distress, even if it appears successful in terms of revenue growth.

In this chapter, we will explore:

- The **difference between profitability and cash flow**, and why understanding both is essential for financial stability.
- **Key strategies for improving cash flow**, ensuring a business always has enough liquidity to meet its obligations.
- **Cash flow forecasting methods** that allow businesses to plan ahead and mitigate financial risks.
- A **practical exercise** that walks through the process of creating a **cash flow statement**, reinforcing the importance of monitoring and managing cash movement effectively.

By mastering cash flow management and forecasting, businesses can **enhance financial resilience, make better investment decisions, and avoid unnecessary debt or financial crises**.

## The Difference Between Profitability & Cash Flow

Many business owners assume that if their company is profitable, they have nothing to worry about. However, **profitability and cash flow are not the same thing**.

## 1. Profitability: Measuring Business Performance

Profitability is the amount of **money left after subtracting all expenses from revenue**. It is typically measured through:

- **Gross Profit** (Revenue – Cost of Goods Sold)
- **Operating Profit** (Revenue – Operating Expenses)
- **Net Profit** (Total Revenue – Total Expenses)

A profitable business generates more revenue than it spends on operating costs, taxes, and other financial obligations. However, **profitability does not account for when cash is actually received or spent**, which can create financial challenges.

## 2. Cash Flow: The Movement of Money

Cash flow refers to the **actual movement of money into and out of a business**. It is categorized into three main activities:

- **Operating Cash Flow**: Money generated from core business activities (e.g., sales revenue, customer payments).
- **Investing Cash Flow**: Money spent or earned from investments (e.g., buying new equipment, selling assets).
- **Financing Cash Flow**: Cash from financing activities such as loans, issuing shares, or repaying debts.

A business can **be profitable but have negative cash flow** if customers delay payments or if too much money is tied up in inventory. Conversely, a business can **have positive cash flow but still operate at a loss** if it receives a large loan or sells assets without actually making a profit from operations.

### 3. Real-World Example: The Cash Flow vs. Profitability Trap

Imagine a manufacturing company, **ABC Enterprises**, that has a profitable year. Their financials show:

- **Revenue**: $500,000
- **Expenses**: $400,000
- **Profit**: $100,000

At first glance, the company seems financially stable. However, upon reviewing its cash flow:

- $150,000 of revenue is **tied up in unpaid invoices from customers**.
- $80,000 was used to purchase new equipment.
- The company has **only $20,000 in available cash** and struggles to cover its supplier payments.

Despite being profitable, **ABC Enterprises faces a cash shortage**, which could lead to missed payments, supplier disputes, and even potential insolvency.

Understanding the **difference between cash flow and profitability** helps businesses make smarter financial decisions and **avoid liquidity crises**.

## Strategies for Improving Cash Flow

To ensure financial stability, businesses must **actively manage and improve their cash flow**. Below are key strategies to strengthen liquidity and prevent cash shortages.

### 1. Accelerating Receivables: Getting Paid Faster

Delayed payments from customers can **cripple cash flow**. To speed up cash inflows:

- **Invoice promptly** and set clear payment terms.
- Offer **discounts for early payments** (e.g., 2% off if paid within 10 days).
- Use **automated invoicing systems** to send reminders for overdue accounts.
- Implement a **strict collections process** for unpaid invoices.

### 2. Managing Payables: Controlling Outflows Efficiently

Businesses must **balance the timing of cash inflows and outflows** to avoid liquidity gaps.

- **Negotiate longer payment terms** with suppliers.
- Prioritize **essential expenses** and delay discretionary spending.
- Take advantage of supplier **early payment discounts** when possible.

### 3. Reducing Unnecessary Expenses

Cutting costs can **significantly improve cash flow** without harming operations.

- Identify **non-essential spending** and reduce unnecessary overhead.
- Streamline business operations by **outsourcing non-core functions**.
- Reduce excess inventory to free up cash.

### 4. Optimizing Inventory Management

Holding too much inventory ties up **cash that could be used elsewhere**. Businesses should:

- Improve **inventory turnover** by selling off old stock.
- Use **just-in-time (JIT) inventory management** to reduce excess stock levels.
- Forecast demand accurately to avoid over-purchasing.

### 5. Maintaining a Cash Reserve

A business should always have a **cash cushion** to cover unexpected expenses.

- Set aside at least **3-6 months of operating expenses** as a safety net.
- Keep an emergency fund separate from working capital.

### 6. Using Financing Wisely

If a business needs external funding to maintain cash flow, it should:

- Use **short-term loans** or a **business line of credit** for temporary cash shortages.
- Avoid excessive debt that could create long-term financial problems.
- Ensure that loans are used for revenue-generating activities.

By applying these strategies, businesses can **improve cash flow stability** and prevent liquidity crises.

## Cash Flow Forecasting Methods

Cash flow forecasting helps businesses **predict future cash inflows and outflows**, ensuring they are prepared for potential shortfalls. There are two main forecasting methods:

### 1. Direct Method (Short-Term Forecasting)

The direct method forecasts cash flow based on **actual expected cash receipts and payments** over a short period (weeks or months).

**Best for:**

- Businesses with **seasonal revenue fluctuations**.
- Managing **daily or weekly cash flow needs**.

### 2. Indirect Method (Long-Term Forecasting)

This method starts with **net profit** and adjusts for non-cash expenses (e.g., depreciation) to project future cash flows.

**Best for:**

- Companies planning for **long-term investments** or **expansion**.
- Businesses that need to **secure financing** or evaluate profitability trends.

**Example:** A business forecasts that it will receive $100,000 in revenue next month but expects to pay $80,000 in expenses. The projected **net cash flow = $20,000**, helping them determine whether they need external funding.

Effective **cash flow forecasting** ensures businesses can **plan for financial stability, make informed investment decisions, and avoid unexpected cash shortages**.

## Practical Exercise: Creating and Analyzing a Cash Flow Statement for a Retail Business

Understanding how cash flows in and out of a business is **essential for financial health and long-term stability**. This exercise will guide you through the process of preparing a **cash flow statement**, analyzing the results, and providing actionable recommendations to improve the business's financial situation.

## Scenario: Retail Clothing Store Financial Transactions

You own a **retail clothing store**, and you are reviewing your cash flow statement for the month. Below is a summary of your financial activities:

***Cash Inflows (Money Coming In)***

- **Sales Revenue**: $50,000
- **Loan Received**: $10,000

***Cash Outflows (Money Going Out)***

- **Rent**: $5,000
- **Payroll**: $12,000
- **Inventory Purchases**: $20,000
- **Utilities**: $1,500
- **Loan Repayment**: $3,000

Using this information, we will calculate:

65. **Total cash inflows**
66. **Total cash outflows**
67. **Net cash flow** (cash inflows minus cash outflows)
68. **Interpretation of whether the business has a positive or negative cash flow**
69. **Recommendations for improving cash flow**

## Step 1: Preparing the Cash Flow Statement

A cash flow statement is divided into three sections:

70. **Operating Activities** (day-to-day business transactions)
71. **Investing Activities** (purchasing assets, selling investments)

72. **Financing Activities** (loans, dividends, issuing shares)

Since this business primarily involves operating and financing activities, we will focus on those.

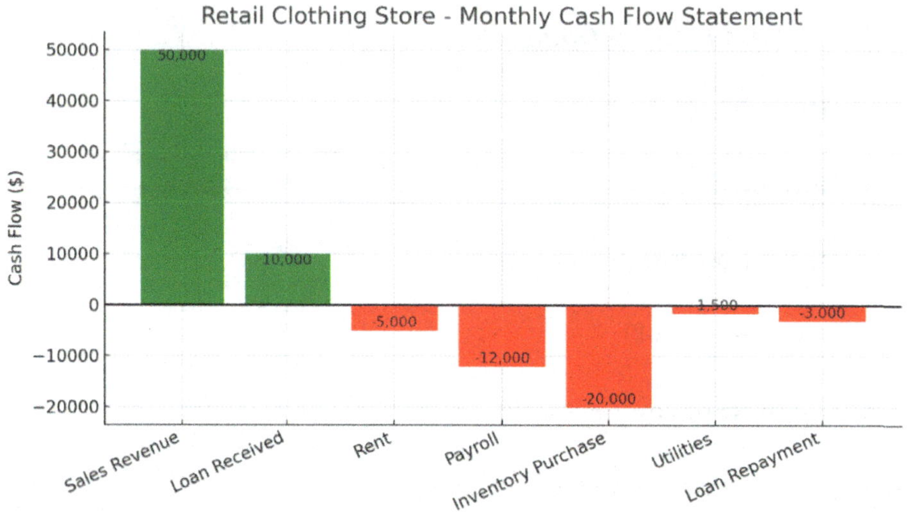


## Step 2: Interpreting the Cash Flow Statement

The **total net cash flow** for the month is **+18,500**, meaning the business **ended the month with more cash than it started with**. However, **this does not necessarily mean financial stability**, as part of the positive cash flow comes from an external loan rather than operating profits.

Here's what we can observe:

73. **Operating cash flow is positive (+$11,500)**

- The business generated more cash than it spent through core operations, which is a **good sign**.
- However, a **large portion of cash ($20,000) is tied up in inventory**, which may not immediately turn into cash.

74. **The business relied on external financing (+$10,000 loan)**

- While the cash flow appears strong, the **loan artificially inflated the cash balance**.
- Without the loan, the business's net cash flow would have been **only +$8,500**, which is **much weaker**.
- This means that the business might struggle with cash flow **if it cannot sustain positive operations without loans**.

75. **Loan repayment of $3,000 affects available cash**

- While taking a loan helped with liquidity, **debt repayments will continue affecting cash flow in future months**.
- This business needs a strategy for **repaying loans without straining cash reserves**.

## Step 3: Recommendations for Improving Cash Flow

To maintain **healthy cash flow**, the business should consider the following strategies:

### *1. Improve Inventory Turnover*

- **Issue promotions or discounts** to sell excess inventory faster and convert it into cash.
- Reduce the amount of inventory purchased in future months to **avoid tying up too much cash**.
- Consider **drop shipping** or other inventory management methods to reduce upfront stock costs.

*2. Increase Operating Cash Flow*

- Implement a **loyalty program or marketing campaign** to boost cash sales.
- Focus on **high-margin products** that generate more profit per sale.
- Offer **limited-time deals** to encourage faster purchases from customers.

*3. Reduce Unnecessary Expenses*

- Review payroll expenses to see if **labor efficiency** can be improved.
- Negotiate with landlords or suppliers for better terms on **rent and inventory costs**.
- Cut non-essential expenses like excessive marketing spend that does not generate a **direct return on investment**.

*4. Manage Debt More Efficiently*

- Prioritize **higher-interest debt repayments** to reduce long-term costs.
- If cash flow improves, consider **early repayment of loans** to minimize interest expenses.
- Avoid taking on more debt unless necessary for **business expansion or revenue growth**.

*5. Build a Cash Reserve*

- Set aside **a portion of profits each month** as an emergency fund.
- Maintain at least **3-6 months of operating expenses** in a separate

account.

- This ensures the business has a safety net for **unexpected downturns** or slow sales periods.

## Step 4: Adjusting for Future Growth

Based on the cash flow statement, the business is currently **managing cash flow well**, but it still relies on **external financing** to stay liquid. To ensure **long-term financial health**, the company should:

76. **Increase sales and revenue without increasing debt.**
77. **Improve inventory management** to ensure cash is not tied up unnecessarily.
78. **Plan for future loan repayments carefully**, ensuring debt does not become a financial burden.
79. **Maintain strict control over expenses** to improve net cash flow without sacrificing growth.

By regularly monitoring cash flow, adjusting expenses, and increasing revenue generation, the business can move toward **self-sufficiency and financial sustainability** without relying on external financing.

## Final Takeaways from the Exercise

This exercise reinforces key **cash flow management principles**:

- **Positive net cash flow is essential for business survival**—but it must come from **operations, not just loans or external financing**.
- **Liquidity is more important than profitability in the short**

**term**—a profitable business can still fail if cash is mismanaged.

- **Effective cash flow forecasting** allows businesses to **anticipate financial needs and adjust spending accordingly**.

By regularly analyzing cash flow statements, businesses can **make informed decisions, avoid financial surprises, and sustain long-term growth**.

### Next Steps: Creating Your Own Cash Flow Statement

Now that you have completed this exercise, try applying the same principles to **your own business or a different industry**.

- Choose a business (restaurant, e-commerce store, consulting firm, etc.).
- List its key **cash inflows and outflows** for a month.
- Prepare a **cash flow statement** and analyze whether it has **positive or negative cash flow**.
- Identify potential risks and strategies to **improve liquidity and financial stability**.

Mastering **cash flow analysis and forecasting** will give you the tools needed to make **smarter financial decisions and grow your business sustainably**.

## Industry-Specific Cash Flow Challenges & Solutions

Different industries experience **unique cash flow challenges**, requiring **customized strategies** to maintain liquidity and financial stability. Below, we explore **how businesses in various sectors manage cash flow and improve financial resilience**.

## Retail & E-Commerce: Managing Inventory and Seasonal Demand

Retail and e-commerce businesses must balance **high inventory costs, seasonal fluctuations, and consumer demand changes**.

### Common Cash Flow Challenges

- **Tying up cash in excess inventory** – Large stock purchases can limit available working capital.
- **Slow-moving inventory** – Products that don't sell quickly reduce liquidity.
- **High marketing expenses** – Heavy spending on ads and promotions can strain cash reserves.
- **Seasonal fluctuations** – Sales spike during peak seasons (e.g., holidays) but drop off in slower months.

### Solutions

- Implement **Just-in-Time (JIT) inventory** to **avoid overstocking** and reduce storage costs.
- Offer **flash sales or bundle deals** to move inventory faster and free up cash.
- Negotiate **extended payment terms** with suppliers to ease cash flow strain.

- Use **AI-driven sales forecasting tools** to predict demand and optimize stock levels.

## Real-World Example

An online clothing retailer experiences a **drop in sales after the holiday season**, but they still have **$200,000 worth of unsold winter apparel**. To improve cash flow, they:

- Launch **clearance sales with discounts** to turn excess stock into cash.
- **Negotiate supplier contracts** for flexible payment terms.
- Use predictive analytics to ensure **better inventory planning for next year**.

## Manufacturing: Balancing Production Costs and Payment Cycles

Manufacturers often have **long production cycles**, meaning **cash is spent on raw materials, labor, and operations before revenue is received**.

## Common Cash Flow Challenges

- **Delayed customer payments** – Clients may take **30 to 90 days** to pay invoices.
- **High upfront costs for raw materials and machinery** – These expenses must be paid before production even begins.
- **Production delays** – If supply chains are disrupted, revenue generation is delayed.

## Solutions

- Offer **early payment discounts** to encourage faster invoice payments.
- Arrange **supplier financing** to spread the cost of raw materials over multiple months.
- Implement **contract manufacturing** to reduce internal production costs.
- Optimize production scheduling to **reduce idle time and wasted resources**.

## Real-World Example

A furniture manufacturer spends **$500,000 upfront** on materials but won't receive payment from retailers for **90 days**. To **maintain liquidity**, they:

- Offer **2% early payment discounts** for customers who settle invoices in 15 days.
- Negotiate **longer payment terms with wood suppliers** to reduce upfront expenses.
- Lease specialized equipment instead of purchasing it outright.

## Service-Based Businesses: Managing Irregular Revenue Streams

Consulting firms, freelancers, and agencies rely on **client payments** for cash flow, but these payments are often **delayed or inconsistent**.

## Common Cash Flow Challenges

- **Unpredictable client payments** – Clients may take longer to settle invoices.
- **Project-based income** – Revenue is not always consistent month to month.
- **Over-reliance on a few large clients** – Losing one major client can significantly impact cash flow.

## Solutions

- Introduce **retainer-based contracts** for steady income.
- Use **automated invoicing software** to issue reminders for overdue payments.
- Diversify client base to **reduce dependency on one or two large clients**.
- Require **partial upfront payments** before starting work.

## Real-World Example

A digital marketing agency struggles with **delayed client payments**, affecting payroll and operational expenses. To fix this, they:

- Shift to a **50% upfront, 50% on completion payment structure**.
- Automate invoice follow-ups using **payment tracking software**.
- Offer subscription-based services for **predictable monthly revenue**.

**The Role of Technology in Cash Flow Management**

Technology is **transforming cash flow management**, allowing businesses to **automate processes, forecast financial trends, and improve liquidity management**.

## AI-Powered Cash Flow Forecasting

Machine learning tools analyze **historical transactions and trends** to **predict future cash flow**, helping businesses plan ahead.

## Automated Invoicing & Payment Reminders

Software like **FreshBooks, QuickBooks, and Xero** sends automatic invoice reminders, **reducing late payments**.

## Real-Time Cash Flow Monitoring

AI-powered dashboards provide **instant updates** on cash flow, alerting businesses to potential shortfalls.

## Real-World Example

A construction company using **AI-based forecasting** sees that **cash reserves will be low in three months due to delayed project payments**. With this insight, they:

- **Secure a temporary credit line** to cover payroll.
- **Negotiate faster payments from clients**.
- **Adjust project expenses to improve liquidity**.

**How Economic Conditions Impact Cash Flow**

## Recessions & Market Downturns

- Declining consumer demand reduces **sales and revenue.**
- Increased risk of **delayed customer payments.**

**Strategy**: Build an emergency fund and **diversify revenue streams** to reduce reliance on a single market.

## Inflation & Rising Costs

- Higher costs for **raw materials, labor, and transportation** affect profitability.
- Reduced purchasing power leads to **lower consumer spending.**

**Strategy**: Adjust pricing strategies **without alienating customers** and lock in **long-term supplier contracts at stable rates.**

## High-Interest Rate Environments

- More expensive loans **increase debt repayment costs.**

**Strategy**: Refinance existing loans to **lower interest rates** and prioritize **debt reduction.**

**Cash Flow Strategies for Scaling & Growth**

## Expanding Too Fast Without Enough Liquidity

- Many businesses invest in **new locations, staff, and inventory** before ensuring steady cash flow.

**Solution**: Use **phased expansion strategies** to **test new markets** before fully committing.

## Delayed ROI on Growth Investments

- Growth often requires upfront spending before seeing a return.

**Solution**: Secure growth-focused financing like **revenue-based loans** rather than draining cash reserves.

### Expanding the Practical Exercise: Cash Flow Simulation for 3-6 Months

Instead of just one month, simulate **three to six months of cash flow** to account for:

- **Seasonal fluctuations** (high/low sales periods).
- **Unexpected expenses** (equipment breakdown, supplier price hikes).
- **Loan repayments and interest costs.**

This will allow businesses to:

- **Adjust spending strategies in advance.**
- **Prepare for slow periods by building cash reserves.**
- **Identify upcoming cash flow gaps and secure financing ahead of time.**

## The Vital Role of Cash Flow Mastery in Business Success

Cash flow is **the lifeblood of any business**, and its effective management is often the difference between success and failure. As we explored in this chapter, **profitability alone does not guarantee financial stability**—even profitable businesses can face serious financial challenges if they do not have sufficient cash on hand to meet their obligations.

One of the most important lessons from this chapter is the **difference between profitability and cash flow**. Many businesses focus on **net profit as a success metric** while overlooking **how and when cash actually moves through their operations**. A company can be profitable on paper but still **struggle with cash shortages if customers delay payments, inventory purchases tie up liquidity, or unexpected expenses arise**. Conversely, a company can have **positive cash flow but still operate at a loss**, particularly if it relies on loans or asset sales to stay afloat.

We also examined **key strategies for improving cash flow**, reinforcing that businesses must be **proactive, not reactive**, when it comes to liquidity management. A strong **cash flow strategy involves accelerating receivables, managing payables strategically, reducing unnecessary expenses, and optimizing inventory turnover**. These techniques ensure that businesses maintain **a healthy balance between incoming and outgoing cash**, reducing financial stress and enabling them to capitalize on growth opportunities.

A critical part of financial success is **cash flow forecasting**, which allows businesses to anticipate future financial needs rather than reacting to shortfalls. We explored **two primary forecasting methods**:

- The **direct method**, which focuses on short-term cash flow planning based on expected cash inflows and outflows.
- The **indirect method**, which adjusts net profit for non-cash

expenses to create a longer-term financial outlook.

By forecasting cash flow, businesses can **prepare for seasonal fluctuations, identify potential liquidity gaps, and make informed decisions about investments, expansion, and financing**. A business that does not forecast cash flow risks **running out of money at a critical moment**, which can result in **missed supplier payments, employee salary delays, or even business closure**.

The **practical exercise in this chapter** demonstrated the importance of tracking **real-life financial transactions** through a **cash flow statement**. This exercise emphasized that businesses must regularly **analyze cash inflows and outflows, identify trends, and adjust their spending habits** to maintain financial health. Through this process, companies can determine whether they are **truly cash-flow positive** or **relying on external funding** to survive.

Another key takeaway from this chapter is that **cash flow management is an ongoing process, not a one-time exercise**. Economic downturns, unexpected expenses, and changes in market conditions can **affect liquidity at any time**. To build resilience, businesses must not only focus on **improving cash flow today** but also ensure they are prepared for **future financial challenges**. Maintaining a **cash reserve**, carefully managing debt, and aligning cash flow with business goals are essential strategies for **long-term success**.

Finally, this chapter reinforced that **financial planning and cash flow management go hand in hand**. A business that integrates **cash flow forecasting into its budgeting process** is better equipped to **make data-driven financial decisions, avoid liquidity crises, and seize new**

**growth opportunities**. In an increasingly uncertain business environment, **cash flow mastery is one of the most valuable skills a company can develop**.

By mastering **cash flow management, forecasting, and strategic liquidity planning**, businesses can:

- **Avoid financial distress and maintain financial stability.**
- **Ensure that they can meet short-term and long-term financial obligations.**
- **Improve operational efficiency by aligning cash inflows with outflows.**
- **Make smarter investment decisions that contribute to sustainable growth.**
- **Reduce reliance on external financing, thereby improving profitability and independence.**

## Looking Ahead: Risk Management & Financial Resilience

As we conclude our exploration of business financing and capital management, it is essential to recognise that securing funding and managing capital effectively are just part of the equation. Even with strong financial structures in place, businesses face a range of financial risks that can threaten profitability and long-term stability. From market volatility and credit risks to operational disruptions and global economic shifts, risk management is a critical component of financial strategy.

In the next chapter, we will explore **Risk Management & Financial Resilience**, focusing on how businesses:

- **Identify and Assess Financial Risks:** Understanding market risks, credit risks, and operational risks that impact financial stability.
- **Develop Risk Mitigation Strategies:** Using financial planning, liquidity management, and contingency planning to navigate uncertainty.
- **Implement Protection Mechanisms:** Leveraging insurance, hedging, and diversification to safeguard financial health.
- **Learn from Real-World Case Studies:** Examining how successful companies have managed financial crises and emerged stronger.

Effective risk management ensures that businesses are not only prepared for unexpected disruptions but also capable of adapting, pivoting, and thriving in challenging economic conditions. By integrating risk management strategies into financial planning, businesses can build resilience and sustain long-term growth, regardless of external pressures.

Let's now turn our focus to **Risk Management & Financial Resilience**, where we will uncover the best strategies to protect and strengthen financial stability in an unpredictable business landscape.

# ETHICS IN FINANCIAL ACCOUNTING

## Introduction: The Role of Ethics in Financial Accounting

Ethics in financial accounting is **more than just compliance with rules and regulations**—it is the foundation of **trust, integrity, and transparency** in business. Without ethical financial practices, businesses risk **losing investor confidence, facing legal penalties, and damaging their reputation beyond repair**. The financial world has seen numerous scandals where companies **manipulated financial data, misrepresented earnings, or engaged in fraudulent activities**, leading to **massive financial collapses**.

Consider the infamous **Enron scandal**—a once-thriving energy company that **collapsed under the weight of accounting fraud**. Executives used unethical financial reporting to **inflate profits**, deceiving investors and employees who lost billions when the company went bankrupt. Similarly, **WorldCom** engaged in one of the largest financial frauds in history, misclassifying expenses to **artificially boost earnings**, only to end in scandal and bankruptcy.

These real-world examples underscore **why ethics in accounting is non-negotiable**. A single instance of unethical accounting can destroy **an entire company**, harm employees, and shake public trust in financial systems. Ethical financial practices ensure that **investors, employees, and the public can rely on accurate and honest financial reporting**.

In this chapter, we will explore:

- **Why ethics is essential in accounting and decision-making**
- **Common ethical dilemmas and how to resolve them**
- **Regulatory frameworks that enforce ethical accounting**
- **The role of auditors in upholding financial integrity**
- **The devastating impact of unethical accounting practices**

## Trust and Credibility: The Backbone of Business Stability

Financial accounting exists as the foundation of transparency in the corporate world. Investors, creditors, employees, regulatory bodies, and the public rely on financial statements to assess a company's stability, profitability, and long-term viability. The integrity of these statements directly impacts decision-making at every level. When financial figures are misrepresented, it creates a false reality that can lead to poor investment decisions, unsound credit extensions, employee uncertainty, and ultimately, financial collapse. Trust in corporate financial reporting is not an automatic privilege but a status that must be earned and maintained through ethical accounting practices.

A company's financial health is scrutinized by a wide range of stakeholders, each of whom relies on accurate and ethical financial reporting to make informed decisions. Investors assess earnings reports, cash flow statements, and balance sheets to determine whether a company is a worthwhile investment. Creditors evaluate debt ratios, revenue streams, and asset valuations to decide whether a business is capable of repaying loans. Employees look to financial reports to gauge the stability of their jobs, future salary expectations, and company growth opportunities. Consumers and the general public consider financial stability when deciding whether to engage with a company's products or services.

If financial information is manipulated, it not only misguides stakeholders but also undermines the foundation of corporate trust. False financial statements can artificially inflate stock prices, creating a dangerous bubble that inevitably bursts when the truth is revealed. Investors who believed in a company's prospects based on fraudulent reports may suffer significant financial losses, while employees may find themselves out of work when the company can no longer sustain itself. Creditors who extended loans under false pretenses may be left with uncollectible debts, and consumers may lose confidence in the brand. The ripple effect of unethical financial reporting is far-reaching, affecting not only the company in question but also the broader economy.

One of the most notorious examples of financial fraud destroying trust is the collapse of Enron. Once considered a Wall Street darling, Enron used complex accounting loopholes and off-the-books partnerships to hide debt and inflate profitability. Investors trusted the financial statements presented by Enron's executives, believing that the company was experiencing record growth. Employees, many of whom had invested their retirement savings in Enron stock, were confident in their financial future. However, when the truth came to light and it was revealed that Enron had engaged in widespread financial fraud, the company collapsed into bankruptcy. Investors lost billions, employees lost their pensions, and public trust in corporate financial reporting was shaken.

By contrast, companies that uphold ethical accounting principles and prioritize financial transparency establish themselves as reliable and trustworthy institutions. Microsoft and Apple, two of the world's largest technology companies, have consistently adhered to ethical financial practices and regulatory compliance. Their commitment to accurate financial reporting has strengthened investor confidence, solidified their reputations, and contributed to long-term financial growth. Microsoft, for example, has regularly provided transparent earnings reports that offer a realistic view of its financial standing, ensuring that investors and analysts have a clear understanding of its revenue streams, expenses, and market strategies. Apple, known for its rigorous financial discipline, has maintained a reputation for clear and honest financial disclosures, ensuring that stakeholders can rely on its financial statements to make informed decisions.

Trust in financial reporting is not built overnight; it is cultivated through years of consistent ethical behavior, accurate disclosures, and regulatory compliance. Businesses that prioritize ethical financial reporting benefit from increased investor confidence, easier access to credit, and a more stable workforce. They are also more resilient in times of financial uncertainty, as stakeholders are more likely to support a company they trust. When financial statements reflect reality rather than a manipulated illusion, businesses can make informed strategic decisions, avoid financial crises, and ensure long-term sustainability.

Maintaining credibility in financial reporting requires more than simply following accounting regulations; it demands a corporate culture that prioritizes ethical decision-making at every level. Corporate governance structures must include strong internal controls, independent audits, and a commitment to transparency. Executives must lead by example, setting a tone of integrity and accountability that extends throughout the organization. Employees should be encouraged to report any unethical practices without fear of retaliation, and regulatory bodies must enforce stringent penalties for those who engage in financial misrepresentation.

Trust and credibility in financial accounting are not just about avoiding scandals or regulatory penalties. They are about fostering long-term business success. Ethical financial reporting allows businesses to attract and retain investors, secure financing at favorable rates, maintain employee morale, and uphold consumer confidence. When companies prioritize integrity, they create a stable and sustainable business environment that benefits not only their own operations but also the broader economic system. Ethical accounting is not just a legal obligation—it is a strategic advantage that separates successful, long-lasting enterprises from those doomed to fail under the weight of financial deception.

## Ethical Decision-Making in Accounting: Navigating Moral Dilemmas in the Corporate World

Ethical dilemmas in financial accounting are not hypothetical scenarios that exist only in textbooks or business ethics discussions. They are real-world challenges faced by accountants, financial controllers, auditors, and executives in businesses of all sizes. Ethical decisions in financial reporting often involve competing pressures—corporate expectations, financial performance demands, personal career risks, and the fundamental duty to uphold transparency and truth in accounting.

Consider a situation where a financial controller is asked by their CEO to **delay recognizing certain expenses** until the next quarter. The reasoning behind this request is clear: by pushing expenses forward, the company's financial statements for the current quarter will appear stronger, increasing profitability on paper. This move could boost stock prices, impress investors, and allow executives to meet performance targets. However, the request is **a direct violation of accounting standards**, specifically the **matching principle**, which requires that expenses be recorded in the same period as the revenue they help generate.

For the financial controller, the situation is a moral and professional dilemma. If they refuse, they may risk alienating upper management, jeopardizing their career, or even losing their job. If they comply, they become complicit in financial misrepresentation, which could have far-reaching consequences for the company, its investors, and their own professional credibility. This type of ethical challenge is not uncommon, especially in highly competitive industries where meeting earnings expectations is a critical factor in executive compensation and shareholder confidence.

Making ethical decisions in financial accounting requires three key principles: **integrity, courage, and transparency**. Integrity means adhering to ethical and legal accounting standards, even when pressured to deviate from them. Courage is necessary to challenge unethical behavior and take a stand, even when facing personal or professional risks. Transparency ensures that financial data remains accurate, unaltered, and reflective of a company's true financial health. These principles are the backbone of responsible financial reporting and are essential for maintaining trust in the accounting profession.

Ethical dilemmas in accounting do not always come in the form of explicit fraud. Sometimes, they present themselves as **"gray areas"**—small adjustments that may seem harmless but ultimately set a precedent for ethical compromises. A slight exaggeration in revenue recognition, an understated liability, or a deferred expense may not seem like a major ethical breach at first glance. However, these small actions can accumulate, leading to systemic financial misrepresentation. Many corporate scandals, including those of **Enron, WorldCom, and Lehman Brothers**, started with seemingly minor ethical lapses that eventually escalated into massive fraud.

A real-world example of ethical decision-making in accounting can be found in the case of **HealthSouth Corporation**, a healthcare services provider that became embroiled in one of the largest corporate fraud scandals in U.S.

history. HealthSouth executives engaged in widespread financial fraud, inflating earnings by **more than $2 billion** to meet Wall Street expectations. Over several years, fraudulent accounting practices allowed the company to appear far more profitable than it actually was. The fraud could have continued unchecked had it not been for the courage and integrity of a former accountant within the company.

Richard Scrushy, the CEO of HealthSouth, had fostered an environment where **financial manipulation was the norm**, and executives were pressured to engage in fraudulent accounting practices to sustain the illusion of profitability. However, an internal accountant identified the fraudulent activities and took the courageous step of exposing the deception. Despite immense pressure and the risk of professional retaliation, he chose to uphold ethical accounting principles. His decision to **blow the whistle** on the fraudulent activities led to **a major investigation, a corporate lawsuit, and the downfall of HealthSouth's top executives**.

The HealthSouth case is a powerful reminder that **ethical lapses in accounting rarely go unnoticed forever**. Fraudulent financial activities may provide short-term gains, but they inevitably unravel, often with devastating consequences. Companies that engage in unethical accounting practices eventually face regulatory scrutiny, lawsuits, loss of investor confidence, and, in extreme cases, bankruptcy. Employees who participate in or turn a blind eye to financial misrepresentation risk damaging their reputations, facing legal penalties, or being barred from the profession altogether.

Ethical decision-making in accounting is not just about avoiding fraud; it is about fostering a **corporate culture of accountability and responsibility**. Companies that prioritize ethical accounting practices invest in strong

**internal controls, independent audits, and a compliance-driven leadership team**. Ethical organizations provide employees with mechanisms to report unethical behavior **without fear of retaliation**, ensuring that ethical concerns can be addressed before they escalate into full-blown financial scandals.

For accountants and financial professionals, maintaining ethical integrity requires vigilance and a strong sense of professional responsibility. Ethical dilemmas may not always present themselves in black-and-white terms, but professionals must be able to **recognize red flags, question questionable accounting treatments, and push back against unethical requests**. This is particularly important in industries where **performance-based compensation and short-term financial targets create pressure to manipulate financial statements**.

Accountants must also consider their **legal and professional obligations**. Regulatory bodies such as the **Financial Accounting Standards Board (FASB), International Financial Reporting Standards (IFRS), and the Securities and Exchange Commission (SEC)** have established strict guidelines to ensure ethical accounting practices. Ignoring or circumventing these standards can lead to legal consequences, including fines, criminal charges, and the revocation of professional certifications.

Companies that embed ethical decision-making into their financial operations gain significant advantages. Ethical businesses are more likely to attract investors, retain employees, and sustain long-term profitability. They avoid costly legal battles, regulatory fines, and reputational damage. They also foster trust among their stakeholders, which is **invaluable in an increasingly transparent business environment**.

The importance of ethical accounting extends beyond individual businesses. The global financial system relies on the credibility of financial statements to maintain market stability. When companies engage in fraudulent accounting practices, they not only harm their own stakeholders but also **undermine trust in financial markets as a whole**. This is why regulatory bodies impose strict penalties on financial misrepresentation and why auditors, analysts, and investors closely scrutinize financial reports.

The challenge for accountants and financial professionals is not just to comply with ethical standards but to **champion them**. Ethical decision-making should not be seen as an obligation but as a responsibility to protect the integrity of financial reporting. In moments of ethical uncertainty, financial professionals must ask themselves: **Will this decision maintain transparency and trust? Will it uphold the integrity of the accounting profession? Will it serve the long-term interests of the business rather than short-term financial gains?** If the answer to any of these questions is no, then the ethical path is clear.

The reality of ethical dilemmas in accounting is that they are often **difficult and uncomfortable**. It takes courage to challenge unethical practices, particularly when the pressure to comply comes from senior executives. However, history has shown that **those who stand by ethical accounting principles ultimately contribute to stronger businesses, healthier financial markets, and a more trustworthy corporate environment**. The price of unethical accounting is always greater than the short-term benefits it might provide. Companies that prioritize ethical decision-making in accounting will always be in a stronger position for **long-term success, stability, and credibility**.

## Regulatory Compliance: Ethics and the Law Go Hand in Hand

Ethical accounting practices are not only essential for maintaining credibility and transparency but are also **legally mandated** to protect investors, creditors, and the public from financial misrepresentation and fraud. Governments and regulatory bodies worldwide enforce strict accounting standards to ensure businesses present accurate financial information. Without these regulations, companies would have unchecked freedom to manipulate their financial statements, potentially misleading investors and damaging economic stability.

Accounting regulations are designed to establish **consistency, comparability, and reliability** in financial reporting. By enforcing ethical financial practices, these laws help prevent fraud, financial misstatements, and corporate scandals that can lead to massive investor losses and economic turmoil. Companies that fail to comply with these regulations not only face severe financial penalties but may also expose their executives to criminal charges.

## The Role of GAAP and IFRS in Ethical Financial Reporting

The **Generally Accepted Accounting Principles (GAAP)** and the **International Financial Reporting Standards (IFRS)** serve as the global benchmarks for ethical financial reporting. These frameworks dictate how financial transactions should be recorded, ensuring that businesses follow a uniform structure in their financial statements.

GAAP is primarily used in the United States and is enforced by the

**Financial Accounting Standards Board (FASB)**. It outlines strict guidelines on revenue recognition, expense classification, asset valuation, and disclosure requirements. Under GAAP, companies must **adhere to principles of consistency, materiality, prudence, and full disclosure**, all of which promote ethical accounting practices.

IFRS, developed by the **International Accounting Standards Board (IASB)**, is the globally accepted alternative to GAAP. Many countries, including the UK, Canada, and most of Europe, follow IFRS standards. Like GAAP, IFRS aims to **enhance transparency and accountability in financial reporting**, ensuring that companies disclose financial information in a way that allows for fair comparison across industries and countries.

Both GAAP and IFRS serve as the **foundation for ethical financial practices**. Companies that manipulate financial data to mislead stakeholders are, by definition, violating these standards. Regulators use these frameworks as the basis for investigating and penalizing companies that fail to comply.

## The Sarbanes-Oxley Act: A Response to Corporate Fraud

One of the most significant regulatory reforms in financial accounting was the passage of the **Sarbanes-Oxley Act (SOX) in 2002**. This legislation was enacted in response to corporate accounting scandals such as **Enron and WorldCom**, both of which involved fraudulent financial reporting that resulted in billions of dollars in investor losses.

SOX introduced **stricter financial disclosure requirements and accountability measures** to prevent similar corporate fraud in the future. Among its key provisions:

- **Increased responsibility for executives** – Corporate executives, including CEOs and CFOs, are now required to **personally certify the accuracy of financial statements**. If a company's financial reports are found to be fraudulent, executives can be held **criminally liable**, facing significant fines and potential imprisonment.
- **Stronger internal controls** – Publicly traded companies must establish **robust internal auditing procedures** to prevent financial misstatements. Independent auditors must **verify financial statements**, ensuring accuracy and compliance.
- **Whistleblower protections** – Employees who report financial fraud within their companies are protected under SOX. This ensures that accountants, auditors, and financial professionals can **speak out against unethical practices without fear of retaliation**.

SOX has played a crucial role in **restoring investor confidence** after the corporate fraud scandals of the early 2000s. By holding executives accountable for financial misstatements and implementing stricter auditing requirements, the law has significantly **reduced the likelihood of fraudulent accounting practices**.

## Regulatory Agencies: Enforcing Ethical Accounting Standards

Several government agencies are responsible for ensuring companies comply with ethical accounting practices. The **Securities and Exchange Commission (SEC)** in the United States and the **Financial Conduct Authority (FCA)** in the United Kingdom are among the most influential financial regulatory bodies worldwide.

The SEC oversees financial reporting by publicly traded companies in the United States. It enforces compliance with GAAP and SOX regulations, ensuring that companies **do not mislead investors with inaccurate financial disclosures**. The SEC investigates financial misconduct, bringing legal action against businesses and individuals that violate accounting standards.

In the UK, the **Financial Conduct Authority (FCA)** plays a similar role. The FCA ensures that companies comply with **IFRS and financial market regulations**. It has the authority to fine corporations, revoke business licenses, and take legal action against executives engaged in fraudulent financial reporting.

Other regulatory bodies worldwide, including **the European Securities and Markets Authority (ESMA), the Australian Securities and Investments Commission (ASIC), and the Monetary Authority of Singapore (MAS)**, work to ensure ethical financial practices within their respective jurisdictions.

## Legal Consequences of Violating Financial Regulations

Companies and executives that fail to adhere to ethical accounting standards face **serious legal consequences**, including:

- **Financial penalties** – Regulatory agencies impose massive fines on companies that misrepresent financial information.
- **Lawsuits from investors** – Shareholders can sue businesses that mislead them with fraudulent accounting practices.

- **Criminal charges for executives** – CEOs and CFOs who sign off on fraudulent financial statements can face **prison sentences**.
- **Loss of business licenses** – Companies found guilty of fraudulent financial reporting may be **barred from operating** in certain industries.

One of the most high-profile examples of regulatory enforcement in recent years was the **Tesla-SEC investigation in 2018**. The case highlighted how even top executives of leading corporations are **not immune to financial misconduct investigations**.

Tesla's CEO, **Elon Musk**, made a public statement on Twitter claiming that he had secured funding to take the company private at $420 per share. This claim **misled investors**, causing Tesla's stock price to fluctuate wildly. The SEC launched an investigation and found that Musk's statements were **false and misleading**, violating securities regulations. As a result, Musk and Tesla were each fined **$20 million**, and Musk was forced to step down as Tesla's chairman for a period of three years.

The Tesla case demonstrated that **financial statements, corporate disclosures, and executive communications must always be accurate and truthful**. Public companies are held to strict legal standards, and any attempt to manipulate financial data, even through social media, can lead to regulatory penalties.

## Ethical Compliance as a Business Imperative

Beyond legal consequences, failing to uphold ethical accounting standards **damages corporate credibility**. Investors lose confidence in companies that engage in fraudulent financial reporting, leading to declining stock prices and reduced access to capital. Customers may lose trust in brands associated with financial misconduct, leading to declining sales and reputational harm. Employees may also feel uncertain about the future of their company, leading to high turnover and a negative workplace culture.

Companies that prioritize ethical compliance benefit from **long-term stability, stronger investor relations, and increased financial resilience**. Ethical financial reporting fosters a culture of **integrity, transparency, and accountability**, ensuring that businesses remain in good standing with regulators and investors alike.

Regulatory compliance is **not just a legal requirement but a strategic advantage**. Companies that follow GAAP, IFRS, SOX, and other accounting regulations can build stronger relationships with stakeholders, avoid costly legal battles, and ensure sustainable financial growth. Ethical financial practices contribute to **market stability, investor protection, and economic security**, reinforcing the critical role that accounting plays in maintaining trust in the global financial system.

As businesses continue to evolve in an increasingly complex regulatory landscape, **staying ahead of accounting compliance requirements is essential**. Ethical accounting is not simply about avoiding penalties; it is about establishing a foundation of **trust, credibility, and financial responsibility** that ensures long-term business success. Companies that prioritize financial ethics will not only protect themselves from regulatory scrutiny but will also build a reputation of reliability, which is invaluable in today's financial markets.

## Common Ethical Issues in Accounting and How to Address Them

Despite strict financial regulations, ethical violations in accounting continue to occur across industries. Companies, executives, and financial professionals sometimes succumb to the pressures of meeting earnings expectations, securing investments, or maintaining competitive advantages. These pressures can lead to unethical accounting practices that mislead investors, regulators, and the public.

Ethical breaches in financial accounting have far-reaching consequences. They can lead to **financial collapses, loss of investor confidence, regulatory penalties, legal consequences, and reputational damage**. Many corporate scandals that have made headlines over the years share common patterns—**misrepresentation of financial data, revenue recognition manipulation, and conflicts of interest**. Understanding these unethical practices and the measures required to prevent them is critical for maintaining financial integrity and ensuring long-term business sustainability.

### Misrepresentation of Financial Data: The Deception of Stakeholders

Misrepresentation of financial data occurs when companies **inflate profits, conceal losses, understate liabilities, or misclassify expenses** to present a more favorable financial picture than reality. This practice misleads investors, lenders, and other stakeholders into believing that a company is financially stable and growing when, in fact, it may be struggling or even on the brink of collapse.

Financial misrepresentation can take various forms. Companies may overstate revenues, exaggerate asset values, manipulate expenses to appear more profitable, or hide significant financial risks. While such actions may provide short-term benefits—such as increased stock prices, easier access to loans, or executive bonuses—they ultimately lead to devastating consequences when the truth is uncovered.

One of the most infamous cases of financial misrepresentation was the collapse of **Lehman Brothers in 2008**. The investment bank engaged in accounting manoeuvres that hid billions of dollars in debt from its balance sheet, creating the illusion of financial stability. By using an accounting trick called **Repo 105**, Lehman Brothers temporarily removed liabilities from its books before reporting earnings, only to bring them back shortly afterward. This deception allowed the company to **misrepresent its financial condition to investors and regulators**. However, when the financial crisis hit and scrutiny increased, Lehman Brothers' real financial situation was exposed. The firm collapsed, triggering a domino effect that contributed to the global financial crisis.

Misrepresentation of financial data is not just a historical issue. Even today, companies that manipulate their financial statements for short-term gains risk regulatory penalties, investor lawsuits, and reputational damage that can take years to recover from.

### *How to Prevent Financial Misrepresentation*

To prevent the unethical misrepresentation of financial data, companies must implement **strict internal controls, independent auditing processes, and transparent reporting practices**.

- **Internal control mechanisms** should be established to ensure financial statements accurately reflect a company's true financial position. This includes requiring multiple levels of approval for financial reporting and ensuring that financial professionals adhere to ethical guidelines.

- **Independent audits** conducted by external auditors play a crucial role in identifying financial misrepresentation. Auditors must be empowered to scrutinize financial statements objectively and report any red flags.
- **Whistleblower protections** should be strengthened to encourage employees to report unethical financial practices without fear of retaliation. Many financial scandals could have been prevented had employees felt safe enough to expose wrongdoing early on.

## Revenue Recognition Manipulation: Artificially Inflating Profits

Revenue recognition is a critical component of financial accounting, as it dictates **when and how companies record revenue**. When companies manipulate revenue recognition, they mislead investors and other stakeholders about their actual financial performance. The goal of revenue manipulation is often to create the illusion of **higher profits, faster growth, or greater stability** than what actually exists.

One common form of revenue manipulation is **premature revenue recognition**, where companies record revenue before it has actually been earned. This is particularly common in industries with long-term contracts, such as construction and software, where revenue is supposed to be recognized over time rather than all at once.

A notable example of revenue recognition fraud occurred with **Xerox**, which was found guilty of **prematurely recognizing $3 billion in revenue**. The company engaged in an accounting scheme where it recognized revenue from multi-year service contracts upfront, rather than spreading it out over the contract duration. This practice artificially inflated Xerox's earnings, misleading investors and analysts about the company's actual performance. When the SEC uncovered the fraud, Xerox faced penalties and was forced to **restate its financial results**, significantly damaging its reputation.

Another form of revenue manipulation is **delayed revenue recognition**, where companies intentionally postpone recognizing revenue until a later period. This tactic is sometimes used when a company wants to **smooth out earnings fluctuations** to appear more stable over time.

***How to Ensure Proper Revenue Recognition***

To prevent revenue manipulation, businesses must strictly follow **GAAP and IFRS revenue recognition standards**, which outline clear guidelines on how and when revenue should be recorded.

- **Financial teams should undergo regular training** on revenue recognition principles to ensure they adhere to industry standards.
- **Regular audits and financial reviews** should be conducted to identify discrepancies in revenue recognition practices.
- **Companies should establish clear policies** that prevent premature or delayed revenue recognition, ensuring that earnings reports reflect real financial activity.
- **Executives should be held accountable** for ethical revenue

reporting, ensuring that financial performance is not manipulated to meet short-term targets.

Regulators and investors pay close attention to revenue recognition policies, and any inconsistencies or misstatements can raise red flags that lead to investigations and legal consequences.

## Ethical Financial Leadership & Corporate Governance: Why Integrity is a Competitive Advantage

Financial integrity is not just a moral obligation—it is a fundamental driver of business success. In an era where corporate scandals, fraudulent financial reporting, and regulatory violations have eroded public trust, companies that prioritize ethical financial leadership and corporate governance distinguish themselves as industry leaders. Ethical accounting practices safeguard long-term profitability, attract investors, and create a culture of accountability that strengthens a company's reputation and market position. Businesses that fail to uphold ethical financial standards, on the other hand, often face regulatory scrutiny, legal penalties, and the loss of stakeholder confidence, leading to long-term financial damage or complete collapse.

Throughout history, financial scandals have demonstrated the devastating consequences of unethical accounting practices. Companies like Enron, Lehman Brothers, and Wirecard manipulated financial data, concealed liabilities, and engaged in fraudulent activities to present an illusion of profitability. While these companies enjoyed short-term gains, their unethical financial decisions ultimately led to corporate bankruptcy, investor lawsuits, and the imprisonment of executives. Conversely, companies that embed ethics into their financial decision-making processes, such as Patagonia, Unilever, and Johnson & Johnson, have consistently outperformed competitors by building sustainable, financially resilient businesses.

This section explores why ethical financial leadership is a business imperative, how organizations can cultivate a culture of financial integrity, and why corporate governance plays a critical role in safeguarding long-term financial health.

## The Business Case for Ethical Financial Leadership

Ethical accounting is not just about avoiding legal trouble—it is a strategic advantage. Companies that prioritize ethical financial practices enjoy increased investor confidence, stronger customer loyalty, and a more motivated workforce. Financial transparency attracts long-term investors who value sustainable business growth over short-term profit manipulation. Banks and financial institutions offer better lending terms to companies with strong governance structures and ethical accounting practices, reducing the cost of capital.

Additionally, businesses that prioritize financial ethics are less likely to face regulatory penalties, lawsuits, or reputational damage. When companies engage in deceptive financial reporting, the damage to their reputation often outweighs any short-term financial gain. A single scandal can wipe out decades of credibility, leading to stock price collapses, loss of key customers, and legal actions that drain financial resources. In contrast, ethical financial leadership fosters trust, builds resilience, and ensures that businesses can withstand economic uncertainties without resorting to deceptive financial practices.

## How to Build a Culture of Financial Integrity in a Business

Financial ethics are not determined solely by regulatory compliance—they are embedded in the company's culture and leadership. To create an organization where financial integrity is a core value, businesses must take proactive steps to ensure that ethical accounting principles are not just followed, but deeply ingrained in the decision-making process at every level.

The first step in fostering a culture of financial integrity is setting clear ethical standards. Organizations should implement a robust financial code of conduct that defines acceptable accounting practices, revenue recognition policies, expense reporting guidelines, and financial disclosure standards. These ethical guidelines must align with international accounting principles such as GAAP (Generally Accepted Accounting Principles) and IFRS (International Financial Reporting Standards).

Leadership plays a pivotal role in establishing ethical expectations. Executives, particularly Chief Financial Officers (CFOs), must lead by example, demonstrating ethical financial behavior and ensuring that finance teams operate with complete transparency. Businesses must provide financial ethics training to accountants, finance teams, and senior management, equipping them with the knowledge to identify and report unethical practices. Employees must be empowered to speak up when they witness unethical financial activities, with strong whistleblower protections in place to shield them from retaliation.

Transparency and accountability mechanisms must be integrated into the company's financial processes. Businesses should implement internal audit programs, conduct independent financial audits, and maintain real-time reporting tools that allow executives and board members to detect financial discrepancies before they escalate. A strong internal audit function serves as a safeguard against financial misreporting, ensuring that ethical accounting principles are consistently upheld.

## The Role of CFOs in Driving Ethical Financial Decision-Making

Chief Financial Officers (CFOs) are the gatekeepers of financial ethics within an organization. They play a critical role in shaping financial policies, ensuring compliance with accounting standards, and preventing unethical financial practices. CFOs must be more than just financial strategists—they must be ethical stewards who prioritize transparency, accuracy, and accountability in all financial reporting activities.

An ethical CFO resists pressure from executives and shareholders who may seek to manipulate financial data for short-term gain. In many high-profile financial scandals, CFOs were complicit in fraudulent accounting schemes because they prioritized immediate stock price increases over long-term financial health. Ethical CFOs, however, recognize that sustainable business success is built on integrity rather than deception.

To reinforce financial integrity, CFOs must implement strong risk management controls that detect and prevent financial fraud. They should leverage financial analytics, automated compliance systems, and AI-driven fraud detection tools to identify irregularities in financial reporting. By fostering a data-driven, transparent financial environment, CFOs can protect their organizations from financial misrepresentation and regulatory violations.

CFOs must also act as financial educators within their organizations, ensuring that non-finance executives understand the ethical implications of financial decision-making. Many corporate leaders lack deep financial expertise and may unknowingly encourage financial practices that violate ethical accounting standards. CFOs should work closely with CEOs, board members, and department heads to create a shared understanding of financial integrity, ensuring that ethical considerations are embedded into every business strategy.

## Corporate Governance & Financial Accountability: Strengthening Oversight to Prevent Financial Misconduct

Corporate governance refers to the system of rules, practices, and processes that direct and control a company's financial operations. Strong corporate governance structures ensure that businesses operate with financial accountability, preventing fraudulent activities, mismanagement, and conflicts of interest.

An effective corporate governance framework starts with a strong, independent board of directors that provides oversight and ensures that financial decisions align with ethical and regulatory standards. Boards should establish audit committees composed of independent financial experts who review financial statements, monitor risk management practices, and ensure compliance with financial reporting laws.

Investor confidence is heavily influenced by a company's corporate governance practices. Institutional investors, such as pension funds and private equity firms, prioritize investments in companies with strong governance structures, knowing that ethical financial management reduces long-term financial risk. Businesses with transparent governance practices attract high-quality investors, leading to improved financial stability and growth opportunities.

Public companies are particularly vulnerable to financial scandals if corporate governance structures are weak. Without strong oversight, executives may engage in earnings manipulation, improper revenue recognition, or aggressive cost-cutting measures that distort financial reality. Enron's downfall in 2001 was largely due to a lack of corporate governance checks, allowing executives to hide debt off-balance-sheet and inflate revenue figures. In contrast, well-governed companies such as Berkshire Hathaway and Unilever have built reputations for financial transparency, reinforcing long-term investor trust.

## Why Ethical Financial Leadership is the Foundation of Sustainable Business Success

Ethical financial leadership is not just about following accounting rules—it is about building a business that stands the test of time. Companies that uphold financial integrity attract better investors, retain top talent, and create long-term value for shareholders. Financial scandals may offer temporary gains, but they ultimately lead to reputational damage, regulatory fines, and business failure.

Businesses that embrace ethical financial leadership do not wait for regulations to dictate their actions. They proactively implement strong governance structures, integrate transparency into financial reporting, and create a culture where financial integrity is non-negotiable. Ethical leadership is not a constraint—it is a strategic advantage that sets companies apart in a marketplace where trust is the most valuable currency.

## Conflicts of Interest in Accounting: Financial Decisions Influenced by Personal Gain

Conflicts of interest arise when **accounting professionals, executives, or employees make financial decisions based on personal incentives rather than the best interests of the company and its stakeholders**. This can occur when individuals manipulate financial statements, approve unethical transactions, or fail to disclose relationships that could influence their objectivity.

A high-profile example of conflicts of interest leading to unethical financial practices was the **Wells Fargo fake accounts scandal**. Under intense pressure to meet aggressive sales targets, Wells Fargo employees created **millions of unauthorized bank and credit card accounts** in customers' names. Employees did so to meet sales quotas and secure bonuses, even though these accounts were fraudulent. The practice resulted in billions in fines, legal penalties, and a **massive loss of trust in the banking institution**.

Another common conflict of interest scenario occurs when **auditors have financial ties to the companies they audit**. When auditors have close relationships with executives or receive high fees for their services, they may be incentivized to **overlook financial misstatements or fraudulent activities**. The **Arthur Andersen accounting firm**, which was once one of the "Big Five" accounting firms, collapsed because of its role in **covering up Enron's fraudulent accounting practices**. Arthur Andersen had a conflict of interest because it was receiving lucrative consulting fees from Enron while also serving as its auditor. Rather than exposing Enron's financial misconduct, the firm helped conceal it. This failure led to Arthur

Andersen's **dissolution and loss of credibility in the industry**.

***How to Address Conflicts of Interest in Accounting***

To prevent conflicts of interest from leading to unethical financial decisions, companies must establish **strong governance frameworks** that prioritize ethical decision-making.

- **Companies should require full disclosure** of financial relationships and conflicts of interest among executives, auditors, and financial professionals.
- **Independent oversight committees** should be responsible for reviewing financial decisions to ensure they align with ethical and regulatory standards.
- **Strict policies should prohibit auditors** from engaging in lucrative consulting work with the same firms they audit, reducing financial dependencies that could compromise their objectivity.
- **Ethical training programs should be implemented** to ensure that employees understand the dangers of conflicts of interest and how to navigate them responsibly.

Conflicts of interest can severely undermine the integrity of financial reporting. When financial decisions are driven by **personal incentives rather than objective analysis**, companies risk financial misrepresentation, regulatory scrutiny, and long-term reputational damage.

## The Importance of Preventing Ethical Violations in Accounting

Ethical breaches in financial accounting—whether through financial misrepresentation, revenue manipulation, or conflicts of interest—have serious consequences. They damage reputations, lead to legal penalties, and, in extreme cases, result in corporate collapse. Organizations that prioritize **transparency, regulatory compliance, and strong ethical policies** safeguard themselves from these risks and build trust with investors, employees, and the public. Ethical accounting is **not just a legal requirement but a fundamental pillar of financial sustainability and corporate responsibility**.

## The Role of Auditors in Ethical Accounting

Auditors are the **gatekeepers of financial integrity**, playing a crucial role in ensuring that financial statements are accurate, unbiased, and free from fraud. As independent evaluators, auditors provide an **objective assessment** of a company's financial health, ensuring that stakeholders—investors, creditors, employees, and regulators—can trust the information presented in financial reports. Without auditors, companies would have **unchecked freedom** to manipulate financial data, leading to misleading financial statements, unethical business practices, and, in extreme cases, financial collapses.

Despite the importance of auditing, **financial scandals continue to emerge**, often due to weak auditing practices, conflicts of interest, or outright negligence. When auditors fail to uphold ethical standards, the consequences can be severe—corporate fraud goes undetected, investors suffer significant losses, and public trust in financial institutions erodes. To prevent such outcomes, auditors must adhere to **strict ethical guidelines**, maintain independence, and report unethical practices when discovered.

## Independent Verification of Financial Statements

At the heart of auditing is the **independent verification** of a company's financial records. Companies are required to prepare financial statements in accordance with accounting standards such as **GAAP and IFRS**, but auditors are responsible for reviewing these statements to **ensure compliance, accuracy, and fairness**. Auditors assess whether financial reports accurately reflect the company's financial position and whether any **red flags indicate potential fraud or misstatements**.

An auditor's responsibilities include:

- **Examining accounting records, transactions, and financial reports** to ensure that they adhere to regulatory standards.
- **Assessing internal controls and risk management processes** to determine whether a company has sufficient safeguards to prevent financial misstatements and fraud.
- **Identifying inconsistencies, irregularities, or signs of financial manipulation** that could indicate unethical behavior.
- **Ensuring transparency in revenue recognition, expense classification, and asset valuation** to prevent misleading financial statements.

Auditors are expected to remain **independent and objective**, avoiding any conflicts of interest that might compromise their ability to conduct an honest and thorough review. If an auditor becomes too closely aligned with the company they are auditing—whether due to financial incentives, personal relationships, or external pressures—their judgment can be compromised, leading to **biased reporting and overlooked financial**

**fraud**.

A failure in independent auditing was evident in the **Enron scandal**, where **Arthur Andersen**, one of the largest accounting firms at the time, failed to report fraudulent accounting practices at Enron. Instead of exposing Enron's misstatements, Arthur Andersen helped the company hide billions of dollars in debt through complex financial structures. When the fraud was eventually uncovered, **Arthur Andersen collapsed**, and Enron filed for bankruptcy—one of the largest corporate bankruptcies in U.S. history. This case demonstrated how **a lack of auditing independence can have catastrophic consequences** for both companies and the auditing profession.

To ensure independence, regulatory agencies have introduced **strict guidelines** regarding auditor-company relationships. The **Sarbanes-Oxley Act (SOX) of 2002**, passed in response to corporate fraud scandals, requires companies to **rotate auditors periodically** and prohibits audit firms from providing **certain non-audit services** (such as consulting) to the same clients they audit. These measures reduce the risk of conflicts of interest and ensure that auditors maintain their role as **impartial evaluators**.

## Reporting Unethical Practices and Financial Misconduct

Auditors have an ethical and legal responsibility to **report unethical practices** when they discover financial irregularities, fraud, or misstatements. If an auditor finds **evidence of financial manipulation, concealed debt, false revenue recognition, or other fraudulent activities**, they must **escalate the issue**—even if it involves top executives.

Failure to report fraud not only **violates professional ethics** but can also lead to **legal consequences** for the auditor. Regulatory agencies such as the **Securities and Exchange Commission (SEC) in the U.S. and the Financial Conduct Authority (FCA) in the UK** impose penalties on auditors who knowingly overlook fraud or fail to disclose financial misstatements.

A high-profile example of auditing failure was the **Wirecard scandal**, which shook the European financial system. Wirecard, a German fintech company, reported billions in profits that **did not exist**. For years, auditors from **EY (Ernst & Young) failed to detect the fraud**, despite numerous warning signs. The company's financial statements showed **phantom profits from fake subsidiaries**, but rather than conducting a thorough investigation, auditors **signed off on the financial reports year after year**. When the fraud was finally exposed in 2020, Wirecard collapsed, leading to **criminal charges against executives, massive losses for investors, and a severe reputational hit for EY**.

The Wirecard scandal highlighted the **importance of auditor diligence and ethical responsibility**. It demonstrated that auditors must be **willing to challenge management**, verify financial data independently, and report any concerns without hesitation. Weak auditing oversight **enables corporate fraud**, while strong ethical auditing **prevents financial misconduct from escalating**.

## Challenges and Pressures Faced by Auditors

Despite their ethical responsibilities, auditors often face **significant pressures** that can challenge their objectivity and effectiveness. Some of the common challenges include:

- **Pressure from clients to approve questionable accounting treatments** – Auditors may face resistance when they question financial irregularities, as executives often seek to present the most favorable financial picture possible.
- **Conflicts of interest and financial incentives** – Some audit firms develop close financial relationships with the companies they audit, creating an environment where reporting negative findings could lead to a loss of business.
- **Regulatory loopholes and weak enforcement** – In some cases, auditors may operate in regulatory environments with limited oversight, allowing companies to manipulate financial reports without facing immediate consequences.
- **Complex financial structures that obscure fraud** – Large multinational corporations often use sophisticated accounting techniques, shell companies, and offshore accounts to hide liabilities and fabricate earnings. Auditors must be **highly skilled and detail-oriented** to detect these deceptive tactics.

While these challenges make auditing a difficult profession, **ethical auditors must resist pressure, uphold accounting standards, and remain committed to financial transparency**.

## Best Practices for Ethical Auditing

To strengthen the role of auditors in ethical accounting, companies, regulators, and audit firms must implement best practices that **enhance accountability, objectivity, and financial integrity**. Some of the key best practices include:

- **Mandatory rotation of audit firms to reduce long-term conflicts of interest** – When auditors work with the same company for too long, objectivity can be compromised. Regularly rotating audit firms ensures **fresh perspectives** and reduces bias.
- **Strict enforcement of whistleblower protections** – Employees and auditors who report financial misconduct must be protected from retaliation to encourage the reporting of unethical practices.
- **Stronger regulatory oversight of audit firms** – Government agencies should conduct independent reviews of audit firms to ensure compliance with professional standards.
- **Greater transparency in auditing procedures** – Publicly traded companies should disclose more details about their audit processes and any disputes between auditors and management regarding financial statements.
- **Use of advanced auditing technologies** – Data analytics, artificial intelligence, and forensic accounting tools can **enhance auditors' ability to detect fraud and financial misstatements**. By integrating modern technology, auditors can improve accuracy, efficiency, and fraud detection capabilities.

## The Future of Ethical Auditing

The role of auditors in ethical accounting is becoming increasingly critical as financial transactions grow **more complex, globalized, and technology-driven**. Regulators, investors, and the public expect auditors to act as **independent watchdogs**, ensuring that financial statements **truly reflect** a company's financial health.

Moving forward, the auditing profession must **evolve to meet new challenges** by embracing stricter ethical guidelines, leveraging **technology-driven auditing techniques**, and maintaining a firm commitment to **financial accountability**. Companies must also recognize that strong, ethical auditing is **not a burden but a benefit**, as it **protects businesses from fraud, strengthens investor confidence, and promotes financial stability**.

The failures of the past—whether Enron, Wirecard, or Lehman Brothers—underscore the **high stakes of unethical auditing**. When auditors fail in their responsibilities, the damage extends beyond a single company; it affects employees, investors, financial markets, and even the broader economy. However, when auditors uphold their ethical duty, they serve as **pillars of financial integrity**, ensuring that businesses operate transparently, investors make informed decisions, and markets remain stable.

Auditors must remain **unwavering in their commitment to ethical financial reporting**, reinforcing the principle that **integrity in accounting is not optional—it is the foundation of a functional and trustworthy financial system.**

## The Impact of Unethical Accounting Practices

Unethical accounting practices have far-reaching consequences, affecting not just the businesses involved but also their employees, investors, customers, and the broader financial system. When companies engage in financial deception—whether through **fraudulent revenue recognition, misrepresenting liabilities, or hiding losses**—they create an illusion of financial stability that can quickly collapse when exposed. The damage caused by unethical accounting extends beyond financial penalties; it results in **reputational ruin, loss of stakeholder trust, regulatory scrutiny, and in many cases, business failure**.

Many of the world's most infamous corporate scandals—**Enron, Lehman Brothers, Wirecard, Volkswagen, and Wells Fargo**—share a common theme: unethical financial practices that ultimately led to **severe legal, financial, and reputational repercussions**. These cases highlight the importance of ethical accounting and the devastating consequences when businesses fail to uphold integrity in financial reporting.

## Financial Consequences of Unethical Accounting

### *Fines, Lawsuits, and Bankruptcy*

One of the most immediate and severe consequences of unethical accounting practices is **legal and financial penalties**. Regulatory agencies such as the **Securities and Exchange Commission (SEC) in the U.S., the Financial Conduct Authority (FCA) in the UK, and the European Securities and Markets Authority (ESMA)** impose **massive fines, sanctions, and legal restrictions** on companies found guilty of financial misconduct. In some cases, unethical financial reporting leads to **class-action lawsuits** from investors, creditors, and other affected parties.

When fraudulent accounting is exposed, companies can quickly find themselves in **financial distress**, unable to recover from regulatory fines and legal settlements. **Many businesses that engage in large-scale financial deception ultimately declare bankruptcy**, as their financial instability becomes evident once unethical accounting practices are corrected.

**Case Study: Enron – One of the Largest Corporate Bankruptcies in History**

One of the most devastating cases of financial fraud was the **Enron scandal** in the early 2000s. Enron, once one of the most valuable companies in the U.S., used **complex accounting loopholes and off-balance-sheet entities to hide billions of dollars in debt** while inflating earnings. When auditors and regulators uncovered the fraud, **Enron's stock collapsed from over $90 per share to less than $1**, wiping out billions in shareholder value.

The financial consequences of Enron's fraudulent accounting practices included:

- **$74 billion in shareholder losses**
- **$40 billion in lawsuits from creditors and investors**
- **The complete collapse of Enron, leading to bankruptcy**
- **Thousands of employees losing their jobs and retirement savings**
- **The downfall of Arthur Andersen, one of the "Big Five" accounting firms, for its role in covering up Enron's fraud**

Enron's case was a **wake-up call for corporate accountability**, leading to **stricter regulations**, including the passage of the **Sarbanes-Oxley Act (SOX) in 2002**, which introduced **stronger auditing requirements and penalties for financial fraud**.

### *Loss of Investor Confidence and Stock Value*

Investor confidence is **one of the most valuable assets** a publicly traded company can have. Investors rely on accurate financial statements to make decisions about **buying, selling, or holding stock**. When a company is caught engaging in **fraudulent accounting or financial misrepresentation**, investors **lose faith in the company's ability to operate honestly and profitably**.

This loss of confidence often results in a **rapid decline in stock value**, as investors rush to sell their shares before further damage occurs. A company that once had access to **capital markets, bank loans, and investment funding** may find itself **unable to raise money**, leading to severe liquidity issues.

**Case Study: Lehman Brothers and the 2008 Financial Crisis**

Lehman Brothers, one of the largest investment banks in the U.S., collapsed in **2008 due to deceptive financial practices that hid billions in toxic mortgage-backed assets**. The firm engaged in unethical accounting tactics—**using repurchase agreements (Repo 105 transactions) to move liabilities off its balance sheet**—creating an illusion of financial stability.

When the truth was revealed, **investors lost confidence in Lehman Brothers overnight**, leading to:

- **A 95% stock price decline within months**
- **Mass investor sell-offs that triggered market panic**
- **A global financial crisis that led to bank bailouts and severe economic downturns**

Lehman Brothers ultimately **declared bankruptcy, marking the largest bankruptcy filing in U.S. history**. The firm's collapse demonstrated how **unethical accounting practices at a single institution could destabilize global markets.**

## Reputation Damage and Public Distrust

### *Loss of Customer and Investor Trust*

A company's **reputation is one of its most valuable assets**, but unethical accounting practices can **destroy years of goodwill and trust in an instant**. When customers, investors, and business partners **discover financial misconduct, they distance themselves from the company**, fearing instability and dishonesty.

A damaged reputation affects **everything from customer loyalty to supplier relationships, employee morale, and future business opportunities**. Companies that have engaged in financial deception often find it **difficult to rebuild trust**, and in some cases, they never fully recover.

**Case Study: Volkswagen Emissions Scandal – A Reputation Crisis**

The **Volkswagen emissions scandal**, also known as **"Dieselgate,"** is a prime example of how unethical corporate behavior can lead to **severe reputational damage**. In 2015, Volkswagen was caught **intentionally programming its diesel vehicles to cheat emissions tests**, making its cars appear more environmentally friendly than they actually were.

When regulators uncovered the truth, Volkswagen faced:

- **More than $30 billion in fines and legal settlements**

- **Criminal investigations into top executives**
- **A sharp decline in stock value**
- **A significant drop in customer trust and vehicle sales**

Even years after the scandal, Volkswagen **struggled to repair its reputation.** Customers who had trusted the brand's commitment to environmental sustainability felt betrayed, and many **switched to competitors**, causing Volkswagen to lose market share.

This case illustrates that **reputation damage from unethical corporate behavior has long-term consequences.** Even with financial recovery, companies often **struggle to regain the trust of consumers, investors, and regulators.**

## The Long-Term Impact of Unethical Accounting

Unethical financial practices do not just affect the companies involved; they have **wider economic and industry implications.** When large corporations engage in financial fraud, **it undermines public confidence in financial markets**, leading to:

- **Stricter regulations and compliance costs for all businesses**
- **Increased scrutiny on accounting firms and auditors**
- **A loss of faith in entire industries (e.g., banking during the 2008 financial crisis)**

Companies that **prioritize ethical accounting and transparency** not only avoid these risks but also **build long-term sustainability.** Ethical financial reporting helps businesses **attract responsible investors, retain loyal customers, and establish a reputation for integrity**—a competitive advantage in today's highly scrutinized business environment.

## The Cost of Unethical Accounting Is Never Worth the Risk

Engaging in **unethical accounting practices may provide short-term financial gains**, but the **long-term consequences are overwhelmingly negative**. Companies that manipulate financial statements to appear more profitable **eventually face exposure, legal action, and reputational damage**. Financial penalties, loss of investor confidence, and destroyed credibility often **lead to corporate collapse**.

History has shown that **companies that operate with integrity, transparency, and financial discipline thrive in the long run**, while those that prioritize **deception, manipulation, and short-term gains ultimately fail**. Ethical accounting is not just a legal obligation—it is **a strategic advantage that fosters trust, growth, and long-term business success**.

Businesses must recognize that **protecting their financial reputation is just as important as generating profits**. The companies that **prioritize ethics today will be the ones that succeed tomorrow**, while those that cut corners will eventually face the consequences. The lessons from Enron, Lehman Brothers, Volkswagen, and Wells Fargo are clear: **ethical financial practices are essential for sustainability, stability, and success in the modern business world**.

## Why Ethics is the Foundation of Financial Accounting

Ethics is the cornerstone of financial accounting. Without ethical principles guiding financial reporting, the entire system collapses—misleading investors, destabilizing markets, and eroding public trust. Ethical accounting is not just about following regulations; it is about ensuring that **financial statements present a true and fair view of a company's financial health**, allowing stakeholders to make informed decisions.

Throughout this chapter, we explored the profound impact of unethical accounting practices and how they can lead to **legal consequences, financial collapse, reputational damage, and investor distrust**. Corporate scandals such as **Enron, Lehman Brothers, Wirecard, and Volkswagen** serve as stark reminders that deception in financial reporting is always uncovered—whether through whistle blowers, regulatory investigations, or financial distress. These cases highlight that while unethical behavior may provide **short-term financial gains**, it inevitably leads to **long-term failure and reputational ruin**.

One of the most crucial lessons from this chapter is that ethical accounting is not just a moral obligation—it is **a fundamental necessity for business sustainability and economic stability**. Companies that prioritize **transparency, integrity, and compliance** not only avoid regulatory penalties but also **build long-term trust with investors, customers, and employees**. Businesses that adopt ethical financial practices benefit from **stronger investor confidence, greater market credibility, and enhanced brand reputation**.

## Key Lessons from This Chapter

**Honest Financial Reporting Protects Investors and Markets** Financial statements are the foundation of investment decisions. When financial data is manipulated, investors allocate capital based on **false information**, leading to disastrous financial consequences. Ethical accounting ensures that investors, creditors, and stakeholders have **reliable financial data to assess risk, value, and future business performance**.

**Compliance with Laws and Regulations Prevents Financial Fraud** Regulations such as **GAAP, IFRS, and the Sarbanes-Oxley Act (SOX)** exist to uphold financial integrity. Companies that fail to comply with these laws face **severe fines, legal action, and restrictions on business operations**. Ethical accounting aligns businesses with **regulatory requirements, reducing risk exposure and ensuring operational longevity**.

**Auditors and Whistle blowers Play a Vital Role in Financial Integrity** Auditors act as **independent watchdogs**, ensuring that companies do not manipulate financial data. However, when auditors fail to fulfill their ethical duty—as seen in **the Wirecard scandal**—fraud can persist for years. Ethical auditors must **remain independent, report misconduct, and hold companies accountable**. Similarly, **whistle blowers** serve as crucial defenders of ethical accounting, exposing fraud that would otherwise go undetected.

**Reputation is Hard to Rebuild After Ethical Violations** Companies caught engaging in financial fraud often **struggle for years to regain public trust**. The **Volkswagen emissions scandal** demonstrated how corporate deception can lead to **billions in fines, executive resignations,**

**and loss of customer loyalty**. Reputation is **one of the most valuable business assets**, and ethical financial practices **protect and enhance corporate credibility**.

**Ethical Accounting Creates Long-Term Business Success** While some executives prioritize **short-term stock price increases**, businesses that focus on **ethical financial management, accurate reporting, and transparent governance** build **lasting financial strength**. Ethical firms attract better investors, maintain strong financial positions, and **survive economic downturns** better than those engaging in fraud.

## Looking Ahead: The Role of Technology in Financial Accounting

As financial regulations evolve and businesses face increasing scrutiny, technology has become an essential tool in maintaining accuracy, transparency, and efficiency in accounting. Ethical financial management is no longer just about human oversight—it is also about leveraging **technology-driven solutions** to prevent fraud, enhance compliance, and improve financial decision-making.

In the next chapter, we will explore:

- **The Rise of Accounting Automation:** How AI and machine learning are transforming financial reporting and eliminating human error.
- **Blockchain & Financial Security:** How decentralized ledgers enhance transparency, fraud detection, and regulatory compliance.
- **Data Analytics in Financial Decision-Making:** How businesses

use financial modeling and predictive analytics to optimize cash flow, budgeting, and investments.

By integrating **cutting-edge technology with ethical financial practices**, businesses can **enhance accuracy, efficiency, and trust** in their financial reporting. Understanding these advancements will ensure that companies remain competitive in a rapidly evolving financial landscape.

# TECHNOLOGY IN FINANCIAL ACCOUNTING

## Technology in Financial Accounting: Transforming the Industry

The evolution of technology has profoundly changed the way financial accounting is conducted. Traditional manual processes, once reliant on physical documentation and human calculations, have been replaced with automated systems, real-time data processing, and advanced analytics. Modern technology has not only improved accuracy and efficiency but also enhanced security and regulatory compliance. From **accounting software solutions and blockchain integration to data**

**analytics, automation, and cybersecurity**, technology plays a crucial role in **streamlining financial operations, reducing fraud, and providing businesses with valuable insights**.

In this chapter, we explore the **major technological advancements shaping financial accounting**, their benefits, challenges, and the future trends that will continue to redefine the industry.

## The Role of Accounting Software Solutions

## Software Types and Features: The Role of Accounting Technology in Modern Finance

The rise of **digital accounting software** has revolutionized financial management for businesses, replacing traditional manual bookkeeping with **automated, real-time, and highly accurate financial reporting tools**. Today's accounting software solutions **enhance efficiency, reduce errors, and ensure compliance with accounting regulations** such as **Generally Accepted Accounting Principles (GAAP) and International Financial Reporting Standards (IFRS).**

Accounting software is no longer just a tool for recording transactions; it serves as a **comprehensive financial management system**, integrating **payroll, invoicing, tax calculations, inventory management, financial analytics, and cash flow tracking**. These tools help businesses maintain **financial transparency, improve budgeting accuracy, and streamline operations**, making them indispensable for companies of all sizes.

## Key Features of Modern Accounting Software

With rapid advancements in technology, accounting software has evolved to offer **highly advanced features** that improve financial management. Some of the most critical features include:

### *1. Automated Data Entry*

Manual bookkeeping is prone to errors, miscalculations, and inefficiencies. **Automated data entry** ensures that:

- Transactions are recorded in real-time with **minimal human intervention**.
- Repetitive data entry tasks are eliminated, reducing processing time.
- Errors in invoices, receipts, and reconciliations are significantly minimized.

This automation leads to **greater accuracy in financial records**, reducing the risk of discrepancies that could cause tax penalties or financial misstatements.

### *2. Cloud-Based Access*

Cloud-based accounting software has **transformed how businesses manage their financial data**, offering benefits such as:

- **Anywhere, Anytime Access** – Business owners and accountants can access financial data **from any device with internet connectivity**.
- **Collaboration in Real Time** – Multiple users can **simultaneously access and update financial records**, making collaboration

between accountants, management, and finance teams more efficient.

- **Automatic Backups & Security** – Cloud solutions ensure **financial data is backed up in secure locations**, preventing data loss due to hardware failures or cyber threats.

Cloud-based accounting software is particularly valuable for **remote teams and businesses with multiple locations**, as it enables **seamless financial management without geographical restrictions**.

***3. Integrated Financial Tools***

Rather than using separate tools for **payroll, invoicing, tax calculations, and financial reporting**, modern accounting software integrates these functions into **one centralized platform**. This integration allows businesses to:

- Automate **salary payments** and **track employee benefits** within the same system.
- Generate and send **electronic invoices** while tracking payments in real-time.
- Calculate **tax liabilities, deductions, and compliance obligations automatically**.
- Run **detailed financial reports** to assess profitability, expenses, and revenue trends.

This comprehensive approach **reduces administrative burden** and ensures financial data remains **consistent across all aspects of business operations**.

### *4. Real-Time Financial Reporting & Analysis*

One of the most **powerful advantages** of modern accounting software is **real-time financial reporting**, which provides immediate insights into a company's financial performance. Benefits include:

- **Instant Cash Flow Monitoring** – Businesses can track **incoming and outgoing transactions** without waiting for end-of-month statements.
- **Live Financial Dashboards** – Customizable dashboards allow businesses to **visualize key financial metrics** such as profit margins, outstanding invoices, and operational expenses.
- **Automated Financial Forecasting** – AI-powered analytics help **predict future revenue trends** based on historical data.

With access to **real-time financial data**, business leaders can **make quicker and more informed decisions** about investments, cost-cutting strategies, and financial planning.

## Impact of Accounting Software on Small Businesses

Historically, **sophisticated financial management tools** were only available to large corporations with **dedicated accounting departments**. However, **cloud-based and AI-driven accounting software** has **democratized access to financial management tools**, enabling small businesses to **automate their financial operations efficiently and affordably**.

## Cost-Effective Solutions for Small Businesses

Small businesses often operate on **limited budgets** and may not have the resources to hire **full-time accountants** or **finance teams**. Accounting software provides a **cost-effective alternative** by:

- Reducing the need for **manual bookkeeping services**.
- Automating **payroll, tax filing, and invoice generation**.
- Providing **affordable monthly subscription models** rather than large upfront costs.

This accessibility allows **small business owners to focus on growing their businesses** rather than managing tedious financial paperwork.

## Improved Financial Compliance

Many small business owners struggle with **regulatory compliance**, as tax laws and financial reporting requirements can be complex. Accounting software helps by:

- **Automatically calculating tax liabilities** based on the latest regulations.
- **Ensuring accurate record-keeping** for financial audits.
- **Preventing costly penalties** by flagging overdue tax payments or non-compliance issues.

By reducing errors in tax filings and ensuring timely compliance, small businesses **avoid financial penalties and legal issues**.

### Better Resource Allocation and Business Growth

By **automating financial tasks**, small businesses can **redirect time and resources** toward more **strategic activities** such as **marketing, product development, and customer engagement.**

With improved financial management, small businesses can:

- **Secure business loans or investments more easily** by providing **accurate financial statements.**
- **Optimize cash flow** by tracking **accounts payable and receivable in real time.**
- **Make data-driven decisions** on **pricing strategies, expansion plans, and cost management.**

Modern accounting software **empowers small businesses** with the same level of **financial intelligence and operational efficiency as large enterprises**, helping them **compete in an increasingly digital economy.**

## Challenges and Considerations When Choosing Accounting Software

Despite the many advantages of **accounting software**, businesses must carefully evaluate their **specific needs and challenges** before selecting a platform.

### Functionality vs. Business Needs

Not all businesses require **highly advanced accounting software** with **AI-powered forecasting and analytics.** Some businesses **overpay for**

**unnecessary features**, while others struggle with **limited functionality**.

- **Start ups and freelancers** may need **basic bookkeeping software** that focuses on **invoicing and expense tracking**.
- **Mid-sized businesses** might require **advanced financial reporting, payroll integration, and tax automation**.
- **Large corporations** may need **enterprise-level solutions** with **multi-department financial tracking, audit support, and AI-driven analytics**.

## Training Requirements

Adopting **new accounting software** often requires **employee training and adaptation**. Companies must:

- Ensure that **employees understand how to use automation features** effectively.
- Invest in **training sessions and software tutorials**.
- Assign **financial oversight roles** to prevent mismanagement or unauthorized access.

## Data Security Concerns

With financial data being **stored digitally**, businesses must prioritize **data security and privacy** to prevent **cyberattacks and financial fraud**.

- **Regularly update security protocols** and use **multi-factor authentication**.
- **Encrypt sensitive financial data** to protect against breaches.

- **Implement strict access controls** to ensure only authorized personnel can access financial records.

## Future Trends in Accounting Software

Technology continues to **reshape the accounting industry**, with emerging trends focusing on **automation, artificial intelligence, and enhanced cybersecurity**.

### 1. AI-Driven Predictive Analytics

- AI-based accounting tools will **analyze financial patterns** and provide **predictive insights into revenue trends and cost fluctuations**.
- Businesses will be able to **proactively manage risks, optimize budgets, and forecast financial performance more accurately**.

### 2. Automation of Repetitive Tasks

- AI-powered automation will **reduce human intervention** in **bank reconciliations, tax calculations, and compliance checks**.
- Routine financial reporting will be **fully automated**, enabling **real-time audits and compliance tracking**.

### 3. Adaptive Learning Software

- Future accounting software will **learn user behavior** and suggest **personalized financial strategies**.
- AI-driven tools will **automatically flag unusual transactions** and

recommend **cost-saving opportunities**.

## The Future of Accounting Technology

The **adoption of advanced accounting software has revolutionized financial management**, enabling businesses to **enhance efficiency, ensure compliance, and make data-driven decisions**. From **cloud-based access and automation to AI-powered analytics and blockchain integration**, accounting technology continues to **evolve rapidly**, transforming financial processes for companies of all sizes.

As businesses embrace **new technologies**, the future of financial accounting will be **faster, more secure, and more intelligent than ever before**.

## Impact of Accounting Software on Small Businesses

Historically, **sophisticated financial management tools** were only available to large corporations with **dedicated accounting departments**. However, **cloud-based and AI-driven accounting software** has **democratized access to financial management tools**, enabling small businesses to **automate their financial operations efficiently and affordably**.

### Cost-Effective Solutions for Small Businesses

Small businesses often operate on **limited budgets** and may not have the resources to hire **full-time accountants** or **finance teams**. Accounting software provides a **cost-effective alternative** by:

- Reducing the need for **manual bookkeeping services**.
- Automating **payroll, tax filing, and invoice generation**.
- Providing **affordable monthly subscription models** rather than large upfront costs.

This accessibility allows **small business owners to focus on growing their businesses** rather than managing tedious financial paperwork.

## Improved Financial Compliance

Many small business owners struggle with **regulatory compliance**, as tax laws and financial reporting requirements can be complex. Accounting software helps by:

- **Automatically calculating tax liabilities** based on the latest regulations.
- **Ensuring accurate record-keeping** for financial audits.
- **Preventing costly penalties** by flagging overdue tax payments or non-compliance issues.

By reducing errors in tax filings and ensuring timely compliance, small businesses **avoid financial penalties and legal issues**.

## Better Resource Allocation and Business Growth

By **automating financial tasks**, small businesses can **redirect time and resources** toward more **strategic activities** such as **marketing, product development, and customer engagement**.

With improved financial management, small businesses can:

- **Secure business loans or investments more easily** by providing **accurate financial statements.**
- **Optimize cash flow** by tracking **accounts payable and receivable in real time.**
- **Make data-driven decisions** on **pricing strategies, expansion plans, and cost management.**

Modern accounting software **empowers small businesses** with the same level of **financial intelligence and operational efficiency as large enterprises**, helping them **compete in an increasingly digital economy.**

## Challenges and Considerations When Choosing Accounting Software

While accounting software has revolutionized financial management, **choosing the right platform** requires a thorough evaluation of business needs, available features, and potential challenges. The wrong choice can lead to inefficiencies, **unnecessary expenses, and cybersecurity vulnerabilities**. Businesses must carefully assess their **size, industry, security needs, and long-term scalability** before committing to an accounting solution.

### Functionality vs. Business Needs

One of the biggest mistakes businesses make when selecting accounting software is **overestimating or underestimating their needs**. Not all companies require the **most advanced AI-powered financial tools**, and purchasing a complex system with unnecessary features can lead to **wasted**

**resources and employee confusion**. On the other hand, choosing software with **limited functionality** can create bottlenecks, forcing businesses to **manually handle tasks that could be automated**.

## Understanding Business-Specific Needs

Different businesses require different accounting software capabilities. The right solution depends on factors such as **company size, industry regulations, and financial complexity**.

80. **Start ups and Freelancers** – These businesses typically require **basic bookkeeping software** with essential functions like:

- **Invoicing and expense tracking** to manage cash flow.
- **Tax calculation and filing** for freelancers and small entrepreneurs.
- **Basic reporting tools** to assess profitability.

81. **Example:** A freelance graphic designer may only need a simple invoicing system, such as **FreshBooks or Wave**, rather than a comprehensive **ERP (Enterprise Resource Planning) system** used by large corporations.

82. **Mid-Sized Businesses** – As companies grow, financial management becomes more complex, requiring:

- **Advanced financial reporting tools** to track revenue and expenses.
- **Payroll integration** for managing employee salaries and tax deductions.
- **Multi-user collaboration** for financial teams to work on the same

data.

83. **Example:** A growing e-commerce company may use **Xero or QuickBooks** to manage sales, expenses, and payroll while integrating with their online store platform.

84. **Large Corporations and Enterprises** – Large businesses require **enterprise-level accounting solutions** to manage:

- **Multi-department financial tracking and consolidation.**
- **Regulatory compliance and audit support.**
- **AI-driven analytics for financial forecasting and decision-making.**

85. **Example:** A multinational corporation would rely on **SAP or Oracle NetSuite**, which can handle **complex financial operations across multiple countries** while maintaining compliance with international regulations.

### Scalability Considerations

A key factor when selecting accounting software is **long-term scalability**. A business that expects rapid growth should choose a platform that **can expand with its needs**. Cloud-based solutions often provide **tiered pricing and feature upgrades**, allowing businesses to start with a **basic package and scale up as needed**.

## Training Requirements

While accounting software automates many processes, businesses must

**invest in proper employee training** to maximize its benefits. Employees who **lack proper training** may use the software incorrectly, **leading to financial inaccuracies, compliance risks, and workflow inefficiencies**.

## Key Training Considerations

86. **Understanding Automation Features** – Employees should be trained to use features such as **auto-reconciliation, expense categorization, and AI-driven insights** to enhance efficiency.
87. **Preventing Mismanagement and Errors** – Without proper oversight, employees may **input incorrect financial data**, leading to misleading financial statements or regulatory violations.
88. **Software Tutorials and Onboarding Programs** – Businesses should:

- Provide **initial training sessions** for new users.
- Offer **refresher courses** as software updates roll out.
- Use **built-in help features and online tutorials** to assist employees.

89. **Example:** A retail company implementing new accounting software may conduct **a week-long onboarding session for accountants and finance staff**, ensuring they understand **how to generate financial reports, manage accounts payable, and use automation tools** effectively.

## Managing Software Integration Challenges

- Employees may **resist adopting new software**, preferring **manual**

**systems** they are familiar with.

- Some software solutions require **third-party integrations**, which may involve a **steep learning curve** for employees.
- Regular software updates may introduce **new features or changes to the interface**, requiring **ongoing training** to maintain efficiency.

Businesses that fail to provide **proper training and change management strategies** risk **underutilizing their accounting software**, negating its potential benefits.

## Data Security Concerns in Accounting Software: Protecting Financial Information in the Digital Age

As businesses transition to **digital and cloud-based accounting systems**, **cybersecurity threats pose significant risks** to financial data integrity, privacy, and compliance. Accounting software houses some of the **most sensitive financial information**, including:

- **Bank account details and financial transactions.**
- **Taxpayer identification numbers (TINs) and Social Security numbers.**
- **Employee payroll data, salaries, and benefits.**
- **Financial statements, revenue reports, and profit margins.**

If this information is compromised, businesses **face severe financial and reputational consequences**, including **data breaches, fraudulent transactions, legal penalties, and loss of investor confidence**. In today's cyber-threat landscape, **cybercriminals actively target financial systems** to **steal confidential data, commit fraud, and extort money through ransomware attacks**.

To safeguard financial information, businesses **must prioritize cybersecurity** when selecting, implementing, and managing accounting software.

## Common Cybersecurity Threats in Accounting Systems

Cybersecurity threats to accounting software **range from external cyberattacks to internal vulnerabilities**. Understanding these risks allows businesses to **develop proactive defense strategies** to protect financial data.

Phishing attacks remain one of the biggest cybersecurity threats to accounting systems. Cybercriminals impersonate trusted contacts or organizations to trick employees into:

- **Clicking on malicious links** that install malware.
- **Providing login credentials** or security information.
- **Downloading fake invoices or financial documents** containing hidden spyware.

**Example:** A phishing email may appear to be from the company's accounting software provider, requesting employees to update their login details. When employees enter their credentials, hackers gain access to **confidential financial data, payroll records, and bank accounts**.

## Ransomware Attacks: Holding Financial Data Hostage

Ransomware attacks involve hackers encrypting financial records and demanding **a ransom payment** in exchange for restoring access. These attacks are particularly damaging to businesses that **do not have proper backup systems**, leaving them vulnerable to data loss.

**Consequences of Ransomware Attacks:**

- Businesses may **lose access to financial records and transactions**.
- **Operations may halt for days or weeks**, affecting cash flow and payroll processing.
- Failure to pay the ransom may result in **permanent data loss**.

**Example:** In 2021, the global Kaseya ransomware attack targeted **financial firms and accounting service providers**, encrypting their clients' financial records and disrupting **hundreds of businesses worldwide**.

## Insider Threats: Risks from Employees and Contractors

Internal threats pose a **significant cybersecurity risk** in accounting. Employees or contractors **with access to financial systems** may:

- **Misuse financial information** for personal gain.
- **Alter accounting records** to hide fraud or mismanagement.
- **Leak confidential data** to competitors or unauthorized third parties.

**Example:** In 2018, a former employee at Tesla **stole confidential financial data** and shared it with competitors after being dismissed. The case underscored the **importance of controlling internal access to sensitive financial records**.

### Unauthorized System Access: Weak Passwords and Poor Security Controls

Many businesses **fail to implement strong authentication measures**, making it easier for hackers to access financial systems. Common vulnerabilities include:

- **Weak passwords** that hackers can easily guess.
- **Failure to implement Multi-Factor Authentication (MFA)**, leaving financial data exposed.
- **Unrestricted employee access** to accounting systems, increasing risk.

**Example:** A small business accountant might reuse the same password for **banking, payroll, and invoicing systems**, making it easier for cybercriminals to access **multiple financial platforms** if one account is compromised.

## Best Practices for Securing Accounting Data

To **protect financial information from cyber threats**, businesses must implement **strong cybersecurity measures** that prevent unauthorized access, detect suspicious activity, and ensure compliance with **data protection laws**.

## Implement Multi-Factor Authentication (MFA)

Multi-Factor Authentication (MFA) adds **an extra layer of security** by requiring users to verify their identity through:

- **Passwords** combined with **SMS/email verification codes**.
- **Biometric authentication** (fingerprint or facial recognition).
- **Hardware security tokens** for secure logins.

## Encrypt Financial Data for Secure Storage

Encryption ensures that **financial records are stored in an unreadable format**, making it **impossible for hackers to interpret stolen data**.

- **End-to-End Encryption:** Protects financial transactions and payment processing.
- **Data-at-Rest Encryption:** Secures stored financial records on **servers and cloud platforms**.
- **Encrypted Backups:** Ensures financial data is protected **even if the primary system is compromised.**

## Keep Software Updated to Prevent Exploits

Cybercriminals often exploit **outdated software vulnerabilities** to access financial data. Businesses must:

- **Regularly update accounting software and security patches.**
- **Use only licensed, legitimate accounting programs** (avoid pirated versions with malware).

- **Enable automatic updates** for accounting software and firewalls.

### Enforce Role-Based Access Controls (RBAC)

Not all employees need access to **sensitive financial records**. Businesses should implement **Role-Based Access Controls (RBAC)** to:

- **Restrict access** to financial systems based on employee roles.
- **Ensure only authorized personnel can modify accounting records.**
- **Monitor and log all system activity** to detect suspicious access.

### Conduct Regular Security Audits and Compliance Checks

Cybersecurity audits **help businesses identify vulnerabilities** and ensure compliance with **financial regulations**, such as:

- **General Data Protection Regulation (GDPR) – European Union.**
- **Sarbanes-Oxley Act (SOX) – United States.**
- **Payment Card Industry Data Security Standard (PCI DSS).**

Regular cybersecurity assessments **reduce financial risks** and **prevent regulatory fines**.

## Cloud Security Considerations for Accounting Software

With many businesses **storing financial data in the cloud**, security measures must **go beyond traditional on-premise protections.**

### Choosing a Secure Cloud-Based Accounting Provider

- **Verify Compliance Certifications:** Select software providers that meet **ISO 27001, SOC 2, and PCI DSS standards.**
- **Ensure End-to-End Encryption:** Protect **data transfers and storage** with advanced encryption protocols.
- **Enable Backup and Disaster Recovery:** Cloud-based solutions should have **redundancy systems** to prevent data loss.

### Backup Protocols for Financial Data Recovery

Businesses should have **regular financial data backups** stored securely in **multiple locations** to prevent:

- **Data loss due to cyberattacks.**
- **Financial system failures.**
- **Accidental deletions or human errors.**

**Best practice:** Schedule **daily automated backups** to ensure that financial data can be **recovered quickly** if a breach occurs.

## Case Study: The Impact of Weak Cybersecurity in Financial Systems

In **2017, Deloitte—one of the world's largest financial consulting firms—suffered a major cybersecurity breach** that exposed **confidential financial data of large multinational clients.**

### What Went Wrong?

- Deloitte failed to **implement Multi-Factor Authentication (MFA)** for employee logins.
- **Misconfigured cloud storage** left sensitive accounting records **exposed to hackers.**
- The breach remained **undetected for months**, amplifying **financial and reputational damage.**

### Lessons Learned

- Cybersecurity **must be a priority, even for large firms.**
- Implementing **MFA and strong access controls** can prevent unauthorized system entry.
- **Regular cybersecurity audits** help detect vulnerabilities before they are exploited.

## Choosing the Right Accounting Software for Long-Term Security

Selecting accounting software **is not just about functionality—it is about security.** Businesses that fail to address **cybersecurity threats, access controls, and compliance measures** risk **severe financial losses, data breaches, and reputational damage.**

To **safeguard financial data**, companies must:

- Implement **MFA, encryption, and regular security audits.**

- Choose **secure cloud-based accounting providers** with **strong compliance standards**.
- Train employees on **cybersecurity awareness and safe financial practices**.

With **proper planning, cybersecurity integration, and continuous monitoring**, businesses can **protect their financial assets, ensure regulatory compliance, and maintain trust in an increasingly digital economy**.

## Future Trends in Accounting Software

Technology continues to **reshape the accounting industry**, with emerging trends focusing on **automation, artificial intelligence, and enhanced cybersecurity**.

### AI-Driven Predictive Analytics

- AI-based accounting tools will **analyze financial patterns** and provide **predictive insights into revenue trends and cost fluctuations**.
- Businesses will be able to **proactively manage risks, optimize budgets, and forecast financial performance more accurately**.

### Automation of Repetitive Tasks

- AI-powered automation will **reduce human intervention** in **bank reconciliations, tax calculations, and compliance checks**.
- Routine financial reporting will be **fully automated**, enabling **real-**

**time audits and compliance tracking.**

### Adaptive Learning Software

- Future accounting software will **learn user behavior** and suggest **personalized financial strategies.**
- AI-driven tools will **automatically flag unusual transactions** and recommend **cost-saving opportunities.**

## The Future of Accounting Technology

The **adoption of advanced accounting software has revolutionized financial management**, enabling businesses to **enhance efficiency, ensure compliance, and make data-driven decisions.** From **cloud-based access and automation to AI-powered analytics and blockchain integration**, accounting technology continues to **evolve rapidly**, transforming financial processes for companies of all sizes.

As businesses embrace **new technologies**, the future of financial accounting will be **faster, more secure, and more intelligent than ever before.**

## Impact of Blockchain on Accounting

### Understanding Blockchain Technology

Blockchain technology is revolutionizing accounting by offering a **decentralized, tamper-proof ledger system.** Instead of relying on a single database controlled by a company, **blockchain records transactions across multiple nodes**, making it nearly impossible to alter past records.

Key advantages of blockchain in accounting include:

- **Transparency** – Every transaction is recorded in a permanent, verifiable ledger.
- **Decentralization** – Reduces the risk of fraud by eliminating centralized control.
- **Smart Contracts** – Automates agreements by executing transactions only when predetermined conditions are met.

## Benefits for Auditing and Fraud Prevention

Auditing is a critical process in financial accounting, but traditional audits are **time-consuming and prone to human error**. Blockchain enables **real-time auditing**, where transactions are verified instantly, reducing the risk of financial fraud.

- **Eliminates Data Manipulation** – Transactions cannot be altered retroactively.
- **Speeds Up Auditing** – Reduces the need for lengthy financial reconciliations.
- **Enhances Stakeholder Confidence** – Investors and regulators can access transparent, verifiable records.

## Industry Applications and Adoption Challenges

Many industries are incorporating blockchain into accounting processes:

- **Supply Chain Finance** – Tracking real-time financial transactions in global trade.

- **Banking and Financial Institutions** – Streamlining cross-border payments.
- **Start ups and Tech Firms** – Integrating blockchain for improved transaction security.

However, widespread adoption faces **regulatory uncertainty, high implementation costs, and technical complexity**.

## Data Analytics for Financial Decision-Making

### Overview of Data Analytics

With the rise of **big data**, financial accounting has moved beyond traditional bookkeeping to incorporate **data-driven insights**. Businesses now rely on **data analytics to track financial performance, identify trends, and make informed decisions**.

Key applications of data analytics in accounting include:

- **Identifying patterns in financial performance.**
- **Providing real-time financial dashboards with key performance indicators (KPIs).**
- **Detecting anomalies that could indicate fraud or errors.**

### Predictive Analysis for Financial Forecasting

Predictive analytics allows businesses to use **historical data and AI-driven algorithms** to forecast future financial outcomes.

- **Budgeting and Forecasting** – Businesses can better allocate resources based on **projected revenue and expenses**.

- **Risk Management** – Identifies financial risks and predicts downturns before they happen.
- **Strategic Planning** – Helps businesses decide when to invest, cut costs, or expand operations.

## Automation in Accounting Processes

### Which Accounting Processes Can Be Automated?

Advancements in AI and **robotic process automation (RPA)** allow businesses to automate many repetitive financial tasks, including:

- **Invoice Processing** – Automatically generates, sends, and reconciles invoices.
- **Payroll Management** – Ensures timely salary payments and tax deductions.
- **Financial Reporting** – Instantly compiles reports for executives and stakeholders.

### Benefits of Automation

- **Increased Efficiency** – Reduces time spent on manual bookkeeping.
- **Enhanced Accuracy** – Minimizes human errors in calculations.
- **Stronger Compliance** – Ensures financial reports meet regulatory standards.

### Challenges of Automation

- **Workforce Impact** – Job roles in traditional bookkeeping are diminishing.
- **Dependence on Technology** – Errors in software implementation can **lead to financial discrepancies**.

## Cybersecurity in Financial Data Management

### Importance of Cybersecurity in Accounting

With financial data moving to digital platforms, cybersecurity is now a **critical concern for businesses**. Cyberattacks targeting financial information can result in **fraud, data loss, regulatory fines, and reputational damage**.

- **Preventing Unauthorized Access** – Ensures financial data is only accessible to authorized personnel.
- **Mitigating Cyber Threats** – Protects against phishing, malware, and ransomware attacks.
- **Regulatory Compliance** – Meets data protection laws such as GDPR and SOX.

### Common Cyber Threats to Financial Data

- **Phishing Attacks** – Cybercriminals attempt to steal financial credentials through deceptive emails.
- **Ransomware** – Hackers encrypt financial data and demand

payment for its release.

- **Insider Threats** – Employees or vendors with access to sensitive financial data may **misuse or leak information**.

## Best Practices for Protecting Financial Data

- **Implement Multi-Factor Authentication (MFA)** – Adds an extra layer of security to sensitive accounts.
- **Regular Security Audits** – Identifies vulnerabilities in financial systems.
- **Data Encryption** – Ensures financial information is protected, even if breached.

## Conclusion: The Future of Technology in Financial Accounting

Technology has revolutionized **financial accounting**, enabling businesses to operate with **greater accuracy, efficiency, and security** than ever before. The integration of **artificial intelligence (AI), blockchain, automation, and data analytics** has transformed traditional accounting practices, allowing businesses to streamline operations, reduce costs, and make **data-driven financial decisions** with unprecedented speed. These advancements have reshaped the way companies handle everything from **financial reporting and forecasting** to **auditing, compliance, and cybersecurity**.

However, as financial technology evolves, **new challenges emerge** that businesses must navigate. **Cybersecurity risks, workforce displacement,**

**regulatory uncertainty, and ethical considerations** require organizations to balance **technological innovation with security, compliance, and ethical accountability**. Businesses that fail to properly implement cybersecurity protections or manage risks associated with **automated financial processes** may face **data breaches, legal consequences, and financial losses**.

The financial industry is at a turning point where **technology is no longer optional but essential**. Companies that **embrace innovation responsibly**—while prioritizing **strong governance, secure digital infrastructure, and compliance with financial regulations**—will gain a **competitive advantage in a rapidly changing financial landscape**. Those that **ignore or poorly implement these technological advancements** will struggle with inefficiencies, regulatory scrutiny, and exposure to financial risks.

## The Key Takeaways from This Chapter

Throughout this chapter, we explored the **impact of technology** on financial accounting and the **strategies businesses must adopt** to stay ahead. The **key lessons** from this chapter reinforce the need for businesses to:

- **Leverage AI and Automation** – Companies can use AI-driven financial analysis, robotic process automation (RPA), and predictive analytics to **improve decision-making, reduce human error, and increase operational efficiency**.
- **Adopt Blockchain for Transparency and Security** – Blockchain technology offers **tamper-proof transaction records, real-time**

**auditing capabilities, and fraud prevention**, making it a powerful tool for enhancing **financial accountability**.

- **Use Data Analytics for Financial Strategy** – The ability to process **massive amounts of financial data** in real time allows businesses to detect patterns, identify risks, and optimize financial planning.
- **Address Cybersecurity and Compliance Risks** – As digital accounting tools become more sophisticated, **financial data security must remain a top priority**. Businesses must **implement robust encryption, access controls, and compliance frameworks** to protect financial records from cyber threats.
- **Balance Technology with Ethical and Regulatory Considerations** – While automation and AI-driven decision-making improve efficiency, **financial accountability and ethical considerations remain crucial**. Organizations must ensure that technology-driven financial decisions **adhere to ethical guidelines and legal frameworks** to prevent fraud and regulatory violations.

## The Path Forward: Technology and the Future of Financial Accounting

The financial industry will continue evolving at a rapid pace, with emerging technologies such as **quantum computing, machine learning, and decentralized finance (DeFi)** further reshaping accounting practices. As businesses prepare for this **next wave of financial innovation**, they must:

90. **Adopt a Future-Focused Mindset** – Businesses that anticipate technological shifts and **invest in adaptable, scalable financial**

**systems** will remain resilient in an increasingly digital economy.

91. **Train and Upskill the Workforce** – While automation is reducing the need for manual accounting tasks, **financial professionals must develop expertise in AI-powered analysis, cybersecurity, and compliance management** to stay relevant.

92. **Strengthen Governance and Risk Management** – Companies must implement **strong internal controls, audit protocols, and cybersecurity measures** to mitigate risks associated with digital financial operations.

93. **Stay Agile and Adaptive** – The most successful businesses will be those that **embrace innovation while remaining flexible and responsive** to new regulations, cybersecurity threats, and evolving market conditions.

## Final Thought: The Role of Financial Leaders in a Tech-Driven Future

The future of financial accounting belongs to businesses that can **integrate cutting-edge technology with strategic financial leadership**. Organizations that **proactively invest in AI, blockchain, data analytics, and automation—while maintaining a firm commitment to security, compliance, and ethical financial reporting—will thrive** in the years to come.

As financial technology continues to evolve, **the role of financial leaders and accountants will become more strategic than ever**. Rather than simply recording and reporting financial data, professionals must leverage **advanced technological tools** to drive **profitability, efficiency, and**

**long-term business sustainability.**

Those who fail to adapt **will fall behind**. Those who **embrace innovation responsibly, secure their financial systems, and prioritize ethical financial governance will lead the way into the future of financial accounting.**

## Looking Ahead: Risk Management & Financial Resilience

As we conclude our exploration of business financing and capital management, it is essential to recognise that securing funding and managing capital effectively are just part of the equation. Even with strong financial structures in place, businesses face a range of financial risks that can threaten profitability and long-term stability. From market volatility and credit risks to operational disruptions and global economic shifts, risk management is a critical component of financial strategy.

In the next chapter, we will explore **Risk Management & Financial Resilience**, focusing on how businesses:

- **Identify and Assess Financial Risks:** Understanding market risks, credit risks, and operational risks that impact financial stability.
- **Develop Risk Mitigation Strategies:** Using financial planning, liquidity management, and contingency planning to navigate uncertainty.
- **Implement Protection Mechanisms:** Leveraging insurance, hedging, and diversification to safeguard financial health.
- **Learn from Real-World Case Studies:** Examining how successful

companies have managed financial crises and emerged stronger.

Effective risk management ensures that businesses are not only prepared for unexpected disruptions but also capable of adapting, pivoting, and thriving in challenging economic conditions. By integrating risk management strategies into financial planning, businesses can build resilience and sustain long-term growth, regardless of external pressures.

Let's now turn our focus to **Risk Management & Financial Resilience**, where we will uncover the best strategies to protect and strengthen financial stability in an unpredictable business landscape.

# FINANCIAL RISK MANAGEMENT

## Introduction: The Critical Role of Financial Risk Management

In an unpredictable world, **every business, regardless of its size or industry, is exposed to financial risks**. These risks stem from **volatile markets, economic downturns, credit defaults, operational failures, geopolitical instability, and even global crises**. No company is immune—whether it's a multinational corporation managing currency fluctuations or a small business struggling with late customer payments, **financial risks can threaten profitability, disrupt operations, and even lead to bankruptcy**.

The difference between businesses that **survive and thrive** versus those that **fail under financial pressure** often comes down to **how well they anticipate, prepare for, and mitigate risks**. Companies that **proactively manage financial risks** can **protect their assets, stabilize cash flow, strengthen investor confidence, and create opportunities for sustainable growth**—even in uncertain times.

However, **ignoring risk** or failing to develop a solid financial risk management strategy can have **catastrophic consequences**. Businesses that rely on **poor financial planning, excessive debt, or outdated risk assessment models** can find themselves in **liquidity crises, unable to meet obligations, and vulnerable to sudden financial shocks**.

In this chapter, we will **explore the different types of financial risks businesses face**, including **market risk, credit risk, and operational risk**. We will then discuss **proven risk mitigation strategies**, from **hedging and diversification to insurance and stress testing**, to help businesses safeguard their financial health. Finally, we will examine **real-world case studies** of companies that successfully navigated financial crises through effective risk management. While risk management strategies can mitigate financial exposure, they are most effective when combined with strong budgeting and cash flow forecasting. Businesses that proactively model financial risks within their budgets and use forecasting to anticipate financial pressures are better prepared for unexpected disruptions. For a deeper dive into forecasting methods and financial planning applications, refer to Chapter 17.

By the end of this chapter, you will understand **why financial risk management is a cornerstone of long-term business success** and how to implement strategies that **protect your company from unforeseen financial threats while positioning it for continued growth**.

## Identifying Financial Risks: Market, Credit, and Operational Risks

Financial risk is an unavoidable reality for businesses of all sizes, and the ability to identify and manage these risks is crucial for long-term success. While every industry faces unique financial challenges, most financial risks fall into three primary categories: **market risk, credit risk, and operational risk**. Each of these risks can significantly impact profitability, cash flow, and overall business stability. By understanding the nature of these risks and developing proactive strategies to mitigate them, businesses can enhance their financial resilience and ensure sustainability in an increasingly unpredictable economic environment.

## Market Risk: The Impact of Economic and Industry Changes

Market risk refers to the potential financial losses caused by external economic factors, including interest rate fluctuations, foreign exchange volatility, stock market declines, inflation, and shifts in commodity prices. Businesses that operate in highly competitive or economically sensitive industries—such as retail, manufacturing, technology, and finance—are particularly susceptible to market risk.

Economic downturns can reduce consumer spending, leading to lower sales and revenue for businesses across industries. A retail company, for instance, may see a decline in sales when consumer confidence is low and discretionary spending decreases. Similarly, a company that relies on international suppliers might suffer financial losses if foreign exchange rates become unfavorable, making imported goods more expensive and squeezing profit margins.

Industries that rely on commodities—such as oil, steel, or agricultural products—are especially vulnerable to price fluctuations. A manufacturing company that depends on imported raw materials may experience increased costs if commodity prices rise unexpectedly, affecting overall profitability.

Market risk can also extend to financial investments and stock market fluctuations. Publicly traded companies face the risk of declining stock prices due to changes in investor sentiment, industry disruptions, or macroeconomic instability. For instance, a technology company may see its stock price plummet if investors believe the sector is overvalued or if regulatory changes introduce new business constraints.

### *How to Manage Market Risk*

Businesses must take a proactive approach to managing market risk by diversifying revenue streams, staying informed about economic trends, and employing financial hedging strategies.

- **Revenue Diversification:** Companies that rely on a single product or market are more vulnerable to economic downturns. Expanding into multiple markets, developing new product lines, or targeting diverse customer segments can help mitigate the impact of economic shifts.
- **Economic Monitoring:** Businesses should regularly analyze market

trends, competitor performance, and economic indicators to anticipate potential risks. By preparing financial models for different market scenarios, companies can create contingency plans to manage economic volatility.

- **Hedging Strategies:** Companies exposed to currency fluctuations, commodity price swings, or interest rate changes can use financial instruments such as futures contracts, options, and forward contracts to reduce potential losses. For instance, an exporter dealing with fluctuating foreign exchange rates may enter into forward contracts to lock in stable currency exchange terms.

## Credit Risk: The Risk of Customers or Partners Failing to Pay

Credit risk arises when businesses extend credit to customers, suppliers, or partners who fail to meet their payment obligations. This can lead to **cash flow shortages, financial instability, and increased debt burdens**. Credit risk is particularly problematic for businesses that rely heavily on customer invoices, delayed payments, or long-term contracts.

A wholesaler that sells products on credit may face financial difficulties if multiple customers delay payments, leaving the business without sufficient cash flow to cover its operational costs. Similarly, a construction company that depends on milestone-based payments may struggle to pay its own suppliers if a major client fails to meet their payment deadline. Even established companies can experience financial distress if too many customers default on their payments.

Start ups and small businesses are particularly vulnerable to credit risk, as they often lack the financial reserves to absorb delayed payments or customer defaults. Without a steady influx of cash, businesses may find it difficult to meet payroll obligations, pay suppliers, or fund growth initiatives.

### *How to Manage Credit Risk*

Managing credit risk involves implementing strict credit policies, conducting due diligence on customers, and exploring alternative financing solutions.

- **Credit Checks & Risk Assessment:** Before extending credit to new customers or business partners, companies should conduct thorough credit evaluations to assess their financial reliability. Credit reports, payment histories, and financial statements can provide insight into a customer's ability to meet obligations.
- **Strict Payment Policies:** Setting shorter payment deadlines and enforcing late fees for overdue invoices can encourage prompt payments. Businesses can also require upfront deposits for large orders or high-risk transactions.
- **Trade Credit Insurance & Invoice Factoring:** Businesses can protect themselves against customer defaults by using trade credit insurance, which covers unpaid invoices in case of non-payment. Invoice factoring, which involves selling unpaid invoices to a third party in exchange for immediate cash, can also help companies manage cash flow while reducing exposure to credit risk.

## Operational Risk: Internal Failures and External Disruptions

Operational risk arises from **internal process failures, human errors, technology disruptions, supply chain failures, and external crises** such as cyberattacks or natural disasters. Unlike market and credit risks, which are often driven by external factors, operational risk is primarily caused by weaknesses within an organization's internal systems and processes.

For instance, a **software company that experiences a major data breach** may face financial losses from regulatory fines, legal disputes, and reputational damage. If customers lose trust in the company's ability to protect sensitive information, long-term revenue may decline. Similarly, a **manufacturing company that depends on a single supplier** for key raw materials may suffer production delays if that supplier encounters financial difficulties, natural disasters, or logistical challenges.

Businesses that rely heavily on technology and automation are also at risk of **system failures**. A retail business that experiences a point-of-sale (POS) system outage may lose thousands in sales during a peak shopping period. An airline facing IT failures in its booking system may experience widespread operational disruptions, leading to flight cancellations and customer dissatisfaction.

### *How to Manage Operational Risk*

To mitigate operational risk, businesses must invest in **strong internal controls, cybersecurity measures, contingency plans, and supply chain diversification**.

- **Cybersecurity & Data Protection:** Given the increasing frequency of cyberattacks, businesses must implement strong cybersecurity measures such as multi-factor authentication, encryption, and regular data backups. Employee training programs on phishing scams and data security protocols can help prevent breaches caused by human error.

- **Business Continuity Planning (BCP):** Companies should develop comprehensive business continuity and disaster recovery plans to ensure operational stability in the event of a crisis. These plans should outline response strategies for natural disasters, cyberattacks, IT failures, and supply chain disruptions.
- **Supply Chain Diversification:** Over-reliance on a single supplier or geographic region for raw materials and inventory can expose businesses to operational risks. Developing relationships with multiple suppliers and securing backup inventory sources can minimize disruptions.

## Why Identifying Financial Risks Matters

Recognizing financial risks before they escalate allows businesses to take **proactive measures rather than reactive responses**. Companies that fail to address financial risks often find themselves in crisis mode, scrambling for solutions when cash flow problems, credit defaults, or operational failures become unmanageable.

By implementing **strong risk management strategies**, businesses can **enhance financial resilience, improve investor confidence, and sustain long-term profitability**. Whether mitigating market volatility, managing credit exposure, or strengthening internal controls, a well-structured risk management plan ensures that businesses are prepared for **uncertainty and financial challenges**.

Successful companies do not eliminate financial risk entirely, but they **anticipate, prepare for, and strategically manage it**. Those that embrace risk management as a core financial strategy are better positioned to weather economic shifts, maintain financial stability, and achieve sustainable business growth in any industry.

## Risk Mitigation Strategies: How Businesses Protect Themselves from Financial Uncertainty

Understanding financial risks is only half the battle. To build resilience and ensure long-term sustainability, businesses must implement proactive risk mitigation strategies. Whether facing market fluctuations, credit defaults, operational disruptions, or unexpected economic downturns, businesses that anticipate risks and prepare accordingly are far better positioned to survive and thrive.

Risk mitigation is not just about avoiding financial disasters—it is about **strengthening financial stability, ensuring cash flow security, and safeguarding business continuity** in any economic climate. Below are some of the most effective strategies businesses use to protect themselves from financial vulnerabilities.

## Financial Planning & Stress Testing: Preparing for Uncertainty Before It Happens

A company that waits until a crisis occurs before taking action is already too late. The most financially secure businesses **forecast potential risks in**

**advance and stress-test their financial models** under different economic conditions.

Financial stress testing involves simulating worst-case scenarios to determine how a business would cope under adverse conditions. This strategy allows businesses to identify their most significant financial vulnerabilities, adjust capital reserves, and strengthen financial planning before a crisis arises.

**How to Implement This:**

- Develop multiple financial models, including **best-case, moderate-case, and worst-case scenarios**.
- Identify the key financial risks that could cause significant losses, such as **supply chain disruptions, inflation spikes, or sudden drops in consumer demand**.
- Adjust liquidity strategies to ensure **sufficient cash reserves** for prolonged economic downturns or industry slowdowns.

For instance, a global hotel chain might conduct a stress test assuming a **30% decline in bookings due to an economic downturn**. If the company's financial projections reveal that it cannot cover operating costs for at least six months under such conditions, it can take preemptive measures, such as reducing non-essential expenditures or securing alternative revenue streams, to enhance financial stability before a crisis hits.

## Liquidity & Cash Flow Management: Ensuring Business Survival in Unstable Times

Liquidity is one of the most critical factors determining whether a business can **survive financial turbulence**. Companies that **run out of cash—regardless of profitability—are at immediate risk of bankruptcy**. **However, strong liquidity is not just about keeping excess cash reserves; it requires an active approach to financial planning. Businesses that integrate risk-based budgeting and dynamic cash flow forecasting into their financial strategies can anticipate potential shortfalls, model crisis scenarios, and take corrective action before liquidity issues become crises.**

Without structured financial forecasting, companies often find themselves reacting to liquidity shortages rather than proactively preventing them. **Strategies such as rolling forecasts, scenario-based budgeting, and real-time cash flow monitoring—which will be explored in depth in Chapter 17—allow businesses to model different financial conditions and adjust their liquidity plans accordingly.**

The most resilient businesses **strategically manage their cash flow** by ensuring that they have enough working capital to sustain operations during economic downturns, industry slowdowns, or unexpected revenue disruptions. Without proper liquidity management, even the most promising businesses can face financial collapse.

**How to Improve Liquidity & Strengthen Cash Flow:**

- **Maintain emergency cash reserves** equivalent to at least **three to six months of operating expenses** to cushion against unexpected financial shocks.
- **Reduce reliance on credit-based transactions** to prevent prolonged payment cycles that delay incoming cash flow.

- **Secure access to credit lines or business loans** before they are needed, ensuring an additional financial safety net if liquidity tightens.

During the **COVID-19 pandemic**, businesses that had **built strong cash reserves before the crisis** were able to **sustain themselves through lockdowns**, pay employees, and cover fixed expenses. In contrast, companies that had **poor cash flow management and no liquidity buffers were forced to shut down** permanently. A restaurant chain that had saved three months of operating expenses pre-pandemic **was able to keep doors open** while competitors that had mismanaged cash flow **ran out of capital and closed.**

## Risk Transfer Strategies: Using Insurance and Contracts to Reduce Financial Exposure

While businesses cannot eliminate financial risks entirely, they can **transfer financial risks to third parties** using **insurance policies, contractual agreements, and strategic partnerships**. Companies that fail to secure proper risk transfer mechanisms expose themselves to **severe financial losses, legal liabilities, and operational disruptions**.

Insurance policies act as a **financial safeguard** by ensuring that a company can recover from unexpected events without facing financial ruin. Similarly, well-structured contracts help businesses **minimize liability risks, protect revenue streams, and ensure legal protection** in business dealings.

**Key Risk Transfer Methods Businesses Use to Protect Themselves:**

- **Business Interruption Insurance** – Provides financial compensation for lost income and operating expenses when businesses are forced to shut down due to **natural disasters, supply chain disruptions, or unexpected crises**.

- **Cybersecurity Insurance** – Covers financial losses, legal costs, and reputation damage caused by **cyberattacks, data breaches, and online fraud**.
- **Trade Credit Insurance** – Protects businesses from **client payment defaults** by ensuring that outstanding invoices are paid, even if a customer goes bankrupt.

A **fashion retailer that suffered a fire in its primary warehouse** was able to **recover quickly and resume operations within months** because it had secured **business interruption insurance**. The insurance covered lost inventory, facility repairs, and employee wages during the shutdown period. In contrast, **competitors who lacked proper insurance coverage struggled to recover financially** and eventually shut down permanently.

## Operational Risk Management: Strengthening Business Continuity & Disaster Recovery Plans

Operational risks, such as **supply chain disruptions, cyber threats, system failures, or labor shortages**, can significantly impact a business's ability to function efficiently. Companies that **fail to plan for operational risks often experience costly production delays, financial losses, and reputational damage**.

Strong **business continuity and disaster recovery planning** ensures that a company can maintain critical operations even during **unforeseen disruptions**.

**How Businesses Reduce Operational Risks & Strengthen Business Continuity:**

- **Diversify suppliers and logistics partners** to avoid reliance on a single vendor or region, minimizing supply chain disruptions.
- **Invest in cybersecurity infrastructure and employee training** to prevent **ransomware attacks, data leaks, and online fraud**.
- **Develop robust crisis response plans** that outline clear protocols for handling **emergencies, system outages, and operational failures**.

A **global pharmaceutical company that depended on a single supplier for critical raw materials** suffered major **production halts when that supplier experienced financial trouble**. In contrast, another pharmaceutical firm that had proactively **diversified its supplier network** was able to **seamlessly shift production to alternate suppliers, preventing financial losses and maintaining steady product distribution**.

## Regulatory Compliance & Financial Governance: Protecting Businesses from Legal & Financial Penalties

Many financial risks arise from **non-compliance with tax regulations, accounting standards, and industry-specific financial laws**. Businesses that fail to meet regulatory requirements can face **substantial fines, legal penalties, and reputational damage**.

Companies that prioritize **financial governance and compliance strategies** ensure that their financial reporting, tax obligations, and legal structures align with both **domestic and international regulatory requirements**.

**How Businesses Strengthen Financial Governance & Compliance:**

- Implement **internal audits and financial oversight** to prevent errors, fraud, or non-compliance issues.
- Stay informed on **changing tax laws, accounting standards, and financial reporting obligations** to ensure full compliance.
- Establish **anti-fraud protocols, whistle blower protection programs, and financial transparency policies** to uphold ethical accounting practices.

A **multinational tech company faced billions in fines for failing to comply with international tax regulations** due to improper financial reporting. However, another industry competitor that had invested in **strong financial governance and compliance programs** avoided legal penalties and maintained investor confidence.

## Building a Resilient Business Through Strategic Risk Management

Financial risk is an inherent part of doing business, but **companies that implement proactive risk mitigation strategies** gain a significant advantage in **navigating uncertainties, preventing financial crises, and securing long-term stability**.

From stress-testing financial models and strengthening liquidity management to **transferring risk through insurance policies and ensuring regulatory compliance**, businesses must be prepared for

**economic downturns, operational disruptions, and market volatility.**

Companies that **ignore financial risk management operate in a fragile state**, where any unexpected crisis can lead to **irreversible financial losses.** In contrast, businesses that **prioritize risk mitigation build financial resilience, attract investor confidence, and maintain stability through changing economic conditions.**

## Insurance, Hedging, and Diversification: Essential Strategies for Financial Risk Management

Risk is an unavoidable reality in business, but companies that proactively **protect their financial stability through insurance, hedging, and diversification** can safeguard themselves against unpredictable losses, volatile markets, and economic downturns. While some risks can be mitigated through internal controls and financial planning, others—such as natural disasters, market fluctuations, and legal liabilities—require **strategic risk transfer and financial buffering** to prevent catastrophic consequences.

By implementing **comprehensive insurance coverage, sophisticated hedging techniques, and a well-balanced diversification strategy**, businesses can ensure **long-term resilience, financial security, and sustainable growth** even in uncertain conditions.

## Insurance: Protecting Businesses from Unpredictable Financial Losses

Insurance serves as a critical **risk transfer mechanism**, ensuring that businesses can recover quickly from unexpected events without suffering severe financial damage. Whether it's **property damage, legal liability, employee injuries, or cyber threats**, the right insurance policies act as a financial safeguard that absorbs losses and provides the resources needed to **restore operations, cover legal expenses, and compensate for lost income**.

A business without proper insurance is constantly vulnerable to financial disasters that can arise at any moment—one **fire, lawsuit, or market disruption could result in crippling losses**. The right insurance coverage **does not just protect assets—it protects the company's future**.

**Key Types of Business Insurance for Risk Management:**

- **Property Insurance** – Protects physical assets, such as office buildings, warehouses, machinery, and inventory, from **fire, theft, vandalism, and natural disasters**.
- **Liability Insurance** – Covers legal claims against the business due to **accidents, product defects, professional negligence, or customer injuries**.
- **Workers' Compensation Insurance** – Provides financial protection for employees who suffer **work-related injuries or illnesses**, covering medical expenses and lost wages.
- **Cybersecurity Insurance** – Protects against **data breaches, hacking attempts, and cyber fraud**, ensuring that financial and customer data remains secure.
- **Business Interruption Insurance** – Compensates for **lost revenue and operating costs** when a business is forced to shut down due to unforeseen disruptions.

**Real-World Example:**

A **manufacturing company that suffered a warehouse fire** was able to **resume operations within months** because it had secured **comprehensive property and business interruption insurance**. The insurance covered the costs of rebuilding, replacing damaged inventory, and covering lost revenue while the facility was being restored. In contrast, **a competitor without adequate coverage** faced **severe financial losses and ultimately declared bankruptcy**.

**Why Insurance Matters:**

- Prevents **unexpected financial disasters** from derailing business growth.
- Protects against **legal liabilities** that could result in expensive lawsuits.
- Ensures **employee safety and financial security** through proper coverage.
- Provides a **financial safety net** that allows companies to recover quickly from crises.

## Hedging: Reducing Financial Risk in Volatile Markets

While insurance protects against **physical and legal risks, hedging** is a strategy businesses use to protect against **financial risks, such as currency fluctuations, interest rate volatility, and commodity price changes**. Hedging involves using financial instruments—such as **options, futures, and forward contracts**—to offset potential losses and maintain financial stability.

For businesses that rely on **global markets, fluctuating commodity prices, or interest rate-sensitive investments**, failing to hedge financial risks can result in **huge losses that erode profit margins, destabilize operations, and lead to financial crises.**

**How Hedging Works:**

- **Futures Contracts** – Lock in the price of raw materials or goods today to avoid **unexpected cost increases in the future**.
- **Options Contracts** – Give businesses the right (but not the obligation) to buy or sell assets at a predetermined price, protecting against **market swings.**
- **Foreign Exchange Hedging** – Shields companies from **currency fluctuations** when conducting international business.
- **Interest Rate Hedging** – Reduces the impact of rising or falling interest rates on **business loans and investments.**

**Real-World Example:**

A **coffee company that imports coffee beans** from international suppliers is vulnerable to **commodity price fluctuations.** If a poor harvest leads to a **global shortage**, the price of coffee beans will skyrocket, significantly increasing the company's costs. To **protect against this risk**, the company can use a **futures contract** to lock in current coffee bean prices for the next year, ensuring **predictable costs and stable profit margins** regardless of future market conditions.

**Why Hedging Matters:**

- Shields businesses from **unexpected financial losses** due to market volatility.

- Ensures **cost stability and profitability**, even in fluctuating economic conditions.
- Reduces **uncertainty in financial planning**, enabling better investment decisions.
- Protects against **foreign exchange risks**, making international transactions safer.

## Diversification: Strengthening Financial Stability by Expanding Revenue Streams

While **insurance protects against losses** and **hedging safeguards against financial volatility, diversification ensures that businesses do not become over-reliant on a single revenue source, product, or market**. Diversification is a fundamental strategy for **risk reduction, long-term sustainability, and financial security**, allowing businesses to **spread risk across multiple areas** rather than concentrating financial exposure in one vulnerable segment.

A company that **relies too heavily on a single product, market, or customer segment** is highly vulnerable to **shifts in consumer demand, economic downturns, or industry-specific disruptions**. By **expanding product lines, entering new markets, and developing diverse revenue streams**, businesses **minimize risk, improve resilience, and create new opportunities for growth**.

**Key Ways Businesses Diversify to Reduce Financial Risk:**

- **Expanding Product or Service Offerings** – Avoid relying on a

**single product or market segment** by developing new product lines or complementary services.

- **Entering New Geographic Markets** – Reduce reliance on **one country or region** by expanding into **global markets.**
- **Building Multiple Customer Segments** – Serve **different customer demographics and industries** to **reduce dependency on one group**.

**Real-World Example:**

A **tech company that originally built hardware products** recognized the risks of relying solely on **physical product sales**, which were subject to **supply chain disruptions, production costs, and consumer demand shifts**. To **diversify revenue**, the company expanded into **subscription-based cloud software and digital services**, ensuring **steady income even during economic downturns**.

**Why Diversification Matters:**

- Reduces **dependency on one product, market, or revenue stream**, making businesses **more resilient to economic fluctuations**.
- Protects against **market-specific downturns**, ensuring **consistent financial performance**.
- Encourages **innovation and new revenue opportunities**, driving **long-term profitability**.

## Building a Resilient Business Through Comprehensive Risk Management

Risk is an inevitable part of running a business, but companies that **combine insurance, hedging, and diversification strategies** create **a powerful financial shield that minimizes exposure to unpredictable losses, market volatility, and industry-specific disruptions**.

Insurance acts as a **financial safety net**, ensuring that businesses can recover from **property damage, lawsuits, and operational shutdowns**. Hedging reduces **financial volatility**, protecting against **commodity price swings, currency fluctuations, and interest rate changes**. Diversification strengthens **long-term financial stability**, ensuring that businesses are **not overly reliant on a single revenue source, customer base, or geographic region**.

## Uncovering Financial Red Flags: Ensuring Business Stability Through Proactive Analysis

A business's financial health is not always reflected accurately in its profit and loss statements. Many companies appear profitable on paper while facing underlying liquidity issues that threaten long-term sustainability. Understanding the warning signs of financial instability—such as hidden liquidity problems, over-leveraging, accounting manipulation, declining profit margins, and unusual accounting adjustments—is essential for business owners, investors, and financial professionals who want to make informed decisions and prevent financial crises before they occur.

One of the most deceptive financial challenges is hidden liquidity issues. A company may report strong revenues and even increasing profitability, yet struggle with cash flow shortages that make it difficult to cover short-term expenses such as payroll, supplier payments, and loan obligations. This often happens when too much revenue is tied up in receivables, excessive inventory, or long-term contracts with delayed payments. Businesses that fail to actively monitor liquidity can quickly find themselves unable to meet financial obligations despite appearing financially successful on paper.

Over-leveraging is another critical risk that businesses often overlook until it is too late. While taking on debt can be a strategic move to finance growth, excessive borrowing can create significant financial strain, especially if revenues decline or interest rates increase. Companies that rely too heavily on borrowed capital may struggle to meet their repayment obligations, leading to deteriorating credit ratings, higher borrowing costs, and potential insolvency. Recognizing when debt levels become unsustainable is crucial for maintaining financial stability and avoiding long-term financial distress.

Accounting manipulation tactics are another area of concern, as some businesses engage in misleading financial reporting to present a more favorable picture to investors, lenders, and stakeholders. This can include inflating revenue figures through premature revenue recognition, understating expenses to artificially boost profits, or using off-balance-sheet financing to hide liabilities. While these tactics may temporarily enhance a company's financial position, they ultimately erode trust, damage credibility, and lead to severe consequences when uncovered. Understanding the signs of financial manipulation—such as sudden revenue spikes without a corresponding increase in cash flow, unexplained reductions in expenses, or discrepancies between reported earnings and actual cash flow—can help prevent costly investment mistakes and regulatory scrutiny.

Declining profit margins and operational inefficiencies also serve as warning signs that a business may be in trouble. When a company's costs begin to rise faster than its revenues, profitability erodes, making it harder to sustain long-term operations. This can be due to poor pricing strategies, rising production costs, increased competition, or inefficient resource allocation. Businesses must continuously monitor their cost structures and implement efficiency improvements to maintain healthy profit margins. Ignoring these signals can lead to mounting financial losses, reduced competitiveness, and eventual business failure.

Unusual accounting adjustments can also indicate deeper financial issues. When companies make frequent, unexplained changes to their accounting policies or adjust financial figures in ways that deviate from industry norms, it often raises red flags about the accuracy of their financial reporting. These adjustments may be used to manipulate earnings, defer losses, or obscure financial weaknesses. Investors and financial professionals must scrutinize financial statements for inconsistencies, unexplained changes in accounting estimates, and adjustments that lack transparency to ensure they are working with accurate and reliable financial data.

Recognizing these financial warning signs is critical for maintaining stability and avoiding financial crises. By staying proactive, businesses can identify risks early, implement corrective measures, and protect their financial health. Whether it is liquidity management, debt oversight, operational efficiency, or financial transparency, taking a detailed and disciplined approach to financial analysis ensures that businesses remain resilient, adaptable, and positioned for long-term success.

## Case Study: How Companies Survived Financial Crises

### Case 1: Apple's Survival After Near Bankruptcy (1997)

Apple faced severe financial struggles in the 1990s due to poor product sales. However, it **restructured its operations, secured funding from Microsoft, and focused on innovation**, leading to the launch of the iMac and iPod. This turnaround cemented Apple's **dominance in the tech industry**.

### Case 2: Airlines During COVID-19 (2020)

During the pandemic, airlines faced severe cash flow problems. Those with **strong liquidity reserves and government-backed loans** (such as Delta Airlines) were able to **weather the crisis**, while others struggled.

### Case 3: Netflix's Shift from DVD Rentals to Streaming

In the early 2000s, Netflix faced competition from **Blockbuster Video** but mitigated risk by **shifting to a subscription-based streaming model**, ensuring long-term profitability and reducing reliance on physical DVD sales.

### Conclusion: Building a Strong Financial Risk Management Strategy

Every business, regardless of its size or industry, will inevitably face **financial risks**—but those that implement **robust risk management strategies** can protect their assets, maintain financial stability, and position themselves for **long-term success**. In this chapter, we explored **how businesses identify, assess, and mitigate financial risks**, using a combination of strategic planning, financial tools, and real-world examples.

One of the key takeaways from this chapter is that **not all risks are the same**. We classified financial risks into **three major categories**:

- **Market risk**, where businesses are vulnerable to external economic changes, currency fluctuations, interest rate shifts, and commodity price volatility.
- **Credit risk**, where delayed payments or bad debts from customers can lead to severe cash flow constraints.
- **Operational risk**, where internal failures, technological disruptions, supply chain issues, or unexpected disasters can severely impact business continuity.

Each of these risks requires **proactive risk mitigation strategies**. For market risks, businesses can **diversify revenue streams, hedge against financial losses, and monitor economic trends** to stay ahead of fluctuations. To manage credit risk, businesses should **implement strict credit policies, conduct due diligence on customers, and use trade credit insurance to protect against defaults**. Operational risk, on the other hand, requires **strong internal controls, cybersecurity protection, supply chain resilience, and business continuity planning** to ensure the company can continue functioning even in the face of unexpected disruptions.

We also examined **how businesses can prepare for financial uncertainties** through **liquidity management, stress testing, and**

**financial forecasting**. Businesses that maintain **adequate cash reserves and access to reliable credit facilities** are far better equipped to navigate financial shocks than those that operate without a safety net. Companies that engage in **stress testing**—by simulating worst-case financial scenarios—are also able to make better, more informed decisions when crises arise.

A key risk management tool that businesses often overlook is **insurance**. We explored how different types of insurance—such as **business interruption insurance, liability insurance, and cybersecurity insurance**—can provide critical financial protection against potential losses. Similarly, **hedging strategies**, such as futures contracts or currency hedging, help businesses **reduce exposure to unpredictable market movements**, ensuring financial stability even when external conditions fluctuate.

We also discussed the importance of **diversification** as a risk reduction strategy. Businesses that rely too heavily on **one revenue stream, one supplier, or one key customer** put themselves at significant financial risk. By diversifying products, markets, and supply chains, companies can **spread their risk exposure** and build resilience against unexpected disruptions.

One of the most insightful parts of this chapter was the **real-world case studies** that demonstrated how businesses have successfully navigated financial crises. From **Apple's turnaround in 1997**, to **airlines surviving the COVID-19 pandemic**, and **Netflix's shift from DVD rentals to streaming**, these case studies highlighted how effective risk management can determine whether a company thrives or fails in the face of adversity.

The overarching lesson from this chapter is that **risk management is not**

**about avoiding risks altogether, but about preparing for them in advance**. Companies that have **a clear risk mitigation strategy in place, maintain financial flexibility, and continuously monitor economic conditions** are better positioned to **withstand financial uncertainties and emerge stronger**.

# CRISIS MANAGEMENT & BUSINESS RESILIENCE

## Understanding Financial Crises: How Businesses Get Caught Off Guard

In business, uncertainty is the only certainty. Economic downturns, financial crises, global pandemics, and industry disruptions can put immense strain on companies, often exposing vulnerabilities that were previously hidden beneath strong revenue figures and seemingly stable financial statements. Many businesses do not struggle due to a lack of profitability but rather because they fail to anticipate financial shocks, manage liquidity effectively, or pivot quickly enough in response to changing conditions. Businesses that survive are those that proactively prepare for crises, build financial contingency plans, maintain adaptable cash flow management, and develop response strategies that allow them to sustain operations even under extreme circumstances.

Some companies collapse within months of an unexpected downturn, while others emerge stronger, more competitive, and better equipped for future challenges. The difference between survival and failure often comes down to financial discipline, strategic foresight, and the ability to make swift, calculated decisions under pressure. The global financial crisis of 2008, the COVID-19 pandemic, and rapid technological disruptions have reshaped entire industries overnight. While some organizations succumbed to these forces, others navigated through them by maintaining liquidity, restructuring their operations, and capitalizing on emerging opportunities. The following sections explore how businesses can prepare, adapt, and recover from financial crises, ensuring long-term resilience and sustainability.

### ***Preparing a Financial Contingency Plan to Withstand Economic Shocks***

A financial contingency plan is a structured, proactive approach that ensures a business can continue operations despite economic shocks, market volatility, or external disruptions. Instead of scrambling for solutions once a crisis unfolds, businesses that establish contingency plans in advance can minimize financial shocks, reduce the impact of revenue losses, and preserve operational stability even in the most adverse conditions.

Businesses that effectively prepare for financial crises begin by maintaining substantial cash reserves. Companies that hold six to twelve months' worth of operating expenses in accessible reserves can weather unexpected downturns without needing to resort to excessive borrowing or cost-cutting measures that may damage long-term profitability. One of the most well-documented examples of this strategy is Apple, which maintains over $100 billion in cash reserves, allowing it to sustain operations and continue investing in innovation even during economic downturns.

Revenue diversification is another critical element of financial resilience. Businesses that rely heavily on a single revenue source, a limited customer base, or one geographical market are significantly more vulnerable during economic contractions. By expanding into multiple markets, leveraging digital platforms, and developing new product or service offerings, companies can mitigate risks associated with industry-specific downturns.

Cost structure flexibility is equally important. Companies that carry high fixed costs, such as long-term leases, expensive payroll structures, and inflexible supplier contracts, often find it difficult to adapt to sudden changes in revenue. Businesses that negotiate variable cost structures, explore leasing rather than purchasing equipment, and implement scalable workforce models can reduce expenses quickly when needed, preserving cash flow without drastic layoffs or business disruptions.

Another key component of financial contingency planning is securing access to emergency credit lines before they are needed. During times of crisis, lenders often tighten credit conditions, making it difficult for businesses to secure funding. Those that establish credit lines in advance ensure they have immediate access to liquidity, allowing them to cover operational expenses even when cash flow declines unexpectedly.

## Survival Strategies for Businesses Facing Economic Recession

Recessions force businesses to rethink their financial priorities, optimize resource allocation, and cut unnecessary costs without sacrificing long-term stability. Poorly managed companies often resort to reactionary decisions such as mass layoffs, drastic budget cuts, or excessive price reductions that ultimately weaken their market position. In contrast, businesses that make strategic financial adjustments, focus on core operations, and maintain customer loyalty can emerge from recessions even stronger.

During economic downturns, successful businesses prioritize their most profitable products and services, reallocating resources away from secondary operations that do not generate significant returns. Amazon, for example, has successfully navigated multiple recessions by focusing on its core e-commerce business and cloud computing division while scaling back on less profitable experimental projects.

Reducing debt exposure is another vital survival strategy. Companies that proactively pay down high-interest debt, refinance loans at lower rates, and avoid excessive financial leverage position themselves to endure financial downturns with greater stability. Businesses that enter a crisis with minimal debt obligations have the flexibility to adjust their cost structures without facing immediate solvency concerns.

Maintaining strong customer relationships is equally critical in a downturn. Economic uncertainty often leads to decreased consumer spending and heightened price sensitivity. Businesses that offer loyalty programs, flexible payment plans, and superior customer service can retain their existing clients, ensuring a steady revenue stream even in challenging market conditions.

Pricing and promotion strategies must also be adjusted carefully. Rather than engaging in aggressive price reductions that erode profit margins, businesses should focus on targeted promotions, bundling offers, and value-driven pricing that appeals to cost-conscious consumers while preserving financial sustainability.

## Scenario-Based Financial Planning for Economic Uncertainty

Scenario-based financial planning allows businesses to anticipate different financial conditions and develop actionable strategies for each situation. Companies that engage in scenario planning create multiple financial models to determine how they will respond to various levels of economic impact.

A best-case scenario assumes minimal disruption to revenue streams, allowing business expansion and ongoing investments. A moderate downturn scenario, in contrast, forecasts revenue declines of 15 to 30 percent, requiring businesses to reduce costs and delay expansion plans while preserving core operations. The worst-case scenario prepares businesses for revenue losses of 50 percent or more, requiring them to implement emergency cost-cutting measures, restructure operations, and seek alternative funding sources to maintain solvency.

Businesses that prepare for multiple financial outcomes can avoid knee-jerk reactions, ensuring they implement well-thought-out financial strategies that preserve long-term stability rather than focusing solely on short-term survival.

## Case Studies: Companies That Successfully Navigated Financial Crises

Some of the world's most successful companies have faced near-collapse due to financial crises but emerged stronger due to effective financial management and strategic adaptability.

Apple was on the verge of bankruptcy in the late 1990s, suffering from declining sales, poor financial management, and high production costs. Under the leadership of Steve Jobs, Apple streamlined its product offerings, secured emergency funding, and prioritized innovation, eventually becoming the most valuable company in the world.

During the COVID-19 pandemic, Airbnb lost 80 percent of its revenue in just a few weeks. Instead of shutting down, the company pivoted its business model to focus on long-term rentals, significantly reducing operational costs while shifting marketing efforts toward people seeking temporary relocation options. By the end of 2020, Airbnb had not only recovered but had one of the most successful IPOs in history.

Netflix is another example of a company that adapted to industry disruption. Initially a DVD rental service, Netflix faced an existential threat when digital streaming emerged. Instead of resisting change, the company invested in digital infrastructure, built a subscription-based revenue model, and expanded into original content production. By embracing change, Netflix became a global leader in entertainment while competitors like Blockbuster collapsed.

## Crisis-Proofing a Business for Long-Term Success

No business is immune to financial downturns, global disruptions, or industry changes, but those that proactively manage risks, build financial buffers, and plan for uncertainty can navigate crises with confidence. Companies that anticipate potential financial risks, maintain financial flexibility, and make disciplined financial decisions are far better positioned to survive and thrive in any economic climate.

The most successful businesses do not merely endure crises; they leverage them as opportunities for reinvention and long-term growth. By implementing strong financial resilience strategies, optimizing resource allocation, and embracing adaptability, businesses can transform economic challenges into a foundation for future success. The ability to crisis-proof an organization is not just about survival—it is about building a business that remains strong, competitive, and capable of sustained financial health, regardless of external circumstances.

# BUSINESS FINANCING & CAPITAL MANAGEMENT

## Introduction: The Power of Smart Financing in Business Growth

Every great business—whether a **small start up or a global corporation**—relies on **strategic financing** to grow, innovate, and stay competitive. Without sufficient capital, even the most **promising business ideas** can stall before they gain momentum. Financing is the **fuel** that powers expansion, sustains operations, and enables businesses to weather economic uncertainty. However, securing capital is not just about **getting money**—it's about making the **right financial decisions** that align with business objectives and long-term success.

The financing decisions a company makes today will **shape its future**. A well-structured financial strategy can provide the necessary funds to **launch new products, expand into new markets, invest in technology, or increase operational capacity**. But making the wrong financing choices—whether through **excessive debt, poor cash flow management, or giving up too much equity too soon**—can lead to **financial instability, reduced profitability, and even business failure**.

This chapter explores **the different ways businesses can access capital**, focusing on the two primary funding options: **debt financing and equity financing**. We will break down their **advantages, risks, and when to use each**, helping you decide which financing method best suits your business needs. We'll also delve into the **importance of working capital management**, showing how businesses can **optimize cash flow, manage short-term assets and liabilities, and maintain financial flexibility**.

Beyond securing funding, we'll explore how businesses can **evaluate loan options, build strong investor relationships, and make financing decisions that fuel long-term success**. We'll also examine **real-world case studies** of companies that have successfully leveraged financing to scale their operations—offering valuable lessons that you can apply to your own financial strategy.

By the end of this chapter, you will have a **deep understanding of business financing and capital management**, empowering you to make

**smart, informed financial decisions** that drive growth, stability, and long-term profitability. Whether you are seeking **a business loan, negotiating with investors, or managing cash flow**, the insights from this chapter will help you navigate the financial challenges and opportunities ahead.

## The Psychology of Financial Decision-Making: How Behavior Shapes Business Success

Financial management is not purely a numbers-driven exercise—it is deeply influenced by **human behavior, cognitive biases, and emotional decision-making**. Even the most experienced business leaders and financial professionals are not immune to psychological tendencies that **distort financial reasoning, impact strategic planning, and lead to costly mistakes**.

Understanding the **psychological factors that influence financial decisions** is just as important as understanding financial statements, budgeting, and forecasting. Many businesses fail—not because of **a lack of revenue, poor products, or weak markets**—but because of **misguided financial decision-making, often driven by bias, emotional impulses, and short-term thinking**.

By recognizing these psychological traps and implementing **disciplined, data-driven financial strategies**, businesses can improve financial performance, minimize risks, and achieve sustainable long-term profitability.

## Cognitive Biases in Financial Decision-Making: Why Smart People Make Costly Mistakes

Cognitive biases are **mental shortcuts that influence decision-making**—

and in financial management, they can lead to **overestimating revenues, underestimating risks, or making irrational investment choices**. Business leaders, investors, and financial managers must actively identify and **counteract these biases** to avoid poor financial outcomes.

### *1. Overconfidence Bias: Thinking You Know More Than You Do*

Many business owners and executives **overestimate their ability to predict financial outcomes, market trends, and investment returns**. This often leads to **risky financial decisions, excessive debt, and unrealistic revenue projections**.

A CEO might assume that a new product launch will be an immediate success based on **gut instinct rather than detailed financial projections**. This can result in **over-expansion, misallocated resources, and unmet sales targets**—leading to significant financial losses.

**How to Overcome It:**

- Base all financial decisions on **data, historical trends, and thorough analysis**, not personal confidence or intuition.
- Consult **multiple perspectives**—including financial analysts, accountants, and industry experts—before making major financial moves.
- Regularly **stress-test financial models** to prepare for worst-case scenarios.

### *2. Loss Aversion: The Fear of Losing Prevents Smart Investments*

Loss aversion refers to the **tendency to fear losses more than valuing equivalent gains**. Business owners often **avoid necessary risks or refuse**

**to cut losses on failing projects** due to emotional attachment.

A company may continue investing in an underperforming marketing campaign, product line, or business unit simply because of the **time and money already spent**—even when financial data clearly indicates it should be discontinued.

**How to Overcome It:**

- Separate **emotions from financial analysis**—focus on facts, not past investments.
- Conduct regular **cost-benefit analyses** to determine when to pivot or cut losses.
- Accept that **not every investment will succeed** and recognize that redeploying resources effectively is a sign of financial intelligence.

### *3. Anchoring Bias: Getting Stuck on Initial Numbers*

Anchoring occurs when **people rely too heavily on the first piece of information they receive**, even if it is outdated or irrelevant. This often leads to **pricing errors, inaccurate valuations, and misguided budget decisions**.

For example, a business that **initially priced its product at $200 per unit** may resist lowering the price—even when customer demand and competitive analysis suggest that a **$150 price point would maximize revenue**.

**How to Overcome It:**

- Continuously **re-evaluate financial decisions based on updated data**.

- Compare financial estimates with **industry benchmarks and external market conditions**.
- Avoid **fixating on past financial figures**—adjust strategies based on real-time performance.

## Why Businesses Ignore Financial Data—And How to Fix It

Many businesses fail to act on financial data, even when it clearly signals a **need for change**. Whether it's an **unprofitable business model, rising debt levels, or declining cash flow**, companies often delay necessary financial adjustments due to **denial, ego, or resistance to change**.

Ignoring financial data is often a result of **confirmation bias**—where leaders only focus on information that supports their existing beliefs while disregarding evidence that suggests financial trouble.

A restaurant owner might **ignore declining profit margins and instead focus on positive customer reviews**, convincing themselves that the business is thriving when financial reports indicate otherwise.

**How to Fix This:**

- Make **financial data a central part of decision-making**, not an afterthought.
- Schedule **regular financial reviews** with accountants, investors, or advisors.
- Accept that **financial numbers do not lie**—and adjust strategies accordingly.

## Emotional Spending vs. Strategic Investment

Businesses that **prioritize emotional spending over strategic investment** often struggle with profitability. Emotional spending occurs when **leaders make financial decisions based on personal preferences, status, or impulse rather than financial necessity**.

Examples include:

- **Overinvesting in luxury office spaces, branding, or unnecessary perks** to create an illusion of success—while struggling with cash flow.
- **Expanding too quickly** without a clear financial strategy, leading to operational inefficiencies and debt burdens.
- **Spending aggressively on marketing campaigns** that lack clear return on investment (ROI) metrics.

**Strategic investment, on the other hand, is based on:**

- **Financial analysis and ROI calculations.**
- **Aligning spending with long-term growth and profitability goals.**
- **Focusing on business fundamentals rather than short-term appearances.**

**How to Avoid Emotional Spending:**

- Always **justify major expenses with financial data and expected returns**.
- Separate **personal desires from business needs**.

- Set clear **financial thresholds and approval processes** before making large investments.

## Short-Term vs. Long-Term Financial Thinking

A major challenge in financial decision-making is the **tension between short-term survival and long-term financial sustainability**. Many businesses prioritize **immediate gains**, sacrificing future stability in the process.

Examples include:

- **Cutting costs excessively** (e.g., laying off employees, slashing marketing budgets) to boost short-term profits—while damaging long-term growth.
- **Maximizing quarterly earnings** by delaying necessary investments in research, technology, or infrastructure.
- **Taking on excessive debt** to expand quickly without a clear repayment strategy.

Businesses that focus **only on short-term results** often find themselves in financial trouble when market conditions shift. On the other hand, those that prioritize **long-term financial health** by investing in **strategic growth, sustainability, and operational efficiency** tend to be more resilient.

**How to Balance Short-Term & Long-Term Thinking:**

- Develop a **multi-year financial strategy** that accounts for both immediate needs and future goals.

- Focus on **building sustainable revenue streams** rather than chasing short-term spikes in profit.
- Allocate resources to **long-term investments**, such as employee training, technology, and innovation.

## The Impact of Financial Discipline on Long-Term Profitability

At the heart of financial success is **discipline**—the ability to **make data-driven decisions, resist impulsive spending, and commit to long-term financial planning**. Businesses that embrace financial discipline consistently outperform those that operate with **loose financial oversight and reactive decision-making**.

Financially disciplined businesses:

- Maintain **healthy cash reserves** to navigate economic downturns.
- Focus on **profitability and efficiency** rather than unsustainable growth.
- Use **clear financial KPIs** to measure and track performance.
- Continuously **refine strategies based on financial insights**.

A company that **practices strong financial discipline can weather economic crises, seize market opportunities, and maintain investor confidence**, while undisciplined businesses often collapse under financial mismanagement.

### Final Thoughts: Developing a Strategic, Data-Driven Financial Mindset

The difference between financial success and failure is **not just about revenue—it's about how financial decisions are made**. Businesses that recognize and **correct cognitive biases, avoid emotional spending, balance short- and long-term financial thinking, and maintain strong financial discipline** are far more likely to **achieve sustained profitability and financial resilience**.

By shifting from **reactionary financial decisions to strategic, data-driven planning**, businesses can **maximize financial stability, mitigate risks, and create long-term value**—ensuring that financial management is **a tool for success rather than a source of failure**.

## Types of Business Financing: Debt vs. Equity

When businesses require additional funds, they typically choose between **debt financing and equity financing**. Each financing method comes with **advantages and risks**, and selecting the right one depends on the company's **growth stage, financial health, and long-term strategy**.

### Debt Financing: Leveraging Borrowed Capital for Growth

Debt financing is one of the most common ways businesses raise capital. It involves **borrowing money from external sources—such as banks, private lenders, or investors—under the agreement that it will be repaid over time, typically with interest**. Unlike equity financing, which requires **selling ownership stakes** in the company, debt financing allows businesses to **retain full control while securing the funds necessary for growth, expansion, or operational stability**.

Many businesses, from **start ups to multinational corporations**, use debt financing to **invest in new equipment, expand operations, increase inventory, acquire assets, or cover short-term cash flow gaps**. However, while debt can provide **quick access to funds**, businesses must carefully manage their repayment obligations to avoid financial strain.

## Key Features of Debt Financing

94. **Fixed or Variable Interest Rates** – Lenders charge interest on borrowed funds, which can be fixed (remains the same throughout the loan term) or variable (fluctuates based on market conditions).

95. **Principal Repayment** – The loaned amount (principal) must be repaid according to a **structured payment plan**, which could be monthly, quarterly, or annually.

96. **Maturity Period** – The repayment duration varies based on the type of loan. Short-term loans typically last **one to three years**, while long-term loans can span **10 to 30 years**.

97. **Collateral Requirement** – Some forms of debt financing require businesses to **pledge assets as collateral** in case of loan default.

98. **Legal and Financial Obligations** – Borrowers must adhere to contractual terms, which may include **financial performance requirements (covenants)** and restrictions on how the funds are used.

## Types of Debt Financing

Businesses can access debt financing through various instruments, depending on their **financial needs, business stage, and repayment capacity**.

### *Traditional Bank Loans*

**Bank loans** are one of the most common debt financing options. They typically require **strong creditworthiness, financial history, and collateral**.

✅ **Best for:** Established businesses with stable revenue streams and good credit history.

✅ **Common Uses:** Expanding operations, purchasing equipment, hiring staff.

### *Business Lines of Credit*

A **business line of credit** functions like a credit card, allowing businesses to **borrow only what they need and repay with interest only on the amount used**. It provides flexibility for **short-term cash flow management**.

✅ **Best for:** Businesses that need **on-demand** funding for operational expenses.

✅ **Common Uses:** Covering payroll, seasonal inventory purchases, unexpected costs.

### *SBA Loans (Government-Backed Loans)*

Government agencies, such as the **Small Business Administration (SBA)**

**in the U.S.**, offer loans with **lower interest rates and favorable terms** to help businesses grow.

✅ **Best for:** Small businesses needing affordable financing with lower risks.

✅ **Common Uses:** Expanding a small business, real estate purchases, refinancing debt.

***Corporate Bonds***

Larger businesses can issue **corporate bonds**, which allow them to raise capital from investors who lend money in exchange for **regular interest payments and repayment at maturity**.

✅ **Best for:** Established corporations needing significant capital for **large-scale expansion or infrastructure investments**.

✅ **Common Uses:** Expanding product lines, international expansion, acquisitions.

***Merchant Cash Advances (MCAs)***

A **merchant cash advance** provides businesses with a **lump sum payment** in exchange for a percentage of future sales. While **quick and accessible**, MCAs often come with **high fees and interest rates**.

✅ **Best for:** Businesses with **strong daily sales but limited access to traditional loans**.

✅ **Common Uses:** Urgent working capital needs, covering short-term expenses.

## Advantages of Debt Financing

Debt financing can be a **powerful tool** for businesses seeking capital while maintaining ownership. Key benefits include:

**Full Ownership Retention** – Unlike equity financing, debt financing does not dilute ownership or decision-making power. Business owners remain in **full control** of their operations.

**Predictable Payment Structure** – Loans have **fixed repayment schedules**, making it easier for businesses to plan and **budget for expenses**.

**Potential Tax Benefits** – **Interest payments on debt are often tax-deductible**, reducing a company's taxable income.

**Enhances Business Credit** – Successfully repaying loans helps **build a company's credit profile**, making future financing more accessible.

**Flexibility for Short-Term or Long-Term Needs** – Businesses can choose between **short-term loans for operational expenses** or **long-term loans for capital investments**.

## Disadvantages and Risks of Debt Financing

While debt financing offers many benefits, **mismanaging debt can create serious financial problems**.

**Repayment Obligation Regardless of Profitability** – Loans must be **repaid on schedule**, even if the business is struggling financially.

**High Interest Costs** – Some debt instruments, such as **merchant cash advances**, come with high-interest rates that can **significantly impact**

**cash flow**.

**Collateral Requirements** – Many loans require businesses to pledge **property, inventory, or assets** as collateral, increasing financial risk if the business fails.

**Restrictive Loan Terms** – Lenders often impose **financial covenants,** restricting how businesses can spend funds or requiring them to maintain **specific financial ratios**.

## When Should a Business Use Debt Financing?

Debt financing is **not one-size-fits-all**. A business should consider debt financing when:

- **It has stable and predictable revenue streams** to manage repayments.
- **The cost of debt is lower than the return on investment (ROI)**—meaning the borrowed capital will generate more profit than the interest costs.
- **It needs funding for a specific, high-impact investment**—such as acquiring new technology, expanding production, or entering a new market.
- **It has strong financials and can qualify for low-interest loans** from banks or government programs.

## Real-World Case Study: Amazon's Use of Debt Financing to Scale Operations

Amazon is a prime example of how a business can **strategically use debt**

**financing** to fund expansion while maintaining ownership control.

- In **1999**, Amazon **issued $1.25 billion in corporate bonds** to fund its warehouse expansion and technology infrastructure.
- The company used **bank loans and credit lines** to support logistics and inventory management as it expanded globally.
- Despite initial losses, Amazon **reinvested borrowed funds into long-term growth**, leading to **massive profitability in later years**.

***Key Takeaway:***

Amazon's strategy illustrates how **debt financing can be a growth accelerator** if managed properly. The company took on debt **at the right time**, ensuring that borrowed capital **generated higher returns** than the cost of financing.

## Conclusion: Using Debt Financing as a Growth Tool

Debt financing provides businesses with **valuable capital for expansion, operational stability, and long-term investments**. By borrowing strategically, businesses can **leverage funds for growth without giving up ownership**. However, **debt must be carefully managed**—over-reliance on borrowing, high-interest costs, or cash flow mismanagement can lead to **financial distress and business failure**.

**Successful businesses treat debt as a tool, not a burden**. They carefully **evaluate repayment obligations, consider interest costs, and ensure that borrowed funds generate a positive return**. By **aligning debt financing with business goals, managing risks, and maintaining financial discipline**, businesses can **maximize growth potential while**

**avoiding the pitfalls of excessive debt.**

## Equity Financing: Raising Capital Through Investors

Equity financing is a powerful tool for businesses looking to **raise significant capital without incurring debt obligations**. Unlike debt financing, where businesses borrow funds and commit to repayment, equity financing involves **selling ownership stakes** in exchange for funding. This means investors become **part-owners of the business**, sharing both the risks and the rewards.

For many start ups and high-growth companies, **equity financing is essential to scaling operations, entering new markets, or funding research and development**. However, it comes at a cost—business owners must be prepared to **share decision-making power, distribute profits, and align their vision with investors' expectations**.

In this section, we will explore:

- **The different types of equity financing** and when to use them.
- **The advantages and disadvantages of equity financing** compared to debt financing.
- **How businesses can attract the right investors** and negotiate favorable terms.
- **Real-world examples of successful equity financing strategies.**

## How Equity Financing Works

When a business opts for equity financing, it **issues shares or ownership stakes** to investors in exchange for capital. Investors, whether individuals, venture capitalists, or institutions, provide funding in hopes of **earning a return on their investment (ROI)** through dividends, appreciation in stock value, or an eventual sale of their shares.

### Common Forms of Equity Financing

Different types of equity financing are available depending on the **business's size, stage, and funding needs**.

#### 1. Angel Investors

#### – Early-Stage Funding from Wealthy Individuals

Angel investors are **high-net-worth individuals** who provide capital to start ups in exchange for equity. They typically invest **during the early stages of a business**, when risk is high, but the potential for returns is significant.

✅ **Best for:** Start ups and small businesses in the pre-revenue or early-growth phase.

✅ **Common Investment Range:** $25,000 to $500,000.

✅ **Examples:** Jeff Bezos, founder of Amazon, was an angel investor in Google before it went public.

## 2. Venture Capital (VC) Firms

## – Scaling Through Institutional Funding

Venture capital firms invest in **high-growth start ups** with the potential to become industry leaders. They **take equity stakes** in businesses and often provide **strategic guidance, networking opportunities, and mentorship**.

✅ **Best for:** Companies with high scalability and disruptive innovation.

✅ **Common Investment Range:** $500,000 to $100+ million.

✅ **Examples:** Facebook, Uber, and Airbnb all secured venture capital in their early years.

## 3. Private Equity (PE) Firms

## – Investing in Established Businesses

Private equity firms invest in **mature businesses** that require capital for expansion, restructuring, or acquisitions. Unlike venture capital firms, private equity firms often **buy significant ownership stakes or acquire full control of a business**.

✅ **Best for:** Mid-sized and large companies looking for capital to expand or restructure.

✅ **Common Investment Range:** $10 million to $500+ million.

✅ **Examples:** Dell Computers went private in a $24.4 billion private equity deal to restructure its business.

### 4. Initial Public Offering (IPO) – Entering the Stock Market

An **IPO is when a private company sells shares to the public for the first time**, allowing it to raise capital from stock market investors. IPOs can generate **large-scale funding**, but they come with strict **regulatory, financial, and transparency requirements**.

✅ **Best for:** Businesses with strong financials and growth potential.

✅ **Common Investment Range:** Can raise **hundreds of millions or even billions of dollars**.

✅ **Examples:** Tesla raised $226 million through its IPO in 2010, fuelling its global expansion.

## Advantages of Equity Financing

Equity financing offers **several strategic advantages**, especially for businesses that require **large-scale funding and operational flexibility**.

### 1. No Debt Obligation

One of the biggest benefits of equity financing is that **businesses do not have to repay investors in fixed instalments**. Unlike loans, which require **monthly payments and accrue interest**, equity financing allows businesses to **use capital for growth initiatives without immediate financial pressure**.

### 2. Access to Strategic Expertise and Networks

Investors, particularly venture capitalists and private equity firms, bring more than just money—they provide:

- **Industry knowledge and mentorship** to help businesses scale.
- **Connections to key stakeholders, suppliers, and potential customers.**
- **Operational guidance** to improve efficiency and profitability.

### 3. More Flexible Funding for High-Risk Ventures

Start ups and innovative companies often struggle to secure traditional bank loans due to a **lack of credit history or tangible assets**. Equity financing provides **greater flexibility**, allowing businesses to **pursue long-term projects, R&D, and market expansion without immediate repayment pressure**.

### 4. Stronger Financial Stability

Since equity financing does not involve **fixed debt payments**, businesses can **navigate economic downturns, invest in long-term growth, and reinvest profits into operations** without the risk of defaulting on loans.

## Disadvantages of Equity Financing

While equity financing offers **debt-free capital**, it comes with **trade-offs that business owners must carefully consider**.

### 1. Loss of Ownership & Control

Equity financing requires business owners to **give up a portion of ownership** in exchange for funding. Investors may want **decision-making authority**, which can impact:

- **Company vision and strategic direction.**
- **Hiring and operational decisions.**
- **Future financial and exit strategies.**

### 2. Profit Sharing & Dilution

When a company issues new shares, existing ownership stakes are **diluted**. This means that original founders and shareholders **own a smaller percentage of the business** over time. Additionally, investors expect **financial returns**, which may reduce retained earnings available for reinvestment.

### 3. Time-Consuming & Complex Process

Raising equity financing is **not as fast as securing a bank loan**. The process often requires:

- **Investor due diligence** – Financial, operational, and market assessments.
- **Legal agreements and term negotiations.**
- **Regulatory compliance, especially for IPOs.**

For companies seeking **quick funding**, equity financing may not always be the best option.

## When Should a Business Use Equity Financing?

Equity financing is **most beneficial for businesses that:**

- Require **significant funding** for expansion, innovation, or acquisitions.
- Operate in **high-risk industries**, such as technology and biotech, where debt financing may be too restrictive.
- Have **limited collateral** or credit history, making traditional loans difficult to obtain.
- Want to **leverage investor expertise and networks** to accelerate growth.
- Are preparing for **IPO or large-scale investor funding rounds**.

## Real-World Case Study: Facebook's Venture Capital Success

Facebook, now one of the most valuable companies in the world, **relied heavily on equity financing to fuel its growth**.

- In **2004**, Facebook secured **$500,000 from angel investor Peter Thiel**, its first major equity investment.
- Over the next few years, Facebook raised **hundreds of millions from venture capital firms, including Accel Partners and Greylock Partners**.
- By **2012, Facebook launched its IPO**, raising **$16 billion**—one of the largest IPOs in history.

### Key Takeaway:

Facebook's equity financing strategy allowed it to **scale rapidly, expand globally, and invest heavily in product development**—all without taking on **burdensome debt**.

## Leveraging Equity Financing for Long-Term Growth

Equity financing is a **powerful tool for businesses that need substantial capital without the constraints of debt repayment**. By selling ownership stakes, businesses can **secure funding, gain strategic expertise, and expand operations**. However, business owners must be **prepared to share decision-making power and distribute profits**.

For businesses seeking **long-term scalability, industry connections, and financial flexibility**, equity financing provides a **pathway to sustained growth, innovation, and global market expansion**. However, it's essential to **strategically choose investors, negotiate favorable terms, and ensure that funding aligns with the company's long-term vision**..

**Managing Working Capital Effectively & Evaluating Business Loan Options and Investor Relations**

## Managing Working Capital Effectively

**Working capital is the lifeblood of a business.** It ensures that a company has enough short-term assets to cover **short-term liabilities**, allowing smooth day-to-day operations and financial stability. Poor working capital management can lead to **cash flow crises, late payments, loss of**

**business opportunities, and even insolvency**.

A company's ability to **balance receivables, payables, and inventory** effectively determines whether it can sustain operations without relying on external financing. Businesses with **strong working capital strategies** not only maintain stability but also **gain a competitive advantage** by reinvesting surplus funds into growth and innovation.

## 1. Key Components of Working Capital

Understanding the **fundamentals of working capital** is essential to implementing strategies that keep a business financially agile. A **positive working capital balance** means the company can cover its short-term obligations, whereas a **negative balance** signals financial strain. The key components of working capital include:

***Current Assets (Short-Term Resources)***

- **Cash & Cash Equivalents** – The most liquid asset, used to cover immediate expenses.
- **Accounts Receivable (AR)** – Money owed by customers for products or services provided.
- **Inventory** – Raw materials, finished goods, and in-progress work waiting to be sold.

***Current Liabilities (Short-Term Obligations)***

- **Accounts Payable (AP)** – Amounts owed to suppliers for goods/services purchased on credit.
- **Short-Term Loans** – Bank overdrafts, credit lines, or business

loans due within a year.

- **Payroll & Employee Benefits** – Salaries, bonuses, and other short-term employee costs.

A well-managed working capital system ensures that **current assets exceed current liabilities**, providing financial flexibility and business resilience.

## 2. Strategies for Improving Working Capital

Maintaining **healthy working capital** requires optimizing the movement of money within a business. Companies that **streamline receivables, manage payables wisely, and optimize inventory levels** can maintain a **strong cash position** and avoid unnecessary borrowing.

### *Optimizing Cash Flow*

- **Accelerate Receivables Collection** – Businesses should implement **incentives for early payments, stricter credit policies, and automated invoicing systems** to speed up cash inflows.
- **Strategically Delay Payables** – Extending payment terms with suppliers without damaging relationships allows businesses to **hold cash longer** and improve liquidity.

### *Inventory Management*

- **Avoid Overstocking & Dead Stock** – Holding excessive inventory ties up cash that could be used elsewhere. Implementing **just-in-time (JIT) inventory systems** helps free up working capital.
- **Improve Demand Forecasting** – Businesses should analyze sales

trends to ensure **optimal stock levels** and reduce unnecessary capital tied up in unsold goods.

***Reducing Unnecessary Expenses***

- **Identify Cost-Cutting Opportunities** – Businesses should periodically review expenses and eliminate **non-essential costs** that do not contribute to revenue generation.
- **Negotiate Supplier Discounts** – Bulk purchasing and long-term contracts with suppliers often lead to **better pricing and extended payment terms**, reducing cash outflows.

When working capital is **optimized**, businesses have more **financial flexibility** to **invest in growth initiatives, avoid costly emergency loans, and maintain operational stability during economic downturns.**

## 3. The Impact of Poor Working Capital Management

Failing to manage working capital effectively can lead to **serious financial distress**. If a business's current liabilities exceed its current assets, it faces:

- **Cash Flow Shortages** – Businesses may struggle to **pay suppliers, employees, and creditors on time**, leading to **late payment penalties and damaged relationships**.
- **Difficulty Securing Financing** – Lenders and investors closely monitor **working capital ratios** to assess financial health. Poor ratios can **reduce creditworthiness** and **hinder loan approvals**.
- **Missed Growth Opportunities** – A lack of liquidity means businesses cannot **take advantage of bulk discounts, invest in expansion, or acquire new assets**, limiting long-term success.

**Example:** A retail business that over-invests in seasonal inventory may find itself with excess stock after peak shopping periods. If sales slow, the business may **struggle to pay its suppliers**, leading to cash shortages and **potential insolvency**.

To avoid these risks, companies must adopt **proactive working capital management strategies** that balance short-term liquidity needs with long-term profitability.

## Evaluating Business Loan Options and Investor Relations

Choosing the right financing source is **critical for business sustainability**. Whether a company seeks a **loan from a financial institution** or **capital from investors**, it must evaluate financing terms carefully and maintain strong relationships with stakeholders.

### 1. How to Evaluate Business Loan Options

Businesses considering debt financing should analyze key factors to **ensure affordability and sustainability**.

***Key Considerations Before Taking a Loan***

- **Interest Rates** – Compare **fixed vs. variable interest rates** to determine the most cost-effective option.
- **Repayment Terms** – Evaluate loan **tenure, instalment flexibility, and prepayment penalties** to align with cash flow cycles.
- **Lender Reputation & Conditions** – Some loans come with **restrictive covenants** (e.g., maintaining a minimum cash balance).

Businesses must **read all loan agreements carefully**.

***Types of Business Loans***

- **Term Loans** – Best for long-term investments (e.g., expanding operations, purchasing equipment).
- **Lines of Credit** – Flexible borrowing for covering short-term operational expenses.
- **Invoice Financing** – Helps businesses with slow-paying customers by using unpaid invoices as collateral.

A company must **only borrow what it can afford to repay** while ensuring that financing decisions **align with its strategic goals**.

## 2. Building Strong Investor Relations

Investor relations go beyond just securing funding. **Investors provide capital, strategic insights, and industry connections**—but maintaining their confidence is essential for long-term collaboration.

***Key Principles of Investor Relations***

99. **Transparency & Communication**

- Investors expect **regular updates** on business performance, risks, and market conditions.
- Companies should provide **quarterly reports, investor calls, and financial disclosures** to maintain trust.

100. **Delivering Consistent Returns**

- Investors want to see **growth and profitability**, whether through

**capital appreciation or dividend payouts.**

- Businesses should **set realistic goals and meet financial targets** to retain investor confidence.

101. **Aligning Business Goals**

- Not all investors align with a company's long-term vision. **Choosing investors who share strategic objectives** prevents future conflicts.
- Founders must negotiate funding terms carefully to **maintain control over critical business decisions.**

**Example:** A tech start up that raises funding from venture capitalists must balance **growth expectations with sustainable business strategies.** Over-promising and under-delivering can **erode investor trust**, making future fundraising more difficult.

## The Role of Smart Capital & Working Capital Management

Effective **working capital management and strategic financing decisions** are critical for long-term business success. Businesses must ensure they have enough **liquid assets to cover short-term liabilities** while avoiding cash shortages that could **hinder growth or lead to financial distress.** In this chapter, we explored:

- **The key components of working capital** and why balancing assets and liabilities is essential.
- **Strategies to optimize cash flow, inventory, and expenses** to

maintain strong liquidity.

- **The consequences of poor working capital management**, such as missed growth opportunities and difficulty in securing financing.
- **How businesses evaluate loan options and maintain investor relationships** to secure sustainable funding.

Ultimately, businesses that **balance working capital effectively, secure the right financing, and build strong investor confidence** position themselves for **financial stability, growth, and long-term success**. By applying these principles, companies can **navigate economic challenges, scale strategically, and create long-term value for stakeholders.**

## Real-World Case Study: Funding a Business for Growth

### Real-World Case Studies: How Businesses Successfully Managed Financing

*Case Study 1: Tesla – A Masterclass in Strategic Financing*

Tesla's journey from a **high-risk start up to a dominant force in the automotive industry** is a testament to **smart financing and capital management**. In its early years, Tesla faced **significant funding challenges** as it attempted to disrupt the highly competitive car industry with electric vehicles.

To sustain operations and fund its ambitious production goals, Tesla leveraged **multiple financing sources**, including:

- **Venture Capital**: Early investors, including **Elon Musk**, contributed millions to keep the company afloat.

- **Government Loans**: In 2010, Tesla secured a **$465 million loan from the U.S. Department of Energy**, allowing it to scale production and refine its technology.
- **Equity Financing & IPO**: Later in 2010, Tesla raised **$226 million through an initial public offering (IPO)**, gaining the capital needed to expand.
- **Corporate Bonds & Stock Offerings**: Tesla continued to raise billions through **stock sales and bond offerings** to finance the launch of new models, such as the Model S, Model X, and Model 3.

## Lesson Learned:

Tesla's financing strategy demonstrates how businesses can combine **venture capital, government-backed loans, equity financing, and corporate debt** to achieve growth. The key takeaway is that companies must **align financing choices with long-term expansion goals** and **diversify funding sources** to reduce financial risk.

***Case Study 2: Airbnb – Scaling Through Investor Confidence & Adaptive Financing***

Airbnb started in **2008 as a struggling start up**, founded by **Brian Chesky, Joe Gebbia, and Nathan Blecharczyk**. The company was on the verge of failure when it implemented a **creative financing approach** to raise funds.

- **Bootstrapping & Crowdfunding**: In its earliest days, Airbnb sold **custom-designed cereal boxes ("Obama O's" and "Cap'n**

**McCain's") during the 2008 U.S. presidential election, raising $30,000** to sustain operations.

- **Angel Investors & Seed Funding**: Recognizing the company's potential, **Y Combinator invested $20,000** in 2009, followed by additional angel investments.
- **Venture Capital Funding**: Airbnb later secured **$600,000 from Sequoia Capital**, a crucial turning point that allowed the company to scale globally.
- **Private Equity & Later-Stage Funding**: Airbnb raised billions from investors, including **Andreessen Horowitz, Tiger Global, and Founders Fund**, to solidify its global presence.
- **Going Public**: In 2020, Airbnb launched its **IPO**, raising **$3.5 billion**—one of the biggest IPOs of the year.

## Lesson Learned:

Airbnb's financing story highlights **the power of investor confidence, adaptability, and creative funding strategies**. The company **leveraged multiple funding rounds, built strong investor relationships, and used capital efficiently** to scale into a **multi-billion-dollar global enterprise**.

***Case Study 3: Starbucks – Managing Debt & Equity for Expansion***

Starbucks, now a **global coffee giant**, had **humble beginnings as a single Seattle coffee shop in 1971**. The company's growth was fueled by **a strategic mix of debt financing, equity financing, and reinvested earnings**.

- **Early Expansion Through Bank Loans**: In its early years,

Starbucks took out **small business loans** to open additional locations.

- **Venture Capital Infusion**: In the late 1980s, Starbucks attracted **private investors**, allowing it to expand beyond Seattle.
- **Initial Public Offering (IPO) in 1992**: Starbucks went public and raised **$271 million**, funding rapid expansion across the U.S. and international markets.
- **Smart Debt Management**: Unlike many companies that over-leverage, Starbucks **carefully balanced its debt and equity,** ensuring it never took on excessive financial risk.
- **Ongoing Stock Buybacks & Dividends**: Over the years, Starbucks has **repurchased billions in company stock** while still investing in store expansions, technology, and employee benefits.

### Lesson Learned:

Starbucks' financing strategy showcases the importance of **gradually scaling financing options**—starting with **small business loans, attracting private investors, leveraging IPO capital, and using long-term debt responsibly**. The company's disciplined approach to **capital management** ensured **sustainable growth while minimizing financial risk**.

### Key Takeaways from These Case Studies

102. **Diversifying Financing Sources is Key** – Tesla, Airbnb, and Starbucks all used a mix of **venture capital, bank loans,**

**private equity, and IPOs** to fund their growth.

103. **Investor Confidence Matters** – Companies that **demonstrate strong growth potential** (like Airbnb and Tesla) attract investors willing to commit significant funding.

104. **Smart Debt Management Prevents Over-Leveraging** – Starbucks carefully managed its **debt-to-equity ratio**, ensuring that borrowing did not create financial instability.

105. **Creative Funding Approaches Work** – Airbnb's ability to **bootstrap** and raise early capital through **unconventional methods** gave it the breathing room to grow.

106. **Long-Term Planning Ensures Success** – Successful companies focus on **strategic financial planning**, ensuring they raise **capital when needed and avoid financial distress**.

These real-world case studies demonstrate that **smart capital management, strategic financing, and careful debt-equity balance are essential for scaling a business successfully**.

## The Importance of Smart Capital Management

The ability to **secure financing and manage capital effectively** is a critical skill that determines whether a business can grow, innovate, and survive economic challenges. Throughout this chapter, we explored **how businesses raise capital, manage working capital, and build financial resilience** through strategic decision-making. **Understanding and applying capital management principles is essential for maintaining stability, attracting investors, and ensuring sustainable business**

**expansion.**

One of the most important takeaways from this chapter is the distinction between **debt and equity financing**. Each method has its advantages and risks, and choosing the right one depends on a company's **growth stage, cash flow position, and risk tolerance. Debt financing** allows businesses to raise funds without giving up ownership but requires structured repayments that can become a financial burden if not managed properly. **Equity financing**, on the other hand, provides access to long-term capital without immediate repayment obligations but often comes at the cost of **shared ownership and profit dilution**. Businesses must carefully weigh these factors when seeking funding to ensure their financial strategy aligns with their long-term goals.

Another critical concept we explored is **working capital management**, which ensures a company has sufficient liquidity to cover short-term obligations. **Poor working capital management can lead to cash flow shortages, missed payments, and an inability to seize growth opportunities.** We examined strategies such as **accelerating receivables, optimizing inventory, and negotiating better payment terms with suppliers** to maintain a healthy cash flow balance. **Businesses that manage their working capital effectively can improve operational efficiency, reduce financial stress, and remain agile in uncertain market conditions.**

Additionally, we discussed **how businesses evaluate loan options and investor relations** when seeking financing. Business loans can provide necessary funding, but choosing the wrong type of loan or failing to account for high-interest rates can create long-term debt traps. Companies must carefully assess their **repayment capacity, interest obligations, and**

**alternative funding sources** before committing to any financial agreement. On the other hand, businesses that **cultivate strong investor relationships** can access funding with fewer financial risks while benefiting from strategic guidance, mentorship, and networking opportunities.

A key case study in this chapter was **Tesla's financing journey**, which demonstrated how a company can successfully **combine multiple financing sources** to scale and innovate. By securing **venture capital, government loans, and IPO funding**, Tesla was able to establish itself as a dominant player in the electric vehicle industry. This case study highlights the importance of **strategic funding decisions** and the ability to **adapt financial strategies to business needs and market conditions**.

Ultimately, **businesses that manage their capital wisely can scale their operations, invest in innovation, and navigate financial uncertainties with confidence**. Poor financial planning, on the other hand, can lead to over-leverage, financial distress, and missed opportunities. The most successful businesses are those that **balance financial discipline with growth-oriented decision-making, ensuring they have both the capital and the flexibility to thrive in competitive markets.**

# ADVANCED FORECASTING TECHNIQUES & FINANCIAL PLANNING APPLICATIONS

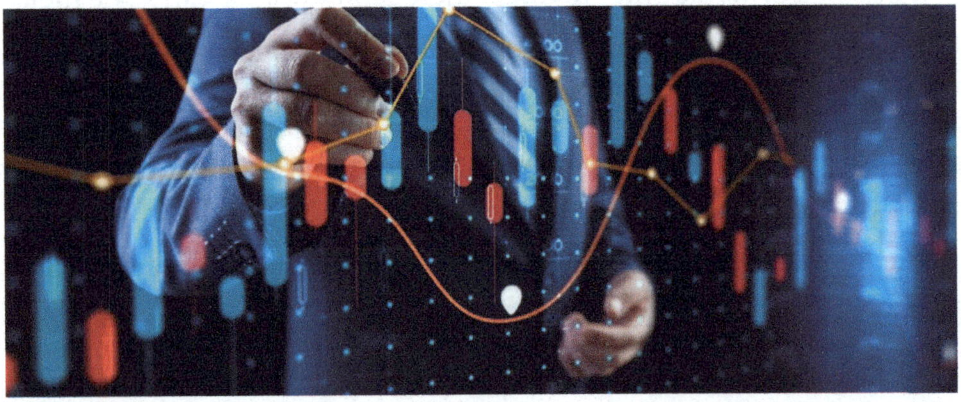

## Introduction: The Power of Forecasting in Financial Strategy

In today's fast-paced and unpredictable business landscape, financial forecasting is more than just a tool—it is a strategic necessity. While budgeting provides a financial roadmap, forecasting takes planning to the next level, offering **data-driven insights that help businesses anticipate future financial performance, mitigate risks, and seize**

**growth opportunities**.

A well-structured forecasting system allows businesses to **adapt quickly to market shifts, plan for different financial scenarios, and optimize decision-making based on real-time data.** Companies that rely solely on traditional budgeting methods risk making outdated assumptions, whereas those that leverage advanced forecasting can adjust their strategies dynamically, ensuring financial stability and long-term growth.

This chapter delves into the most **effective forecasting techniques, from predictive analytics to scenario modeling**, helping businesses transition from reactive decision-making to proactive financial planning. We will explore:

- How **advanced forecasting builds on traditional budgeting** to provide more accurate financial insights.
- The role of **AI and automation in enhancing forecasting accuracy** and decision-making.
- How businesses use **scenario-based forecasting** to prepare for best-case, moderate, and worst-case financial conditions.
- The difference between **short-term forecasting for cash flow management and long-term forecasting for strategic growth**.

By the end of this chapter, you will understand how to move beyond static financial planning and leverage dynamic forecasting techniques to drive business success, **improve risk management, and ensure sustainable financial growth.**

## How Budgeting Drives Financial Success

A budget is more than just a financial plan—it's a **powerful decision-making tool** that enables businesses to **spend wisely, manage cash flow efficiently, and stay ahead of financial risks**. Whether a company is launching a new product, expanding operations, or navigating uncertain market conditions, budgeting **ensures financial stability and strategic resource allocation**.

### Controlling Expenses and Allocating Resources Efficiently

Without a budget, businesses risk **overspending in some areas while neglecting critical investments**. Budgeting ensures that every dollar has a purpose, directing resources toward **the highest-impact areas** while preventing wasteful expenditures.

**Spending with Purpose:**

A well-planned budget helps businesses prioritize spending, ensuring that funds are allocated where they will generate the most value—**product development, marketing, technology upgrades, and operational efficiency**

**Maintaining Financial Discipline:** By setting clear spending limits, budgets prevent impulse decisions that can strain cash flow. Instead of reacting to financial shortfalls, businesses can **plan proactively and allocate resources efficiently**.

**Ensuring Liquidity for Growth:** A business that **manages expenses wisely** has more flexibility to invest in **innovation, expansion, and long-term projects** without jeopardizing short-term financial stability.

**Example:** A tech start up carefully budgets its marketing expenses, ensuring that **customer acquisition costs remain sustainable**. By tracking spending and reallocating funds to the most effective campaigns, the company maximizes **ROI while staying within financial limits**.

**Predicting Cash Flow Needs and Avoiding Liquidity Shortages**

A business can be profitable on paper but still struggle with **cash flow shortages** if it doesn't manage inflows and outflows effectively. A budget acts as a **cash flow roadmap**, helping businesses:

**Ensure On-Time Payments:**

By forecasting income and expenses, businesses can **plan ahead for payroll, supplier invoices, rent, and loan repayments** reducing the risk of missed payments.

**Prepare for Seasonal Variations:** Businesses with **fluctuating revenue**—such as retail stores, tourism companies, and agricultural businesses—can use budgeting to **set aside reserves during peak seasons** to sustain operations during slower periods.

**Anticipate Financial Gaps:** A well-structured budget highlights potential cash shortfalls in advance, allowing businesses to secure financing, **adjust spending, or increase revenue efforts before a crisis arises**.

**Example:** A landscaping business experiences **lower revenue in winter** but plans for this by setting aside a portion of summer profits. Through careful budgeting, the company maintains **enough cash to cover expenses during slow months**, avoiding the need for emergency loans.

**Measuring Performance: Turning Financial Data into Action**

A budget isn't just a **prediction tool**—it's a **performance benchmark** that helps businesses assess how well they are managing their finances. By comparing **actual financial results to budgeted projections**, managers can identify:

**Spending Overruns:**

If costs exceed budgeted amounts, businesses can investigate the cause and adjust spending accordingly.

**Underutilized Resources:** If certain departments **consistently underspend**, it may indicate inefficiencies or missed growth opportunities.

**Profitability Gaps:** Budget variances highlight **whether sales targets, profit margins, and cost-cutting initiatives are on track** or need adjustments.

**Example:** A restaurant budgeted **$10,000 per month** for food supplies but discovers actual costs have risen to **$12,500** due to **supplier price increases**. The management team responds by negotiating better pricing, adjusting portion sizes, and revising menu prices to protect **profit margins without sacrificing quality**.

**Why Budgeting is Essential for Business Longevity**

Without a clear financial plan, businesses **operate in the dark**, making decisions based on guesswork rather than data. Budgeting provides **clarity, control, and confidence**, ensuring that financial resources are **used wisely, cash flow remains stable, and performance is continuously measured and improved**.

By integrating budgeting into financial strategy, businesses can: **Maintain financial stability and avoid unnecessary debt. Identify growth opportunities and optimize spending. Ensure sustainable cash flow**

**and long-term success.**

**Bottom Line:** A well-planned budget transforms **financial uncertainty into strategic financial control**, helping businesses **stay competitive, adapt to market conditions, and achieve sustainable growth**.

### Real-World Example: The Importance of Budgeting

A **small restaurant chain** creates a **quarterly budget** to plan for expenses like food inventory, employee wages, and marketing campaigns. By **monitoring actual expenses against the budget**, the owner discovers that food costs are **10% higher than projected** due to supplier price increases. The business responds by:

- **Negotiating new contracts with suppliers to reduce costs.**
- **Adjusting menu prices slightly to maintain profitability.**
- **Exploring cost-saving measures such as reducing food waste.**

By using budgeting to **identify financial inefficiencies**, the restaurant avoids unnecessary losses and improves its **financial health**.

## Common Budgeting Techniques

Businesses use different budgeting approaches depending on their **size, industry, and financial strategy**. Choosing the right budgeting method ensures that businesses **allocate funds effectively, plan for uncertainties, and stay financially stable**.

## Incremental Budgeting – Adjusting Past Budgets for Expected Growth

Incremental budgeting involves **taking last year's budget and making adjustments** based on expected revenue changes, inflation, or company goals.

- **Advantages:**
- Simple and easy to implement
- Works well for **stable businesses with predictable expenses**.
- **Disadvantages:**
- **Does not encourage cost efficiency**—departments may continue receiving unnecessary funding
- **fail to account for changing business needs** or market shifts.

**Example:** A manufacturing company increases its budget by **5% annually** to account for **inflation and labor costs**, without reviewing whether all previous expenses are still necessary.

## Zero-Based Budgeting – Justifying Every Expense from Scratch

Zero-based budgeting (ZBB) requires businesses to **re-evaluate all expenses each year, rather than automatically increasing budgets based on previous spending**.

- **Advantages:**
- Forces managers to **justify every expense**, preventing wasteful

spending.

- Encourages **cost-cutting and efficiency**.
- **Disadvantages:**
- Time-consuming, requiring **detailed analysis** and justification of all costs
- Can disrupt business operations if **essential expenses are overlooked**.

**Example:** A software company using ZBB may decide to **eliminate low-performing marketing channels** while increasing investment in **social media ads that generate higher ROI**.

## Rolling Budgets – Continuous Updates Based on Real-Time Financial Data

Rolling budgets are **dynamic budgets that are updated periodically (monthly, quarterly) instead of being fixed for an entire year**.

- **Advantages:**
- Allows businesses to **adjust spending based on actual performance** and market conditions
- Reduces **forecasting errors** by continuously revising financial projections.
- **Disadvantages:**
- Requires **constant monitoring** and financial adjustments, making it resource-intensive.

**Example:** A tech start up **updates its budget every three months**, adjusting marketing and hiring plans based on its latest sales growth and funding status.

## Forecasting for Financial Planning

Budgeting alone is **not enough**—businesses must also **forecast future financial trends** to stay ahead of **market shifts and economic fluctuations**. Forecasting provides a **data-driven approach** to predicting future revenue, expenses, and profitability.

### Qualitative vs. Quantitative Forecasting

**Qualitative Forecasting – Expert Opinions & Market Research**

Used when **historical data is unavailable or unreliable** (e.g., launching a new product).

Involves input from **industry experts, customer surveys, and market trends**.

Commonly used in **start ups, emerging industries, and fast-changing markets**.

**Example:** A new electric car manufacturer consults **industry experts and analyzes consumer demand trends** to estimate future sales.

**Quantitative Forecasting – Statistical & Financial Data Analysis**

Uses **historical financial data** to predict future revenue and expenses.

Includes **trend analysis, regression models, and time-series forecasting**.

More accurate for **established businesses with consistent financial trends**.

**Example:** A retail chain uses past sales data and seasonal trends to forecast **holiday sales projections** for inventory planning.

## How Budgeting and Forecasting Work Together

**Budgeting and forecasting are complementary tools:**

- **Budgeting** sets **spending limits** and helps businesses **allocate resources** based on planned financial goals.
- **Forecasting** provides **updated financial predictions** based on real-time data, allowing businesses to **adjust their budgets as needed**.

### Example: Retail Business Budgeting & Forecasting Integration

A **clothing retailer** creates an **annual budget** based on last year's sales. However, after **six months**, market trends indicate that **consumer demand for sustainable fashion is rising**. The company **updates its sales forecast** and **shifts marketing and inventory budgets toward eco-friendly clothing**, ensuring they **capitalize on market trends rather than sticking to outdated projections**.

## Best Practices for Effective Budgeting & Forecasting

**Use Real-Time Data** – Businesses should leverage **modern accounting**

**software and financial dashboards** to track spending and update forecasts.

**Involve Multiple Departments** – Collaboration between **finance, marketing, operations, and HR** ensures budgets reflect **real business needs**.

**Set Flexible Budgets** – Companies should **leave room for unexpected costs** or revenue fluctuations.

**Review and Adjust Regularly** – A budget is a **living document** that should be revisited **monthly or quarterly** to reflect changing market conditions.

## Conclusion: How Budgeting & Forecasting Drive Business Success

Budgeting and forecasting are **more than just financial tools**—they are the **cornerstones of strategic business management**. They provide the foundation for **financial stability, informed decision-making, and long-term growth**. Without a structured approach to budgeting and forecasting, businesses risk **overspending, cash flow shortages, and missed opportunities for expansion**.

A well-designed budgeting system **ensures that financial resources are allocated efficiently**, while forecasting allows businesses to **anticipate future financial needs, identify potential risks, and adjust strategies proactively**. Whether a business is a **startup trying to manage initial capital**, an **established company planning expansion**, or a **corporation navigating an uncertain economy**, mastering budgeting and forecasting is essential for **financial resilience and long-term profitability**.

## Key Lessons from This Chapter:

**Budgeting Creates Financial Discipline & Accountability**

A structured budget ensures that every dollar spent is **aligned with business objectives** and that financial resources are **used efficiently**.

Businesses that practice disciplined budgeting **avoid unnecessary expenses**, improve cost control, and ensure sustainable cash flow.

**Choosing the Right Budgeting Method is Critical for Success**

Different businesses require different budgeting approaches—**incremental budgeting works for predictable expenses**, while **zero-based budgeting** is ideal for companies looking to **eliminate inefficiencies**.

**Rolling budgets provide flexibility**, allowing businesses to adjust financial plans based on real-time market data.

**Forecasting Enhances Financial Agility**

- Forecasting allows businesses to **predict revenue trends, estimate expenses, and adjust financial strategies based on market shifts**.
- By combining **qualitative insights** (expert opinions and market research) with **quantitative analysis** (historical data and financial modeling), businesses can make **proactive, data-driven decisions**.

**Budgeting & Forecasting Work Best When Integrated**

- Budgeting **sets financial boundaries**, while forecasting **helps businesses adjust to changing conditions**.
- Companies that continuously update budgets based on **forecasted**

**financial data** are better prepared to **respond to unexpected challenges, seize opportunities, and maintain profitability**.

**Businesses that Master Budgeting & Forecasting Achieve Long-Term Financial Stability**

- Companies that **align budgeting and forecasting with their business goals** experience greater financial control, improved decision-making, and higher profitability.
- A strong budgeting and forecasting process enables businesses to **secure funding, manage risks, and optimize resource allocation for long-term success**.

## Why Advanced Forecasting is Essential for Business Success

Forecasting is not about predicting the future with certainty—it is about preparing for multiple possible outcomes and making informed financial decisions based on the best available data. **Businesses that master forecasting gain a significant competitive edge, as they can adjust quickly to market conditions, minimize financial risk, and optimize resource allocation.**

Throughout this chapter, we have explored how businesses can **move beyond traditional budgeting and integrate advanced forecasting techniques,** including:

- **Data-driven forecasting models** that use past financial trends to anticipate future performance.
- **Predictive analytics and AI-powered forecasting tools** that

improve accuracy and automate decision-making.

- **Scenario-based financial planning**, which helps businesses prepare for different market conditions.
- **Short-term vs. long-term forecasting**, ensuring businesses maintain both immediate liquidity and long-term financial stability.

The companies that **embrace forecasting as a core financial strategy are the ones that thrive in dynamic markets.** Whether navigating economic downturns, expanding into new markets, or optimizing operational costs, **forecasting enables businesses to act proactively rather than reactively.**

Looking ahead, **forecasting is closely linked to financial performance measurement.** In the next chapter, we will explore **Ratio Analysis for Business Growth,** where we will break down the key financial ratios that businesses use to **assess profitability, liquidity, efficiency, and risk.** These ratios allow businesses to **quantify the effectiveness of their forecasting strategies and make data-driven adjustments for sustainable success.**

## Key Takeaways

- **Forecasting builds on budgeting, allowing businesses to prepare for multiple financial scenarios.**
- **AI, predictive analytics, and automation improve the accuracy and efficiency of financial forecasting.**
- **Scenario planning helps businesses create adaptable financial strategies that minimize risk.**

- **Companies that integrate forecasting with financial planning gain greater control over cash flow, investments, and resource allocation.**
- **The next step in financial strategy is measuring forecasting effectiveness using ratio analysis, ensuring businesses stay financially strong and competitive.**

# RATIO ANALYSIS FOR BUSINESS GROWTH

## Introduction: The Power of Financial Ratios in Business Decision-Making

Ratio analysis is a cornerstone of financial management, providing business leaders, investors, and stakeholders with valuable insights into a company's financial health. By evaluating key financial ratios, businesses can measure liquidity, profitability, efficiency, and overall performance. These ratios help in identifying strengths, weaknesses, and potential risks, allowing for informed decision-making and strategic planning.

Understanding financial ratios is essential for businesses of all sizes, from start ups looking to secure investment to established corporations aiming to optimize performance. Ratios serve as a diagnostic tool, revealing whether a company is maintaining strong cash flow, generating sufficient profit, or using assets efficiently. When used effectively, financial ratios provide a roadmap for sustainable growth, guiding businesses in areas such as pricing strategies, expense management, and capital allocation.

A well-performing business does not rely solely on revenue figures or net profits; it closely monitors financial ratios to assess whether operations are efficient, whether it is adequately managing liabilities, and whether its financial strategies align with long-term goals. Companies that ignore these ratios may find themselves facing unexpected liquidity crises, declining profitability, or operational inefficiencies that erode market competitiveness.

This chapter explores key financial ratios, how to interpret them, and their role in decision-making. It also presents a real-world case study demonstrating how a business leveraged ratio analysis to uncover financial vulnerabilities and implement corrective measures. The chapter concludes with a practical exercise designed to reinforce the application of financial ratio analysis.

# Key Financial Ratios: Liquidity, Profitability, and Efficiency Metrics

## Liquidity Ratios: Measuring Financial Stability

Liquidity ratios determine whether a business has enough short-term assets to cover immediate obligations. These ratios are critical for evaluating a company's ability to meet day-to-day financial commitments and avoid cash flow crises.

The **current ratio** compares current assets to current liabilities, helping businesses assess their short-term financial health. A current ratio below **1.0** may indicate liquidity risk, while an excessively high ratio could suggest that assets are not being utilized effectively.

The **quick ratio**, also known as the acid-test ratio, is a more stringent measure of liquidity because it excludes inventory. This ratio is particularly relevant for businesses with slow-moving inventory, such as manufacturers or wholesalers, where assets may take time to convert into cash.

A company with a declining liquidity ratio may need to **improve its cash flow, renegotiate supplier terms, or secure additional working capital** to avoid financial distress.

## Profitability Ratios: Assessing Business Performance

Profitability ratios measure how efficiently a company converts revenue into profit. These ratios help businesses determine whether their pricing strategy is effective and whether costs are being managed appropriately.

The **gross profit margin** calculates the percentage of revenue remaining after accounting for the cost of goods sold. A company with a declining gross profit margin may be experiencing rising production costs or price competition in the market.

The **net profit margin** accounts for all expenses, including operating costs, interest, and taxes, providing a clearer picture of overall profitability. A company with a high net profit margin relative to competitors may have a competitive advantage through **cost control or premium pricing strategies**.

Another critical profitability ratio is **return on assets (ROA)**, which measures how efficiently a business utilizes its total assets to generate profit. A declining ROA may indicate inefficient asset usage or poor investment decisions.

For investors, the **return on equity (ROE)** is an essential metric, as it reflects how much profit a company generates from shareholder investments. A low or declining ROE may suggest that the company is not maximizing shareholder value.

## Efficiency Ratios: Optimizing Business Operations

Efficiency ratios, also called activity ratios, assess how well a company uses its assets to generate revenue. These ratios are particularly valuable for understanding **inventory management, receivables collection, and asset utilization**.

The **inventory turnover ratio** measures how quickly a company sells its inventory. A **low inventory turnover** may indicate slow-moving products, excessive stock levels, or weak demand. In contrast, a **high inventory turnover** suggests strong sales and efficient inventory management.

The **accounts receivable turnover ratio** evaluates how effectively a company collects payments from customers. A **declining receivables turnover ratio** may signal that the business is offering overly lenient payment terms or experiencing delays in collections, potentially leading to cash flow problems.

The **asset turnover ratio** measures how efficiently a company uses its assets to generate revenue. A high asset turnover ratio indicates that a business is making good use of its assets, while a low ratio suggests underutilization.

By regularly monitoring efficiency ratios, companies can **identify operational inefficiencies, improve cash flow, and refine business strategies** to enhance financial performance.

## Benchmarking and Industry Comparisons

Financial ratios become even more meaningful when compared against **industry benchmarks and competitors**. A ratio that appears strong in isolation may be **below average for a specific industry**, indicating underperformance.

For example, a **grocery retailer** with a net profit margin of **4%** might be performing well in an industry where margins are typically **2-3%**, whereas a **software company** with a **10% net profit margin** may be underperforming if industry peers average **20%**.

Investors and lenders rely on industry comparisons to **assess financial risk and growth potential**, making benchmarking an essential part of financial analysis.

## Limitations of Ratio Analysis

While financial ratios provide valuable insights, they should not be viewed in isolation. Several external factors can influence ratio results, including **economic conditions, seasonal fluctuations, and changes in business strategy**.

Ratios also do not account for **non-financial factors** such as **brand reputation, employee productivity, and innovation**, which can significantly impact a company's long-term success.

Additionally, businesses can **manipulate financial ratios** through accounting adjustments, making it essential to analyze ratios in conjunction with other financial statements and operational data.

## Case Study: How a Business Used Ratios to Spot Financial Issues

A mid-sized manufacturing company specializing in industrial equipment experienced declining profits despite steady sales. Management was unsure of the cause, as revenue remained stable, but operational costs appeared to be rising. To diagnose the issue, the company conducted a detailed **financial ratio analysis**.

The **gross profit margin** had dropped significantly over the past two years. Further analysis revealed that the **cost of raw materials had increased**, but the company had not adjusted its pricing strategy.

The **inventory turnover ratio** showed that products were staying in stock longer than usual, indicating **overproduction** and **poor inventory management**.

The **accounts receivable turnover ratio** revealed that customers were **taking longer to pay invoices**, affecting cash flow. This was due to **looser credit terms** and inadequate follow-up on overdue payments.

Armed with these insights, the company **adjusted its pricing strategy, reduced inventory levels, and tightened credit policies**. Within six months, **profitability improved, cash flow stabilized, and inventory turnover increased**.

This case study highlights how **financial ratios can uncover inefficiencies and drive proactive decision-making**.

## How to Interpret and Use Ratios for Decision-Making

Interpreting financial ratios requires more than simply calculating them; businesses must analyze trends, compare ratios against industry benchmarks, and use them to inform strategic decisions. Financial ratios provide context, enabling businesses to assess their performance over time and relative to competitors.

For example, a retail company with a declining gross profit margin might investigate whether rising production costs, excessive discounting, or supply chain inefficiencies are eroding profitability. A manufacturer with a low inventory turnover ratio may need to adjust its purchasing strategy or streamline production to avoid excess stock and obsolescence. A technology firm with a high accounts receivable turnover ratio may have a strong cash collection process, but if sales growth is stagnant, it may need to revisit its pricing model or market expansion strategy.

Ratios are also critical in identifying financial red flags before they escalate into major problems. A company with a deteriorating current ratio may face liquidity challenges, indicating that it should reduce expenses, renegotiate supplier terms, or secure short-term financing to maintain stability. A declining return on equity could suggest that the company is not using its shareholders' investments effectively, prompting management to re evaluate capital expenditures or explore new revenue streams.

In the investment world, financial analysts and creditors use ratios to assess a company's risk profile. Banks examine liquidity ratios before approving loans, ensuring that businesses have the capacity to meet debt obligations. Investors compare profitability and efficiency ratios to determine which companies are best positioned for long-term growth and sustainable earnings. Businesses that actively monitor and interpret their financial ratios gain a competitive edge, allowing them to make proactive decisions that drive profitability and operational efficiency.

## Practical Exercise: Financial Ratio Analysis in Decision-Making

### *Company Profile*

The company operates in the **consumer electronics industry**, specializing in **home appliances and smart devices**. Over the past two years, it has **expanded operations**, investing heavily in **inventory and marketing** to increase market share. Despite **steady revenue growth**, the company has **seen rising production costs** and **customer payment delays** affecting cash flow.

*Financial Data*

- **Total Revenue:** $5,000,000
- **Cost of Goods Sold:** $3,000,000
- **Net Profit:** $500,000
- **Total Assets:** $10,000,000
- **Total Liabilities:** $4,000,000
- **Current Assets:** $2,500,000
- **Current Liabilities:** $1,500,000
- **Inventory:** $800,000
- **Accounts Receivable:** $600,000
- **Dividends Paid:** $100,000
- **Operating Expenses:** $1,200,000
- **Interest Expense:** $50,000

*Industry Benchmarks (Hypothetical Averages for the Consumer Electronics Sector)*

- **Gross Profit Margin:** 45%
- **Net Profit Margin:** 12%
- **Current Ratio:** 2.0
- **Quick Ratio:** 1.2
- **Inventory Turnover Ratio:** 6.0

- **Accounts Receivable Turnover Ratio:** 10.0
- **Return on Assets (ROA):** 8%
- **Return on Equity (ROE):** 15%

## Analysis Questions:

107. **Profitability Analysis:**

- Calculate the **gross profit margin** and **net profit margin**.
- Compare these margins to the **industry benchmarks**.
- What does the company's profitability suggest about **cost management and pricing strategies**?

108. **Liquidity Analysis:**

- Calculate the **current ratio** and **quick ratio** to determine whether the company can **cover short-term obligations**.
- Given the **current financial position**, does the company have sufficient liquidity to manage unexpected costs?

109. **Efficiency Analysis:**

- Determine the **inventory turnover ratio** and **accounts receivable turnover ratio** to assess **how well the company manages inventory and collects payments.**
- Is the company holding **too much inventory**, or are **customers taking too long to pay**?

110. **Investment Decision:**

- Compute **return on assets (ROA) and return on equity (ROE)**.
- Compare these figures to **industry averages**.
- Based on this analysis, would you **invest in this company**, or are there **red flags that need to be addressed**?

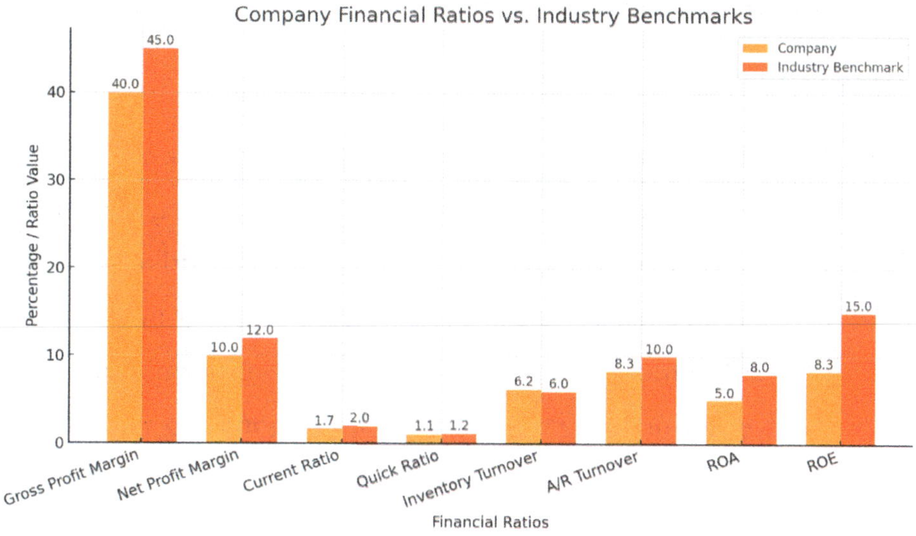


## Analysis of Financial Ratios

### *Profitability Analysis*

- The **gross profit margin** for the company is **40%**, which is lower than the **industry benchmark of 45%**. This suggests that the company is **spending more on production costs relative to its revenue** compared to industry competitors. This could indicate **higher raw material costs, inefficient production processes, or weaker pricing power**. The company may need to **reassess its cost structure** and explore ways to improve efficiency or **increase product pricing** to improve margins.

- The **net profit margin** stands at **10%**, compared to the **industry average of 12%**. While the company is still generating profit, it is slightly below industry standards. This may indicate that **operating expenses, interest payments, or administrative costs are eating into profits**. The business should evaluate its **cost management strategy** to improve net profitability.

*Liquidity Analysis*

- The **current ratio** is **1.67**, slightly below the **industry benchmark of 2.0**. This means that while the company has enough current assets to cover its current liabilities, it is **not as liquid as industry peers**. If an unexpected expense arises, the company may face **cash flow difficulties**. Strengthening liquidity through **improving cash reserves, optimizing receivables, or renegotiating short-term debt** could improve financial flexibility.

- The **quick ratio**, which removes inventory from current assets to measure the company's immediate liquidity, is **1.13**, compared to the **industry standard of 1.2**. Since the quick ratio is slightly below the benchmark, the company **might be relying too much on inventory sales to meet short-term obligations**. A more **aggressive accounts receivable collection strategy or a slight reduction in inventory levels** could improve short-term liquidity.

*Efficiency Analysis*

- The **inventory turnover ratio** is **6.25**, which is slightly above the **industry benchmark of 6.0**. This indicates that the company is **moving inventory efficiently**, likely keeping up with customer demand. However, if turnover is increasing too much, there could be a risk of **understocking or supply chain constraints** affecting sales. Maintaining a **balanced inventory level** is crucial.

- The **accounts receivable turnover ratio** is **8.33**, below the **industry benchmark of 10.0**. This suggests that customers **are taking longer to pay invoices** compared to industry standards, which can lead to **cash flow problems**. The company may need to **tighten credit policies, offer early payment incentives, or follow up more aggressively on overdue invoices** to improve collections.

***Investment Decision***

- The **return on assets (ROA)** is **5%**, compared to the **industry benchmark of 8%**. This means the company **is not utilizing its assets as efficiently as competitors to generate profit**. This could be due to **underutilized machinery, excess cash reserves, or inefficient investment in fixed assets**. Optimizing asset allocation or improving operational efficiency could enhance profitability.
- The **return on equity (ROE)** is **8.33%**, which is significantly lower than the **industry benchmark of 15%**. This suggests that the company **is not providing the same level of returns to its shareholders as its competitors**. Investors may see this as a **red flag**, indicating that the company **is not leveraging equity effectively to generate profit**. Management should consider **better capital allocation strategies, cost-cutting measures, or revenue expansion opportunities** to improve shareholder returns.

***Final Interpretation: Should You Invest?***

Based on the ratio analysis, the company has **stable profitability and good inventory turnover**, but **slightly weaker liquidity, lower efficiency in collecting payments, and underperforming ROA and ROE** compared to industry standards.

If considering an investment, one should be cautious about **lower-than-average profitability and investor returns**. However, if the company can **improve cost management, strengthen liquidity, and optimize asset utilization**, it could become a **stronger investment opportunity**. Investors might want to **wait and see if the company implements these improvements before committing capital**.

## Conclusion: The Significance of Financial Ratio Analysis in Business Growth

Financial ratio analysis is an indispensable tool for understanding a company's **financial health, operational efficiency, and overall business performance**. Throughout this chapter, we have explored how liquidity, profitability, and efficiency ratios provide valuable insights that enable business leaders, investors, and financial analysts to make **informed, data-driven decisions**. A company's financial statements contain an overwhelming amount of raw data, but without proper interpretation through ratio analysis, much of this information remains meaningless. By breaking down financial data into key ratios, businesses can **identify strengths, uncover weaknesses, and implement corrective strategies** to ensure sustainable success.

One of the most critical takeaways from this chapter is the importance of **liquidity management**. The ability to meet **short-term financial obligations** without relying on excessive borrowing is a hallmark of a financially sound company. Liquidity ratios, such as the **current ratio and quick ratio**, allow businesses to assess whether they have sufficient assets to cover liabilities in case of unexpected expenses. A company that fails to maintain a healthy liquidity ratio may face **cash flow shortages**, struggle to pay suppliers, and ultimately weaken its market position. As we have seen in the analysis exercise, even a slightly lower-than-average **quick ratio** can signal potential liquidity risks, emphasizing the need for **proactive financial planning**.

Profitability ratios, on the other hand, provide a clear measure of a company's **ability to generate profit from its operations**. The **gross profit margin and net profit margin** help businesses determine whether they are pricing their products effectively, controlling production costs, and managing operating expenses efficiently. A business with declining profitability must investigate **whether rising costs, inefficient operations, or weak demand** are eroding its margins. The ability to maintain a strong **return on assets (ROA) and return on equity (ROE)** is essential for ensuring **long-term sustainability and investor confidence**. Companies that underperform in these areas may struggle to attract investors, secure financing, or expand their market share.

Efficiency ratios reveal how well a company **utilizes its assets and manages operational processes**. The **inventory turnover ratio** is particularly important in industries that rely on physical products, as it indicates how quickly inventory is being sold and replaced. A business with a low inventory turnover may be **overproducing, experiencing weak**

**demand, or struggling with excess stock**, which can tie up cash that could be used elsewhere. Similarly, the **accounts receivable turnover ratio** highlights how effectively a company is collecting payments from customers. As seen in our analysis, a company that struggles with collecting payments in a timely manner risks **cash flow problems and liquidity constraints**. Businesses must strike the right balance between offering **flexible credit terms** and ensuring **strong cash collection policies** to avoid financial instability.

A key lesson from this chapter is that financial ratio analysis is **not just about numbers**—it is about understanding the **bigger picture of business performance and strategy**. A company with strong liquidity but poor profitability may be at risk of financial stagnation. Conversely, a company with high profitability but weak liquidity may struggle with cash flow issues that could **threaten long-term survival**. Financial ratios must be analyzed **in combination**, rather than in isolation, to gain a **holistic view of business health**.

We also explored how **benchmarking against industry standards** helps businesses **evaluate their competitive position**. A company may appear to be performing well when viewed independently, but if its financial ratios are **significantly lower than industry averages**, it may indicate **competitive weaknesses**. Investors and lenders rely heavily on ratio comparisons to determine whether a business is a **strong candidate for investment or financing**. Businesses that regularly compare their ratios with competitors can **identify market trends, adapt their strategies, and maintain a competitive edge**.

One of the most valuable aspects of ratio analysis is its ability to **detect financial red flags before they escalate into major problems**. By monitoring key financial metrics, businesses can take **preemptive action to resolve inefficiencies, improve liquidity, and optimize profitability**. A declining **net profit margin**, for example, can signal cost inefficiencies or weak revenue generation. A **low return on equity (ROE)** may indicate that a company is **not maximizing shareholder investment**, which can reduce investor confidence. Addressing these issues early allows businesses to **implement corrective strategies, strengthen financial health, and position themselves for long-term growth**.

In the practical exercise, we applied these principles to a real-world financial scenario, demonstrating how financial ratios can **identify potential challenges and guide strategic decision-making**. The results highlighted areas where the company performed well and where improvements were needed. While the company exhibited **stable inventory turnover and profitability**, it lagged behind in **liquidity and accounts receivable collection**, pointing to potential **cash flow risks and inefficient working capital management**. These insights are invaluable, as they provide **concrete data on where adjustments are required** to enhance financial stability.

The broader implication of ratio analysis is that businesses that consistently track and interpret their financial ratios are **better equipped to adapt to market changes, anticipate financial risks, and seize growth opportunities**. Companies that fail to analyze their ratios risk making decisions based on **incomplete or misleading information**, which can lead to **inefficient resource allocation, missed opportunities, and financial distress**.

In today's rapidly evolving business landscape, where competition is fierce and economic conditions fluctuate, the ability to conduct **comprehensive**

**financial analysis** is a crucial differentiator. Companies that use financial ratios effectively can make **data-driven decisions, optimize cost structures, and enhance operational efficiency**, ultimately achieving **long-term sustainability and profitability**.

# BUSINESS VALUATION & EXIT STRATEGIES

## Why Business Valuation Matters

Every business owner, investor, and financial professional will eventually face questions about business valuation. Whether planning to sell, attract investors, or prepare for an IPO, understanding how to assess and maximize a company's value is critical.

Business valuation is not just about numbers—it is about positioning a company for financial success, strategic growth, and a well-executed exit plan.

In this chapter, we will explore the key valuation methods used in the financial world, the strategic planning behind mergers and acquisitions, and the steps required for a successful exit strategy. The ability to accurately value a business gives decision-makers the power to negotiate better deals, attract investment, and build long-term financial stability.

## Methods of Business Valuation

Business valuation is both an art and a science. It involves financial analysis, market conditions, competitive positioning, and future growth potential. There are several widely accepted valuation methods, each applicable to different types of businesses and industries.

### *1. Asset-Based Valuation*

This method determines a company's worth based on the total value of its tangible and intangible assets, minus liabilities. It is commonly used for asset-heavy businesses such as manufacturing, real estate, and retail.

**When to Use It:**

- For businesses with significant tangible assets, such as property, equipment, or intellectual property.
- In liquidation scenarios where the company is being dissolved, and assets are being sold off.

**Challenges:**

- It does not account for future earnings potential.
- Intangible assets such as brand value and customer loyalty may be difficult to quantify accurately.

### *2. Earnings Multiples (Market-Based Valuation)*

This approach values a company based on its earnings, applying a multiple derived from comparable companies in the industry. It is widely used for businesses with strong cash flows and consistent profitability.

**Key Metrics:**

- Price-to-Earnings (P/E) Ratio – Measures how much investors are willing to pay for each dollar of earnings.
- EBITDA Multiple – Evaluates a company's value based on its Earnings Before Interest, Taxes, Depreciation, and Amortization.

**When to Use It:**

- When comparing a business to publicly traded companies or industry benchmarks.
- For companies seeking investors who want to understand profitability and return on investment.

**Challenges:**

- Market fluctuations can impact valuation multiples.
- Does not factor in future growth potential beyond current earnings.

### *3. Discounted Cash Flow (DCF) Analysis*

DCF valuation estimates the present value of a business based on its projected future cash flows. By discounting future earnings to today's value, this method provides a detailed, forward-looking perspective.

**When to Use It:**

- For businesses with long-term growth potential.
- When valuing companies with stable and predictable cash flows, such as subscription-based businesses.

**Challenges:**

- Requires accurate forecasting of future revenues and expenses.
- Small changes in assumptions (discount rate, growth rate) can significantly impact valuation.

### *4. Market Comparisons (Comparable Company Analysis - CCA)*

This method evaluates a business based on similar companies that have recently been sold or acquired. It is widely used in mergers and acquisitions.

**When to Use It:**

- When there are enough comparable businesses to benchmark against.
- In industries where mergers and acquisitions are common, providing recent market valuation data.

**Challenges:**

- No two businesses are exactly alike, making direct comparisons difficult.

- Market conditions at the time of sale influence valuation figures.

## Preparing for Investor Buyouts & Mergers

For business owners looking to attract investors or position their company for acquisition, financial transparency, and strategic positioning are essential.

**1. Strong Financial Reporting** Investors and buyers want to see well-organized financial statements, clear revenue models, and predictable cash flows. Proper financial reporting ensures that a business looks attractive on paper and meets due diligence requirements.

**2. Optimizing Business Operations** A company that demonstrates efficiency, scalability, and profitability is more appealing to buyers. Businesses preparing for acquisition should streamline operations, reduce unnecessary expenses, and maximize cash flow to enhance valuation.

**3. Understanding Buyer Motivations** Strategic buyers seek businesses that complement their existing operations, while financial buyers focus on potential return on investment. Knowing the buyer's goals allows businesses to position themselves for maximum valuation.

**4. Due Diligence Preparation** A thorough due diligence process examines financial health, legal obligations, intellectual property, employee contracts, and customer agreements. Businesses that proactively prepare for due diligence are more likely to secure favorable terms.

## IPO Planning & Public Market Entry

Going public is a major milestone for any company, but it requires rigorous financial preparation and regulatory compliance.

**1. Financial Readiness** Companies planning an Initial Public Offering (IPO) must demonstrate strong revenue growth, profitability, and transparent financial reporting. Investors demand detailed financial projections and risk assessments before committing capital.

**2. Regulatory Compliance** Public companies must adhere to strict financial regulations, including disclosure requirements and governance standards. Compliance with accounting standards such as GAAP or IFRS is non-negotiable.

**3. Investor Relations Strategy** A successful IPO involves attracting institutional and retail investors. Companies must communicate their long-term vision, market opportunity, and financial strength to potential shareholders.

**4. Costs & Risks** Going public involves significant costs, including underwriting fees, legal expenses, and ongoing compliance costs. Companies must weigh the benefits of raising capital against the long-term obligations of public ownership.

## Strategic Exit Planning

Not all business owners intend to run their companies forever. A well-planned exit strategy ensures that ownership transitions are smooth and financially rewarding.

**1. Selling to a Competitor or Strategic Buyer** Some businesses find that selling to a competitor or industry leader is the best exit strategy. These buyers often seek market expansion, intellectual property, or talent acquisition.

**2. Management Buyouts (MBOs)** In a management buyout, existing leadership purchases the company from the owner. This allows continuity in business operations while ensuring a smooth transition.

**3. Family Business Succession** For family-owned businesses, succession planning is crucial. Identifying and training the next generation of leadership ensures long-term stability.

**4. Liquidation as a Last Resort** If a business is no longer viable, liquidation allows owners to sell off assets and close operations. While not ideal, it ensures creditors and stakeholders are compensated.

## Case Studies: Successful Business Valuations & Exits

Examining real-world examples of successful business valuations and exits provides valuable insights into best practices.

**Amazon's Acquisition of Whole Foods (2017)** Amazon's $13.7 billion acquisition of Whole Foods was a strategic move to enter the grocery industry. By leveraging data analytics and e-commerce expertise, Amazon transformed Whole Foods into a more tech-driven retail operation.

**Facebook's Acquisition of Instagram (2012)** Facebook acquired Instagram for $1 billion when it had only 13 employees and no revenue. The acquisition was based on future growth potential rather than current earnings, demonstrating the importance of long-term valuation strategies.

**Tesla's Stock Growth & Market Capitalization** Tesla's stock valuation skyrocketed due to strong investor confidence in its long-term vision, innovation, and revenue potential. Despite early losses, Tesla's ability to scale and maintain profitability made it one of the most valuable companies in the world.

## Conclusion: The Art of Business Valuation & Exit Planning

Business valuation is more than just financial calculations—it is about strategic positioning, future growth, and financial discipline. Whether preparing for investment, acquisition, or an IPO, companies must align their valuation strategies with long-term business goals.

A well-executed exit strategy ensures that business owners maximize returns while securing the company's future stability. By understanding valuation methods, preparing financial reports, and positioning the business for a strong exit, companies can achieve successful transitions that benefit investors, employees, and stakeholders alike.

# THE FUTURE OF ACCOUNTING & FINANCIAL MANAGEMENT

The financial world is evolving at an unprecedented pace, and businesses that fail to adapt risk being left behind. Accounting, once seen as a back-office function focused primarily on compliance and record-keeping, has transformed into a strategic tool for driving business growth, improving financial decision-making, and mitigating risk. As technology advances, global markets shift, and regulations become more stringent, businesses must embrace the next wave of financial management to stay competitive.

**AI & Automation in Accounting** Artificial intelligence is reshaping how financial data is processed, analyzed, and interpreted. Machine learning algorithms can now automate complex accounting tasks, detect anomalies in financial statements, and even provide predictive insights into future financial performance. Automation reduces errors, increases efficiency, and allows finance professionals to focus on strategy rather than routine bookkeeping.

**Blockchain & Financial Transparency** Blockchain technology is revolutionizing financial accountability by creating immutable, verifiable financial records. This is particularly impactful in fraud prevention, audit transparency, and secure financial transactions. As blockchain adoption increases, businesses will need to incorporate decentralized ledgers into their financial systems to ensure real-time verification of transactions and greater stakeholder trust.

**Regulatory & Compliance Challenges** Governments and financial institutions are tightening regulations to ensure businesses adhere to ethical accounting standards. Compliance with tax laws, financial reporting requirements, and international accounting standards will become increasingly complex. Companies must stay ahead of these changes, leveraging compliance automation tools and expert financial guidance to avoid penalties and reputational damage.

**The Rise of Data-Driven Decision-Making** Financial leaders will rely more on big data and analytics to shape business strategy. Instead of simply reporting past financial performance, accounting will play a central role in forecasting future revenue trends, identifying cost-saving opportunities, and optimizing capital allocation. Financial data will no longer be a static record—it will be a strategic asset used to drive competitive advantage.

**Adapting to a Global Financial Landscape** With businesses operating across multiple countries, financial management now requires a global perspective. Exchange rate fluctuations, cross-border taxation, and international regulatory compliance add layers of complexity. Companies that embrace a global financial mindset will be better positioned to scale and capitalize on emerging market opportunities.

The future of accounting is about **more than just numbers**—it's about harnessing technology, maintaining compliance, and using financial data to make smarter, faster business decisions. Those who proactively embrace these changes will thrive in the next era of business finance.

## Key Takeaways from This Book

As we reach the end of this journey through financial accounting, it's important to reflect on the essential lessons that have been covered. This book has provided a **comprehensive framework** for understanding, implementing, and mastering financial accounting principles for business success.

- **Financial accounting is the foundation of a strong business.** Without it, businesses lack visibility into their performance, making it difficult to manage growth, control costs, or make informed decisions.
- **Financial statements tell a company's story.** The balance sheet, income statement, and cash flow statement provide critical insights

into profitability, liquidity, and overall financial health.

- **Cash flow is king.** Many profitable businesses fail due to poor cash flow management. Understanding how to maintain liquidity and optimize working capital is crucial.
- **Budgeting and forecasting drive long-term success.** Businesses that create financial projections, prepare for different scenarios, and track expenses against budgets have a significant advantage.
- **Ethics and financial accountability cannot be compromised.** Companies that engage in financial mismanagement, fraud, or deceptive accounting tactics ultimately suffer financial and reputational consequences.
- **Technology is redefining financial accounting.** Businesses that leverage AI, blockchain, and automation can improve accuracy, enhance efficiency, and remain competitive in an increasingly digital financial world.
- **Risk management ensures financial resilience.** Economic downturns, regulatory changes, and operational risks require businesses to have strong financial contingency plans.
- **Investor confidence depends on strong financial management.** Businesses that maintain clean financial records, reduce debt, and demonstrate profitability are more likely to attract funding and sustain long-term growth.
- **Business valuation is not just for selling—it's for strategic decision-making.** Understanding a company's value helps with financial planning, investment strategies, and preparing for future

growth or transition.

- **Financial mastery is an ongoing journey.** Staying informed about evolving financial trends, new accounting regulations, and emerging technologies will ensure that businesses remain financially agile.

Each of these insights is **a building block** in developing strong financial acumen. By mastering financial accounting, businesses can make smarter decisions, achieve sustainable profitability, and navigate an unpredictable economic landscape with confidence.

## Final Words on Financial Mastery

Financial success is not about luck—it is about preparation, discipline, and **strategic financial management**. The businesses that thrive in today's fast-changing world are those that **understand their financial position**, anticipate risks, and use financial data to make proactive decisions.

Accounting is no longer just about compliance and record-keeping. It is a **powerful business tool** that, when used correctly, can optimize resources, secure investment, and unlock new growth opportunities. Every successful entrepreneur, business leader, and financial executive understands that **numbers drive decisions**, and **decisions drive success**.

This book has given you the knowledge, tools, and insights needed to **take control of your financial future**. Whether you're a business owner looking to scale, an investor assessing opportunities, or a finance professional aiming for mastery, the principles in this book will guide you toward smarter, more strategic financial management.

Now, it is time to put this knowledge into action. **Review your financial statements regularly. Track your cash flow. Develop strong budgets. Leverage technology. Make informed financial decisions.**

Mastering financial accounting is not just about **keeping score**—it is about shaping the future of your business.

# CONCLUSION

## Mastering Financial Accounting for Business Success

Financial accounting is the foundation of any successful business. Throughout this book, we have explored the principles, strategies, and evolving technologies that shape modern financial management. From understanding financial statements to leveraging advanced forecasting techniques, financial accounting is not just about compliance—it is about **empowering businesses** to make informed decisions, manage resources effectively, and build long-term financial stability.

A business that does not understand its financials is like a ship sailing without a compass. Whether it is a startup seeking funding, a growing company optimizing cash flow, or a well-established enterprise navigating risk, **financial accounting is the key to sustainable business growth**. This book has provided a structured approach to mastering financial data, ensuring that every reader—whether a business owner, accountant, investor, or executive—can confidently apply these principles to real-world financial decision-making.

***The Power of Financial Accounting Principles***

At the core of financial accounting are **fundamental principles** that ensure businesses remain transparent, compliant, and financially sustainable. We began by covering **the three key financial statements**—the balance sheet, income statement, and cash flow statement—and how they interconnect to present an accurate financial picture. Understanding **how to read and interpret these statements** allows businesses to assess profitability, monitor financial health, and make data-driven decisions.

Financial reporting is not just a regulatory requirement—it is **a strategic tool** that enables businesses to attract investors, secure financing, and gain credibility with stakeholders. Investors rely on financial statements to **assess profitability**, creditors use them to **evaluate debt repayment ability**, and executives use them to **drive business strategy**. Throughout this book, we have emphasized **the importance of financial transparency**, ethical reporting, and **strategic financial planning** as the cornerstones of financial success.

### *Accounting as the Backbone of Business Decision-Making*

One of the **central themes** of this book has been the role of financial accounting in **business strategy**. Financial data is not just numbers—it is a powerful tool that **guides decision-making** across all levels of an organization. By applying **ratio analysis, working capital management, and forecasting**, businesses can identify risks, seize opportunities, and **drive sustainable growth**.

We explored **financial ratios** and their significance in evaluating **liquidity, profitability, and efficiency**—helping businesses refine pricing strategies, reduce costs, and improve overall performance. Scenario-based financial planning enables organizations to **prepare for multiple financial outcomes**, ensuring resilience in changing economic conditions.

For business leaders and financial professionals, understanding how to apply financial data effectively is **what separates thriving businesses from struggling ones**. A well-informed financial strategy not only safeguards businesses from risks but **positions them for long-term expansion, investment opportunities, and financial success**.

### *The Importance of Ethical and Transparent Financial Reporting*

While financial data is a powerful business tool, **it must be handled with integrity**. We dedicated an entire chapter to ethics in financial accounting, exploring the dangers of **financial misrepresentation, fraud, and unethical accounting practices**. We examined real-world cases where **corporate misconduct led to financial collapses, regulatory scrutiny, and loss of investor confidence**.

One of the **key lessons** from these case studies is that **financial integrity is non-negotiable**. Businesses that prioritize **ethical accounting practices** build stronger relationships with investors, customers, and regulatory authorities. Ethical financial management does not just protect a company from legal consequences—it fosters **a culture of accountability, trust, and credibility** that drives **long-term success**.

### *Embracing Technology in Financial Accounting*

The **evolution of technology** has transformed financial accounting, offering businesses the opportunity to **increase efficiency, accuracy, and security**. As we explored in the technology in accounting chapter, tools like **AI-driven financial forecasting, automation, and cybersecurity advancements** are redefining how companies manage financial data.

AI is helping businesses **predict market trends**, automation is **streamlining financial reporting**, and cybersecurity measures are **protecting businesses from fraud and cyber threats**. However, with these advancements come **new challenges**, such as **regulatory concerns, data security risks, and workforce adaptation**. Businesses that successfully integrate **technology while maintaining compliance and ethical financial practices** will gain **a significant competitive advantage**.

### *Strategic Financial Planning & Business Resilience*

Beyond mastering accounting principles, we explored **advanced financial planning strategies** that enable businesses to **scale, sustain profitability, and mitigate risk**. Budgeting, forecasting, and capital management are **key financial tools** that provide businesses with the insights needed to anticipate challenges, **optimize resources, and drive expansion**.

Working capital management ensures that companies **maintain liquidity, meet financial obligations, and invest in growth opportunities**. We also examined **business financing options**, from debt and equity financing to securing investor backing, ensuring that companies **understand how to raise and manage capital effectively**.

Through real-world case studies, we analyzed **how businesses successfully navigated financial downturns**, managed risk, and leveraged strategic financial planning to **achieve long-term growth**. The lesson is clear: **businesses that proactively manage their financial health are better positioned to thrive in competitive markets**.

***Looking Ahead: The Future of Financial Accounting***

Financial accounting is not static—it is **constantly evolving** due to technological advancements, regulatory updates, and economic shifts. Businesses must **stay ahead of these changes** by **adapting to new financial regulations, leveraging emerging technologies, and maintaining ethical financial practices**.

The role of financial professionals is also changing. Accountants are no longer just responsible for **record-keeping**—they are now **strategic advisors, risk analysts, and financial decision-makers**. The ability to **interpret financial data, provide insights, and forecast future financial performance** has become **a critical skill in today's business world**.

As a reader, you now have a comprehensive understanding of **financial accounting principles and strategies**. You have learned how to:

- Analyze and interpret financial statements to assess business performance.

- Use financial ratios and forecasting to make **strategic business decisions.**
- Optimize budgeting, cash flow, and **working capital management.**
- Navigate **business financing and capital management.**
- Implement ethical financial practices and **ensure regulatory compliance.**
- Leverage technology and automation to improve **financial efficiency.**

With this knowledge, you are **equipped to make better financial decisions, improve business performance, and contribute to the long-term success of any organization.**

***Final Thought: The Road to Financial Success***

Financial accounting is not just about **recording the past**—it is about **shaping the future.** Businesses that master **financial management gain a competitive edge, maintain financial stability, and position themselves for sustainable growth.**

The key to success lies in **continuous learning, strategic financial planning, and a commitment to ethical accounting.** As financial landscapes evolve, **staying informed, embracing innovation, and prioritizing transparency** will be the defining factors that separate thriving businesses from struggling ones.

The knowledge you have gained from this book is **a powerful tool**—one that can **transform the way you approach financial management,**

**business strategy, and long-term success**. Now, it is up to you to apply these principles, **make informed financial decisions, and build a business that is not only profitable but also ethical, sustainable, and resilient**.

Made in United States
North Haven, CT
09 June 2025

69635607R10222